Slavery and Its Consequences:

American Enterprise Institute for Public Policy Research

A DECADE OF STUDY OF THE CONSTITUTION

How Democratic Is the Constitution?

Robert A. Goldwin and William A. Schambra, editors

How Capitalistic Is the Constitution?

Robert A. Goldwin and William A. Schambra, editors

How Does the Constitution Secure Rights?

Robert A. Goldwin and William A. Schambra, editors

Separation of Powers: Does It Still Work?

Robert A. Goldwin and Art Kaufman, editors

How Federal Is the Constitution?

Robert A. Goldwin and William A. Schambra, editors

How Does the Constitution Protect Religious Freedom?

Robert A. Goldwin and Art Kaufman, editors

Slavery and Its Consequences:
The Constitution, Equality, and Race

Robert A. Goldwin and Art Kaufman, editors

Slavery and Its Consequences:

The Constitution, Equality, and Race

Robert A. Goldwin
and Art Kaufman
editors

American Enterprise Institute for Public Policy Research
Washington, D.C.

This book is the seventh in a series in AEI's project "A Decade of Study of the Constitution," funded in part by grants from the National Endowment for the Humanities. A full list of the titles appears on the series page.

Library of Congress Cataloging-in-Publication Data

Slavery and its consequences : the Constitution, equality, and race /
   Robert A. Goldwin and Art Kaufman, editors.
      p.   cm. — (AEI studies ; 469)
   "This book is the seventh in a series in AEI's project 'A decade
of study of the Constitution' ".
      ISBN 0-8447-3649-X (alk. paper).   ISBN 0-8447-3650-3 (pbk. : alk.
paper)
      1. Slavery—Law and legislation—United States—History.
   2. Slavery—United States—History.   I. Goldwin, Robert A.
   II. Kaufman, Art.   III. American Enterprise Institute for Public
Policy Research.   IV. Series.
   KF4545.S5S58   1988
   346.7301'3—dc19
   [347.30613]   88-10359
                                                                            CIP

AEI Studies 469

Printed in the United States of America

Contents

v

The Editors and the Authors

W. B. ALLEN is professor of government at Harvey Mudd College in Claremont, California. He is a member of the California State Advisory Committee to the U.S. Commission on Civil Rights and the National Council on the Humanities. He is program director of the Liberty Fund Bicentennial Project and a visiting tutor at St. John's College Graduate Institute in Liberal Education. Dr. Allen is past president of the Claremont Unified School District Board of Education. His recent publications include *A Washington Reader* (forthcoming), *The Essential Antifederalist* (1985), *Works of Fisher Ames* (1983), and "Slavery in American Politics" (1983).

DON E. FEHRENBACHER is the William Robertson Coe Professor of History and American Studies Emeritus at Stanford University. Dr. Fehrenbacher was a Guggenheim fellow 1959–1960 and 1984–1985, a National Endowment for the Humanities fellow 1975–1976, and a Huntington-Seaver fellow 1985–1986. Among his publications are *The Dred Scott Case: Its Significance in American Law and Politics* (for which he won a Pulitzer Prize in history), *The South and Three Sectional Crises*, and *Slavery, Law, and Politics: The Dred Scott Case in Historical Perspective*.

ROBERT A. GOLDWIN is resident scholar and director of constitutional studies at the American Enterprise Institute. He has served in the White House as special consultant to the president and, concurrently, as adviser to the secretary of defense. He has taught at the University of Chicago and at Kenyon College and was dean of St. John's College in Annapolis. He is the editor of a score of books on American politics, coeditor of the AEI series of volumes on the Constitution, and author of numerous articles, including "Why Blacks, Women, and Jews Are Not Mentioned in the Constitution" and "Of Men and Angels: A Search for Morality in the Constitution."

KENNETH M. HOLLAND is assistant professor of political science at the University of Vermont. Among his numerous publications are "Roger Taney" in *American Political Thought* (1983) and *Courts in Modern De-*

mocracies (1987). Dr. Holland is the chairman of the Vermont Advisory Committee to the U.S. Commission on Civil Rights.

ART KAUFMAN is a research assistant in the Department of Government at Georgetown University. He has served as acting director of educational programs at the Commission on the Bicentennial of the U.S. Constitution, assistant director of constitutional studies at the American Enterprise Institute, program officer at the Institute for Educational Affairs, and assistant editor of *The Public Interest*. He has taught constitutional law at the Catholic University of America and is coeditor of *Separation of Powers: Does It Still Work?* and of *How Does the Constitution Protect Religious Freedom?*, published by AEI.

GLENN C. LOURY is professor of political economy at the Kennedy School of Government, Harvard University. He has previously taught at Northwestern University and the University of Michigan. He has been a visiting scholar at Oxford University, at Tel Aviv University, and at the University of Stockholm. He has also served on the advisory commissions of the National Academy of Sciences, the National Science Foundation, and the National Commission for Employment Policy. He is the author of numerous publications on race problems in the United States.

ROBERT A. SEDLER is professor of law at Wayne State University. He has litigated a large number of civil rights and civil liberties cases. Professor Sedler was the principal author of the amicus curiae brief for the Society of American Law Teachers in the Supreme Court case of *Board of Regents of the University of California* v. *Bakke* (1978). In 1981 he testified on affirmative action in hearings held by the Senate Judiciary Committee Subcommittee on the Constitution. He is the author of numerous articles on constitutional law in law reviews and professional journals.

HERBERT J. STORING was, at the time of his death in 1977, the Robert Kent Gooch Professor of Government and director of the Program on the Presidency of the White Burkett Miller Center for Public Affairs, University of Virginia. His publications include *The Complete Anti-Federalist, Black American Political Thought, What Country Have I? Political Writings by Black Americans,* and *Essays on the Scientific Study of Politics.*

WILLIAM M. WIECEK is Chester Adgate Congdon Professor of Public Law and Legislation in the College of Law, Syracuse University. He is the author of many books and articles, including *Constitutional Development in a Modernizing Society: The United States, 1803–1917* (1985), *Equal Justice under Law: Constitutional Development, 1835–1875* (1982), *The Sources of Antislavery Constitutionalism in America, 1760–1848* (1977), "Chief Justice Taney and His Court" (*this Constitution*), "Dred Scott Case" and "Ex Parte Merryman" (*Encyclopedia of Southern History*, 1979), and "Somerset: Lord Mansfield and the Legitimacy of Slavery in the Anglo-American World" (*University of Chicago Law Review*, 1974).

Preface

This is a book of controversy about the oldest, ugliest, and most persistent American constitutional problem—slavery and the consequences of slavery. The great American paradox is that while slavery and the race problems that followed from it are an integral part of our history, slavery and race discrimination are not part of the fundamental principles of the nation—and never have been.

From the beginning it has not been possible to account for slavery in terms consistent with the American founding principles. The founders could not find a way to square the practice of slavery and the principle that all men are equal in their rights, except to say that it was an unavoidable price to be paid for union. To most of the founders—but not all of them—slavery was abhorrent; they did not condone it, let alone approve of it, but neither did they abolish it. And therein lies the problem.

At a critical moment in the deliberations of the Constitutional Convention in 1787, when the delegates were searching for some way to resolve the seemingly irreconcilable differences between the large and the small states, James Madison spoke about the "great division of interests" among the states that made agreement so difficult. Differences of size and climate, he said, generated conflicting interests, but they were not the main problem. The chief divisions, he argued, resulted from "the effects of their having or not having slaves." "The real difference of interests" stemmed from "the institution of slavery and its consequences."

The delegates to the convention sought to establish a new kind of government that would, for the first time in history, be based on the principles of the primacy and equality of the rights of all human beings. This government was designed for a people devoted to liberty who had nevertheless practiced human slavery for more than a century. The nation was founded on sound principles and in open violation of them. Slavery was the flaw, and its consequences are still with us. After ratification, the slavery issue, especially the question of its extension to new states, dominated American politics, nearly destroyed the union, and led to problems that are still with us today in the myriad forms that race problems take.

PREFACE

There seems to be little question, therefore, that Madison was right to be concerned about the effects of slavery on the future of America. But there is great dispute about the constitutional status of slavery. Many scholars and political leaders, including some founders, have maintained that the Constitution aimed at the eventual extinction of slavery. But it has also been aruged that because the Constitution did not outlaw slavery and contained circumlocutory references to it, the American founders were insincere in their regard for liberty or had "sold out" to slaveholding interests in framing the Constitution. The Constitution is frequently denounced, therefore, for its departure from the fundamental principles of the nation as they were expressed in the Declaration of Independence, particularly concerning equality.

Whether these charges are well founded is important to national self-understanding. They point to the intense contradiction that slavery posed for the framers of the Constitution, who successfully compromised on so many other issues, such as the federal-state relationship, representation in the legislative bodies, and reelectability of officeholders.

The first several essays in this volume address the intentions of the framers of the Constitution regarding slavery. Was the original Constitution proslavery? Can the slavery provisions be seen as compatible with principles of liberty and equality? What would have been the fate of slavery had the Constitution, framed in 1787, not been adopted by slave states and free states joined within one union?

Because we believe that Madison was right about the paramount importance of "slavery and its consequences," these questions are of more than historical interest; they go to the heart of the meaning of constitutionalism; they raise such matters as the nature of representation, property rights, federalism, and, most of all, citizenship in a racially, ethnically, and religiously diverse society such as ours. One of the authors in this volume argues that the Constitution intentionally perpetuated slavery because slavery was an accepted institution in the fabric of America and was tied to economic progress. Because American society was racist at the time of the founding, the argument goes, there was no question but that black persons were excluded—and were intended to remain excluded—from the Declaration's self-evident truths about the equality of mankind.

Others of these authors argue just the reverse: that because the framers recognized the incompatibility of slavery with the principle of equality, they designed the provisions to start the institution of slavery on the road to extinction, the best they could hope to do given the circumstances of their time. This, they argue, was Lincoln's view as expounded in his Address at Cooper Institute in New York in 1860 (reproduced in the appendix of this volume).

Today, legal devices designed to erase the last vestiges of the consequences of slavery—for example, invidious racial discrimination—are related to our understanding of equality in light of the Reconstruction Amendments, which are, in a sense, our constitutional link to that most basic proposition put forth in the Declaration of Independence "that all men are created equal." The amendments are the result of the contradiction—and the eventual, violent resolution of the contradiction—between that concept and the constitutionality of slavery in America's past.

Affirmative action programs (including the use of numerical goals or quotas), school busing to achieve racial desegregation, and other more recent efforts to improve the condition of many other insular minorities in society are contemporary examples of the continuing debate—intellectual, historical, legal, and, especially, political—over what the principle of equality requires of us.

The last several essays in this volume, therefore, address problems that are properly considered the consequences of slavery. Whether the rights of individuals may be compromised for the sake of compensating groups for past injustices is one of the pressing constitutional and social issues of our time. One of the authors in this volume argues for such compensation, in professional school admissions and employment, for example, to ensure equal participation in society. Another author argues against such group preferences as an unconstitutional deprivation of the rights of individuals.

While arguments for and against affirmative action policies and other devices to integrate society are heard often enough, little attention is paid to possible alternatives to them. The last essay addresses this question. Has enough now been done legally and governmentally to address discrimination in our society within constitutional bounds? What should our expectations be concerning equal social and economic conditions of blacks and other minorities as the result of past measures? Are our only solutions legal ones through which government mandates not only equality of opportunity but equality of results as well?

These and other questions concerning the force of equality in America, past, present, and future, are taken up in this volume. As in the other volumes of AEI's Constitution series, all the authors have been selected for the expertise in the subject they bring to bear and for the differences in views that they represent. Given the often passionate attachment to views that the issue of equality engenders in our society, we believe that the essays in this volume will make a thoughtful and deliberative contribution to the bicentennial of the Constitution.

ROBERT A. GOLDWIN
ART KAUFMAN

1

Slavery, the Framers, and the Living Constitution

Don E. Fehrenbacher

"The Constitution of the United States recognizes, without limitation, the institution of domestic slavery, guarantees its existence, and vindicates the right of the owner to the possession and service of the slave." So spoke Governor Philip Francis Thomas of Maryland in the middle of the nineteenth century, expressing a belief that was held by most southerners and would soon be officially sustained by the chief justice of the United States.[1] But at about the same time, a New York lawyer with abolitionist convictions was asserting that the framers "did not . . . sanction slavery; but, on the contrary, intended to *withhold* all countenance and support of that institution."[2] And a Massachusetts abolitionist went so far as to insist that the Constitution presumed all men to be free and denied the right of property in man, thereby making it "impossible" for slavery to have a "legal existence in *any* of the United States."[3]

Was the U.S. Constitution, as written and ratified two centuries ago, essentially a proslavery or an antislavery document? What were the intentions or expectations of its framers regarding the future of slavery in a nation already dedicated to the principle of human liberty? These two distinct but closely related questions were debated endlessly in the decades preceding the Civil War, and not always as part of the contest between North and South. In the Illinois senatorial campaign of 1858, for instance, Stephen A. Douglas and Abraham Lincoln spent considerable time disputing whether slavery had been visualized by the fathers of the Republic as a permanent or as a temporary institution.[4] But the most elaborate and exhaustive debate on the subject took place within the ranks of the abolition crusade.

The two extremes of abolitionist constitutional theory were dramatically in conflict and have as a consequence received much attention from historians. At one extreme, the Garrisonians saw in the Constitution a document so utterly and irretrievably proslavery that it

1

must be renounced, they said, by all friends of liberty. Their adversaries at the other extreme replied that the Constitution, if properly interpreted, made or could make slavery illegal everywhere in the nation. Emerging in the 1840s, these two irreconcilable expressions of antislavery ultraism were related to the great struggle over the wisdom of political action that had divided the abolition movement. The connection is well illustrated in the changing views of Frederick Douglass. As a young Garrisonian committed to the strategy of moral suasion, Douglass labeled the Constitution "a most foul and bloody conspiracy" in support of slavery. Later, when he broke with Garrison and embraced political.abolitionism, he was able to convince himself that the framers had written an essentially antislavery document.[5]

The Garrisonian interpretation of the Constitution, though developed first in the pages of the *Liberator,* was set forth most cogently in a series of pamphlets by Wendell Phillips.[6] Largely an auxiliary argument formulated to justify the rejection of political action and the advocacy of disunion, it rested on a grimly realistic reading of the document in its historical context. "The Constitution of the United States deals with slavery as a *fact,* and gives it, as such, certain rights," Phillips declared.[7] To him, the framers were a body of able but misguided men who sacrificed the principles of liberty to the needs of sectional compromise by enfolding slavery in the protection of national law. He named five parts of the Constitution in which that protection was given: the apportionment of representation and direct taxes according to population, with slaves counting three-fifths; the twenty-year guarantee against congressional prohibition of the foreign slave trade; the provision for recovery of fugitive slaves; the clause authorizing the use of the militia for suppression of insurrections; and the clause promising the states federal protection against domestic violence.[8] In making these concessions to slavery, Phillips lamented, "our fathers bartered honesty for gain and became partners with tyrants."[9] Stripped of such moral judgments, the Garrisonian doctrine obviously had much in common with proslavery constitutional theory, and many abolitionists found that convergence intolerable.

The doctrines of the anti-Garrisonian extremists, whom one scholar has labeled the "constitutional utopians," reflected a contrary determination to legitimize total political action against slavery within the constitutional system. A diverse group with an abundance of arguments that are not easily summarized, the utopians generally denied that the framers had extended any protection to slavery. One of their number, Joel Tiffany, wrote that the Constitution, while perhaps recognizing the de facto presence of slavery in 1787, did not "legalize, sanction, or in any manner guaranty" its continued existence. Tiffany asserted that the three-fifths clause, far from endorsing human servitude, amounted to a penalty on the slaveholding states. "At this very time," he said, "the south are abated some sixteen members in the Federal Government for permitting the institution of slavery to continue among them." He likewise interpreted the slave-trade clause as an antislavery achievement, suspended for twenty years, to be sure, but ultimately confirming federal authority to prohibit both foreign and interstate traffic in slaves. As for the fugitive-slave clause, which he could not by any logic render advantageous to abolitionism, Tiffany insisted that it conferred no power and imposed no responsibility on the federal government but instead merely forbade state action interfering with the recovery of fugitives.[10] A different and less plausible line of reasoning was pursued by Lysander Spooner, who simply denied that the three clauses were concerned with slavery at all. Spooner contended, for example, that the phrase "free persons" in the three-fifths clause meant *citizens* and that the phrase "other persons" consequently referred, not to slaves, but to *aliens*. "There is, in the whole instrument," he said, "no such word as slave or slavery; nor any language that can legally be made to assert or imply the existence of slavery."[11]

Not content with just defensive strategy, the utopians also maintained that the Constitution, of its own force, made slavery illegal everywhere in the nation, or that it fully empowered the federal government to dismantle the institution everywhere in the nation. There were those who asserted, for instance, that slavery was contrary to the whole spirit of the Constitution and could be abolished in pursuit of any one of the fundamental purposes enunciated in the preamble, such as providing for the common defense or promoting the general welfare. Some said that slavery invaded the rights of U.S. citizenship, which the Constitution extended to all inhabitants of the country except unnaturalized foreigners. Some said that it violated the due process clause of the Fifth Amendment. Some said that it was incompatible with republican principles and could therefore be abolished by virtue of the clause guaranteeing every state a republican form of government. There were some, including Spooner, who even went so far as to argue that slavery had never been legally established within the boundaries of the United States, not by state or national law since 1776 and not by British or colonial law before that time.[12]

To most of their contemporaries, the utopians appeared to be out of touch with reality. Phillips, in a critique of Spooner's work, called it fanciful, logically absurd, and subversive of all sound political principles.[13] Historians, too, with few exceptions, have tended to belittle

3

utopian constitutional thought, while taking Garrisonian theory much more seriously. The Garrisonians, after all, claimed to be talking about the Constitution as it functioned in the real world, whereas the utopians seemed to be talking about the Constitution as it might have been implemented, but never was. With formidable logic, Phillips demanded, "If the unanimous, concurrent, unbroken practice of every department of the Government, judicial, legislative, and executive, and the acquiescence of the whole people for fifty years do not prove which is the true construction, then how and where can such a question be settled?"[14]

Yet there were obvious weaknesses in such reasoning; for the Garrisonians, as a black abolitionist pointed out, had fallen into the error "of making the construction of the constitution of the United States, the same as the constitution itself."[15] The New York abolitionist Gerrit Smith, a strong advocate of political action, likewise distinguished between the document itself and subsequent construction of the document. He asked:

> Why should we regard the Federal Constitution as pro-slavery? Whenever, I read it it presents itself as a noble and beautiful Temple of Liberty. . . . Is the Constitution pro-slavery, because the government of the United States has, almost from its beginning, been administered for the advantage of slavery? As well might you hold the Constitution responsible for any other trampling on its principles. . . . The fact, that the nation, in its national capacity, favors and upholds slavery, proves nothing against the Constitution.[16]

William Jay, who was much more critical of the framers and their work, nevertheless drew a similar distinction. Although the Constitution of 1787 did tolerate slavery, he said, "the evil was partial, and confined within certain limits; and its ultimate extinction, while so confined, *was* inevitable." But the Constitution of the 1840s, "as now mutilated, and used by the slaveholders, would never have been adopted by the people of the United States."[17]

Jay's views were, in this instance, neither Garrisonian nor utopian. They belonged instead to the mainstream of antislavery constitutional thought, which had been largely undisputed until the emergence of extremist doctrines in the 1840s.[18] According to mainstream theory, the Constitution, while implicitly recognizing the existence of slavery and granting it a small measure of protection, gave no sanction to the concept of property in human beings and was generally oriented toward a slave-free nation; furthermore, the federal government, though without constitutional authority to abolish the institution in the southern states, did have power to prevent the territorial expansion of slavery and otherwise indirectly hasten the day of its total eradication. Mainstream abolitionists were thus disposed to consider the Constitution proslavery in certain details but antislavery in underlying purpose and ultimate potential. It was a belief that they could share with free-soilers and other nonabolitionist opponents of slavery, including Charles Sumner, Salmon P. Chase, and, eventually, Abraham Lincoln. Horace Mann, as a Massachusetts congressman in 1851, was dispensing mainstream doctrine when he declared that the Constitution provided "the most comprehensive and fundamental guaranties in favor of freedom, with here and there only an exception in behalf of slavery," and that it was adopted "with the universal understanding that the healing influence of time would purge away the virus of the disease."[19]

Phillips and other Garrisonian abolitionists, by equating the pristine Constitution of 1787 with the living Constitution of the 1840s, were, in effect, holding the framers responsible not only for the original document but for all the gloss that it had acquired over sixty years.[20] Many historians since that time have agreed with the Garrisonians in viewing the Founding Fathers as culpable because they "did not seize the opportunity that then was theirs to implement Revolutionary ideals by acting against slavery."[21] Some have even suggested that the tragedy of the Civil War must be attributed in no small part to the mistakes of the Constitutional Convention. "So firmly etched [in the Constitution] was the guarantee of black bondage," says one writer, "that only a grim and bloody war would begin to expunge it from the laws."[22] Such critics seem to have believed that the framers were relatively free to do whatever they liked about slavery and that the choices they made were rigid in their effect, severely restricting the freedom of later public leaders to deal with the issue. One is reminded of the original transgressions in the Garden of Eden. "Our Fathers, in forming the Federal Constitution, entered into a guilty compromise on the subject of slavery," wrote William Jay in 1839, "and heavily is their sin now visited upon their children."[23]

The legal intent of the Constitution inheres in its text, and not in the purposes of those who wrote it. The "intent of the framers" is, in any case, merely an abstraction linking the multiplicity of individual purposes with the unity of the document. Of course the comments of the framers are often useful in determining the implications and resolving the ambiguities of the text, but they contribute more to a historical understanding of the Constitution than to the interpretation of its legal meaning. Historical understanding depends on general contextual knowledge as well as on a grasp of the specifically relevant facts. In studying the intent of the Constitution with respect to slavery, it is probably best to begin with context and move toward the text.

When the Constitutional Convention assembled in the spring of 1787, slavery was firmly established in the five southernmost states and more than a trivial presence in most of the others. There were, in the nation as a whole, two slaves for every nine free persons and, in the South, two slaves for every four free persons. The slaveholding production of staple crops dominated southern agriculture and eminently suited the nationwide trend toward a market economy. As a racial caste system, slavery was the most distinctive element in the southern social order. Furthermore, slaveholders were playing such a vigorous part in the expansion of the American frontier that their slaves already constituted about one-seventh of the population living in Kentucky and the Southwest. Just ahead, of course, lay the invention of the cotton gin, but even before that historic development, slavery was by several standards a flourishing institution, integral to the prosperity of the nation.

At the same time, slavery was an institution under severe scrutiny, both as a matter of conscience and as a matter of public interest. Many Americans were finding it difficult to square slaveholding with the principles of Christianity, and many were troubled by the contrast between the celebration of human freedom in the Declaration of Independence and the presence of human servitude throughout so much of the Republic. A number of antislavery societies had been organized and could claim some of the nation's leading citizens as members. Abolition had begun in the northern states and was expected to prevail eventually at least as far south as Delaware.[24] Virginia and Maryland had revised their laws in such a way as to facilitate private manumission. Every state except Georgia had taken some kind of action proscribing, inhibiting, or suspending the importation of slaves from abroad. And while the Convention was in session, Congress passed the Northwest Ordinance prohibiting slavery in all federal territory north of the Ohio River.

Yet these gains for freedom, though by no means insignificant, were all on the periphery of American slavery and scarcely touched the central problem, which was the massive concentration of more than 600,000 slaves in the five southern states. No one in the Convention and no one else of any standing in the country favored a frontal attack on that problem. Racial considerations alone were enough to make universal emancipation difficult even to visualize. Among American political leaders of the time, antislavery sentiment was widespread and evidently sincere, but never intense enough to become a prime motive force. Proslavery sentiment, though less prevalent and seldom categorically acknowledged, was more tenacious, being firmly rooted in economic and social interest. The Convention, viewed as an entity, had mixed feelings about slavery and did not consider itself charged with any power or duty to settle the destiny of the institution. Many delegates, to be sure, seem to have believed or hoped that somehow in the flow of time slavery would disappear, and the imprint of that expectation is plainly visible in the document that they finally approved.

Slavery, although not an item on the agenda, intruded frequently on the deliberations of the Convention. The subject could not have been avoided entirely, but for the most part it was a collateral rather than a primary theme. Sometimes, as a matter of debating strategy, slavery was injected into discussion of other issues. James Madison, for example, as a delegate from the most populous state, was determined to secure proportional representation in both branches of the national legislature. He accordingly tried very hard to shift attention from the rivalry between large and small states to the rivalry between slaveholding and free states. In the words of one historian, "he used the issue of slavery as a sectional threat to oppose the adoption of state equality."[25]

As the Convention moved toward establishing proportional representation in at least one house of a bicameral Congress, it could not avoid making a decision of some kind about how slavery fitted into the emerging new design of the federal republic. In the apportionment of representation among the states, were slaves to be counted as part of the population represented? If so, Virginia, for instance, would have about 17 percent of the seats in the House of Representatives; if not, its share would be reduced to about 12 percent. This was a sectional issue on which the sectional lines were never very clearly drawn in the Convention because of complications such as the preference of some delegates for apportionment according to "quotas of requisition" (meaning contributions to the national treasury based on estimated wealth) and the proposal of others that the problem of apportionment be left to the legislature. It is not surprising, in the circumstances, that the delegates were drawn to a familiar solution, one that had been approved by Congress in 1783 as a formula for distributing the expenses of the Confederation, but had never gone into effect.[26] As finally phrased in the Constitution, it provided that representatives and direct taxes should be apportioned among the states according to their respective numbers, determined "by adding to the whole number of free persons, including those bound to service for a term of years, and excluding Indians not taxed, three fifths of all other persons."

The three-fifths compromise, which Phillips labeled "the chief pro-slavery clause in the Constitution," was denounced by Garrisonians and other critics as a constitutional sanction of slavery, a political bonus for slaveholders, and a degradation of the slave to just three-fifths of a human being.[27] No more than partly valid at best, this indictment, by its own inconsistency, pointed up the complexity of the problem that the Convention faced. For if the delegates had chosen to base representation on free population alone (thereby canceling the political bonus for slaveholders), the Constitution still would have carried an implied recognition of slavery. On the other hand, if they had based representation on total population (thereby counting each slave as five-fifths of a human being and avoiding any recognition of slavery), the political bonus would have been retained and increased by 50 percent. In short, there was no way to install proportional representation without taking notice of slavery or making some concession to it, or both.

Of course, neither extreme was politically possible. An apportionment based on total population would have been opposed by most northerners, and an apportionment based on free population would have been unacceptable to most southerners.[28] The delegates had to compromise or give up all thought of proportional representation. They turned to the three-fifths formula because it was ready at hand. The fraction itself had originated four years earlier in congressional efforts to use population as a measure of wealth when making requisitions on the states. More than anything else, it was an estimate of the slave's wealth-producing capacity, compared with that of free men.[29] As adopted by the convention in 1787, the fraction was essentially arbitrary. It did not signify that slaves were only 60 percent human or that they were partly persons and partly property. It had no intrinsic meaning with respect to representation. The delegate who first proposed the three-fifths compromise was James Wilson of Pennsylvania. He did so in order to advance the cause of proportional representation and without giving much thought to slavery. Thus the three-fifths clause, with its concessions to slavery, proved to be part of the price paid for a historic advance toward representative government at the national level.[30]

But precisely what were those concessions? First, the clause acknowledged the presence of non-free persons in the United States (and was the only part of the Constitution to do so). Thus it obliquely recognized the existence of the institution of African slavery, but without any implication of national sanction or protection and without lending any reinforcement to the idea of human property. Second, it was said that the clause conferred an unfair political advantage

8

on slaveholders by giving them representation for their slaves as well as for themselves in one house of Congress and in the electoral college. That complaint rested on the assumption that free population was the only appropriate basis for proportional representation. But as a matter of political theory, it was just as easy to defend apportionment based on the whole population, including slaves, Indians, women, children, and other groups not part of the body politic. So the clause could also be viewed, in the words of Frederick Douglass, as "a downright disability laid upon the slaveholding states," depriving them of "two-fifths of their natural basis of representation."[31] Ironically, emancipation removed that disability in the 1860s, and by the end of the nineteenth century, with blacks disfranchised, white southerners had a greater advantage than ever in the apportionment of congressional and electoral votes.

The prime target of abolitionists in Europe and America at the time of the Constitutional Convention was the foreign slave trade. To many an abolitionist then and later it therefore seemed particularly outrageous that the framers should have extended some measure of protection to the hated traffic. They did so in one long sentence weighted with circumlocution and ambiguity:

> The migration or importation of such persons as any of the states now existing shall think proper to admit, shall not be prohibited by the Congress prior to the year one thousand eight hundred and eight, but a tax or duty may be imposed on such importation, not exceeding ten dollars for each person.

This exemption was then reinforced elsewhere in the Constitution by an exemption from amendment during the twenty-year period.[32] Yet, despite the double lock on its original proslavery purpose, the slave-trade clause is a fine example of how documental intent can stray from authorial intention. Added at the insistence of delegates from the three southernmost states, it nevertheless turned out to be antislavery in its fundamental effect.

The clause was a compromise in itself and also part of a larger compromise involving other aspects of foreign commerce. As the configuration of a stronger national government took shape in the Convention, southern delegates became more concerned about protecting the peculiar interests of their own section. They wanted to prevent taxes on exports and to require a two-thirds vote of Congress for navigation acts. In addition, delegates from the lower South were determined to secure for their states the continuing right, whether exercised or not, to import Negroes from abroad. Some declared themselves unwilling to support a constitution that did not confirm

9

such a right. The Committee of Detail, in converting the various resolutions of the Convention into a first draft of the Constitution, gave the southerners what they had asked for, including a clause that permanently restrained Congress from prohibiting or even taxing the importation of slaves. There followed a sharp debate in which the Virginia delegation led the fight against shielding the slave trade. The other four southern states joined with the three New England states in approving a compromise worked out by a special Committee of Eleven. Designed more or less to split the difference between the commercial and the plantation interests, it retained the ban on export taxes, eliminated the requirement of a two-thirds vote for navigation acts, and exempted the slave trade only temporarily from federal prohibition—until 1800 in the committee report, until 1808 in the final version.[33]

The change from a permanent to a temporary exemption transformed the meaning of the slave-trade clause by setting a target date for federal prohibition of the traffic. The eminent physician Benjamin Rush was just one of many persons who immediately perceived the antislavery implications of the clause. Soon after the Philadelphia newspapers published the text of the completed Constitution, he informed an English friend that in the year 1808 there would be "an end of the African trade in America."[34] Of course, most states had already outlawed or otherwise inhibited the trade, and during the next decade it became illegal everywhere in the country. State enforcement was less than adequate, however, and any state was free to reopen the trade, as South Carolina elected to do in December 1803. Federal intervention was obviously needed for total suppression, but without the slave-trade clause, such intervention might have been resisted by many southerners as a matter of states' rights. The clause, in short, permitted some importation of Africans—indeed, many thousands by South Carolina over a four-year period—but it also fostered a general expectation of federal legislation and federal enforcement at a designated time. When Congress passed the act of 1807 prohibiting importation of slaves, it did so on a schedule set by the Constitution, and the vote in the House of Representatives was 113 to 5.[35]

The slave-trade clause was placed in Article I, section 9, among the enumerated limitations on congressional authority. It temporarily suspended, and thereby plainly acknowledged, federal power to outlaw the foreign slave trade. The power was presumably conferred in the clause authorizing Congress to "regulate commerce with foreign nations." But the same clause invested Congress with equivalent jurisdiction over commerce "among the several states," and if "commerce" included slave traffic in the one instance, it must have done so in the other. That inference was sustained in the act of 1807, which not only forbade the importation of slaves but also placed certain restrictions on that part of the domestic slave trade carried on in coasting vessels. Furthermore, if the power to "regulate" meant the power to prohibit in the one instance, there is no sound basis for argument that it did not mean the same thing in the other. Thus the slave-trade clause, whether or not the framers so intended, recognized congressional power to regulate or even abolish the interstate slave trade at any time after 1807.[36]

Although the clause did not mention slaves or slavery by name, the words "importation" and "duty" came closer than anything else in the Constitution to reflecting the property-holding aspect of the institution. Yet the temporary nature of the clause made it a dubious basis for any defense of slavery after 1807 and seemed to point instead toward restriction and ultimate extinction. In addition, the operation of the clause was restricted from the beginning to the original states, and this, together with the Northwest Ordinance, indicated some disposition to view slavery as the exception rather than the rule in an expanding nation.

The three-fifths clause and the slave-trade clause were side effects of the Convention's progress toward a new constitutional design. One resulted from the introduction of proportional representation at the national level; the other, from the empowering of Congress to regulate foreign commerce; and both were highly controversial. The fugitive-slave clause, in contrast, had no such connections and provoked little argument. Presented late in the Convention by two South Carolina delegates, but certainly not as a sine qua non, it received unanimous approval. The fact that a similar provision had already been incorporated in the Northwest Ordinance no doubt encouraged its ready acceptance.[37] Again the framers chose not to name the thing they were talking about: "No person held to service or labour in one state, under the laws thereof, escaping into another, shall, in consequence of any law or regulation therein, be discharged from such service or labour, but shall be delivered up on claim of the party to whom such service or labour may be due."

The fugitive-slave clause was not placed in Article I with the enumerated powers of Congress but appears instead in Article IV, section 2. That whole article is about states and statehood, and the second section is about interstate comity. Of the three other sections in the article, two expressly confer power on Congress, and the other vests power more generally in the "United States"—meaning, presumably, all three branches of the federal government. There is no such conferral of power in section 2, which lends credence to the view of the fugitive-slave clause as nothing more than a declaratory limitation on state authority.[38] That view, if accurate, goes a long way toward explaining the absence of controversy in the genesis of a clause that became the basis for some of the most controversial legislation ever passed by Congress.

The three-fifths, slave-trade, and fugitive-slave clauses, together with the double lock put on the slave-trade clause, were the only parts of the Constitution written with slavery primarily in mind, and none of them called the institution by its name. Without a doubt, the three-fifths clause, or some equivalent, was essential for the success of the Constitution as we know it. The slave-trade clause may have been a necessary concession to the lower South—one that proved, however, to be antislavery rather than proslavery in its ultimate effect. The fugitive-slave clause was a more gratuitous addition to the Constitution, and it alone provided slaveholders with some measure of protection, though only in vague and passive terms. Each of the three clauses dealt with a marginal feature of slavery that had some claim on national attention. None of the three recognized slavery as having any legitimacy in federal law. On the contrary, the framers were doubly careful to treat it explicitly as a state institution. Most revealing in this respect was a last-minute change in the fugitive-slave clause whereby the phrase "legally held to service or labour in one state" was changed to read: "held to service or labour in one state, under the laws thereof." The revision made it impossible to infer from the passage that the Constitution itself legally sanctioned slavery.[39]

Other parts of the Constitution have sometimes been labeled proslavery, most notably the clauses providing for suppression of insurrections and for protection of the states against domestic violence. Both clauses obviously covered various kinds of resistance to civil authority, including servile rebellion, but the 1780s were not a period of serious disturbances among the slave population. What the framers did have in mind was the alarming series of events in Massachusetts known as Shays's Rebellion, which had come to an end just a few months before the opening of the Convention. Wendell Phillips, writing in the 1840s, conceded that the two clauses were "perfectly innocent in themselves." Futhermore, neither was ever invoked to deal with a slave uprising. Phillips nevertheless insisted that since they were potentially usable for that purpose, the clauses implicated all Americans in "the guilt of sustaining slavery."[40] Perhaps the best way to comment on such reasoning is to ask what alternatives were available to the framers. Should they have excepted slave revolts from the insurrections to be suppressed and from the domestic violence to be guarded against? Any such proposal would have been dismissed as absurd and outrageous. But then the only other option, one that likewise would have received little support in the Convention, was omission or deletion of the two clauses from the text of the Constitution. That would have deprived the federal government of needed authority—authority used as early as 1794 in the Whisky Rebellion and invoked by Lincoln in 1861 to suppress an insurrection, not of slaves, but of slaveholders.

Slavery had a stronger influence on the deliberations of the Convention than on the text of the Constitution. The few concessions to slavery in the text were, as Gerrit Smith maintained, more like eddies in a stream than part of the current.[41] Moreover, the concessions were offset by a stylistic tone of repugnance for the institution and by indications that it could be regarded as something less than permanent in American life. In short, the Constitution as it came from the hands of the framers dealt only minimally and peripherally with slavery and was essentially open-ended on the subject. Nevertheless, because it substantially increased the power of the national government, the Constitution had greater proslavery potential and greater antislavery potential than the Articles of Confederation. Its meaning with respect to slavery would depend heavily upon how it was implemented.

Antislavery implementation was confined largely to two categories, involving three provisions of the Constitution—the territory clause and the commerce clause, reinforced after 1807 by the slave-trade clause. Beginning with reenactment of the Northwest Ordinance in 1789, Congress used its control over federal territories to prohibit slavery in the northern part of the country from the western boundary of Pennsylvania to the Mississippi River, then to the Rocky Mountains, and finally to the Pacific Ocean.[42] Beginning in 1794, Congress prohibited American participation in the foreign slave trade, and in 1807 it passed the first of several laws forbidding the importation of slaves from abroad.[43] Both of these categories of antislavery achievement were plainly within the purview of the Constitution and the expectations of the framers, but each in its own way came to suffer from erosion. Enforcement of the slave-trade law was chronically inadequate, and American complicity in the traffic remained an international issue right up to the Civil War.[44] As for federal exclusion of slavery from the territories, all attempts to extend the ban into southern parts of the country were unsuccessful. Then in the Kansas-Nebraska Act of 1854, Congress virtually repudiated the whole idea, and in the Dred Scott decision three years later, the Supreme Court held such legislation to be unconstitutional.[45]

13

The extraordinary amount of historical attention given to the sectional conflict over slavery in the territories—a conflict in which the antislavery forces managed at least to hold their own—has obscured the fact that an often tacit proslavery interpretation of the Constitution was predominant in the operation of the federal government from 1789 to 1861. A striking case in point is the implementation of the clause empowering Congress "to exercise exclusive legislation in all cases whatsoever, over such district (not exceeding ten miles square) as may, by cession of particular states, and the acceptance of Congress, become the seat of the government of the United States." In 1790, after a long legislative battle, Congress voted in favor of a site on the Potomac River, to be donated jointly by Virginia and Maryland. The decision was made without a word being said about slavery and apparently without any reflection on the possible consequences of locating the national capital within a slaveholding region.[46] Then, when the time came a decade later to provide a system of government for the federal district, Congress avoided a lot of hard work by directing that the laws of Virginia and Maryland should continue in force.[47] Thus, silently and almost casually, in actions a decade apart, slavery was legalized as a federal institution in Washington, D.C. More than that, the city soon became a major center of the domestic slave trade. At the very center of national power, the United States presented itself to foreign visitors and its own citizens as a slaveholding republic.

At the same time, a body of historical and constitutional myth was being fashioned to justify and guarantee slaveholding in the District of Columbia as an inalienable right. Even though the words "exclusive legislation in all cases whatsoever" would seem to have given Congress full power over slavery in the District, abolitionist petitions on the subject were met with emphatic southern denials of such power and, indeed, with much insistence that Congress did not even have the authority to receive such petitions, let alone give them serious consideration.[48] It was asserted, furthermore, that any abridgment of slaveholders' rights in the District would be a breach of faith because the inviolability of slavery had been an implicit condition of the transfer of land from Virginia and Maryland to the United States. The assertion was wholly without foundation, but reiteration made it credible even to many northerners. One finds the argument embraced, for example, in a joint resolution of the New Hampshire legislature, passed in 1839 by a vote of 124 to 21.[49] The southern point of view prevailed throughout the antebellum period. Congress did outlaw the slave trade as part of the Compromise of 1850, but not until a year after the firing on Fort Sumter was slavery itself abolished in the national capital.

Not even Wendell Phillips blamed the framers of the Constitution for the entrenchment of slavery in the District of Columbia. Neither did Phillips attach the label "proslavery" to any of the clauses defining the role of the president in foreign affairs, and yet the actual conduct of foreign relations from 1789 to 1861 could scarcely have been more proslavery if there had been nothing but slaveholding states in the Union. Although the question of whether slaves were property under federal law remained a controversial and unsettled issue in Congress, the Department of State treated them as property from the beginning. One American minister lectured the British foreign secretary at length on the subject in his official correspondence. Under the Constitution, he declared, slaves were fully protected as property and there was "no distinction in principle between property in persons and property in things." Domestic slavery, he added, was "infused" into the laws of the United States and mixed itself "with all the sources of their authority."[50]

The facilities of the State Department were used habitually and assiduously in behalf of slave owners, such as those seeking recovery of slaves who had escaped to Canada and those seeking restitution for slaves liberated in the British West Indies. During the presidency of John Quincy Adams, who later became an antislavery terror in the House of Representatives, the United States made strenuous though unsuccessful efforts to arrange by treaty for the return of fugitive slaves from Mexico and Canada.[51] The government also followed a consistent proslavery policy in refusing for more than fifty years to recognize the black republic of Haiti, which, by the very example of its revolutionary origins and continued existence, posed a threat to every slaveholding society. The South, as Senator Thomas Hart Benton of Missouri frankly explained, could not permit "black Consuls and Ambassadors to establish themselves in our cities, and to parade through our country, and give their fellow blacks in the United States, proof in hand of the honors which await them, for a like successful effort on their part."[52]

The implication of the federal government with slavery extended to all departments. For example, slave labor was often used on federal construction projects, such as military installations and the national Capitol itself.[53] Army troops on the southern frontier frequently lent assistance in the recovery of fugitive slaves.[54] Southern postmasters, with the approval of their superiors in Washington, excluded antislavery literature from the mails.[55] High federal offices were often oc-

15

cupied by proslavery zealots like John C. Calhoun, Roger B. Taney, and Jefferson Davis, whereas no vigorous critic of slavery had the slightest chance of receiving such an appointment. Furthermore, the Supreme Court, with its southern majority reinforced by northern doughfaces, became ever more obviously proslavery in the 1840s and 1850s—until at last it virtually proclaimed that slavery was fully entitled to federal protection and wholly immune from federal restraint.[56]

The difference between the unglossed Constitution of 1787 and the living Constitution of the mid-nineteenth century is nowhere better illustrated than in the implementation of the fugitive-slave clause. As we have seen, the location and phrasing of the clause suggest that it was intended to restrict state authority, not to confer power on Congress. Nevertheless, a fugitive-slave law made its way through Congress in 1793 without much difficulty and was signed by George Washington. The measure provided for a summary process that gave an alleged fugitive almost no legal protection and consequently threatened the security of free Negroes everywhere in the country.[57] Yet the Supreme Court eventually upheld its constitutionality in *Prigg* v. *Pennsylvania.* Justice Joseph Story, who delivered the opinion of the Court, also ruled that responsibility for the enforcement of the fugitive-slave clause rested exclusively with the federal government.[58] The ruling created a need for federal agencies of enforcement in each state and led to passage of the more stringent law of 1850. This step-by-step nationalization of the fugitive-slave problem was accompanied by the persistent growth of a mistaken belief that the fugitive-slave clause had been absolutely necessary for the completion and approval of the Constitution. As Justice Story phrased it in his *Prigg* opinion, the clause was "a fundamental article, without the adoption of which the Union could not have been formed." Four other justices joined Story in paying tribute to the myth. Thus a majority of the Court agreed that the fugitive-slave clause should be placed in a special category as one of the indispensable and therefore "fundamental" provisions of the Constitution.

The Constitution may be called proslavery or antislavery or neutral, depending upon one's definition of terms, but it seems beyond dispute that the document was carefully phrased to treat slavery as an entity owing its legal existence solely to state law. Southerners and most northerners, including mainstream abolitionists, subscribed to that principle, though they differed in the inferences they drew from it. As the years passed, however, slavery tended increasingly to become an institution honored and protected by federal law. That was the most striking difference between the original Constitution and the living Constitution of 1860. Anyone trying to explain the change might begin by pointing out that as the South became progressively more resolute and united in the defense of slavery, it continued to exercise an extraordinary influence on national policy, largely because of southern preponderance in the Jeffersonian and Jacksonian parties. Yet the proslavery bias of the federal government was also the result of northern indifference, and more than that, it was partly the work of northern men like John Quincy Adams, Martin Van Buren, and Daniel Webster, who suffered in varying degrees from the doughface syndrome. Until the emergence of the Republican party in the 1850s, every northerner serving in, or aspiring to, a high executive office in the federal government had to make some kind of peace with slavery. Thus the development of a national party system, which the framers of the Constitution did not foresee, facilitated the growth of a federal policy favorable to slavery. But it appears that the policy also resulted in no small part from the inertial tendencies of government—more specifically, from incremental decision making that was usually perfunctory and unreflective.

Even the Republican movement, despite its vigorous antislavery tone, represented a moral compromise with slavery. Many abolitionists, while complaining about its shortcomings, nevertheless supported the new party as the best political choice available, but there were others like Lewis Tappan who would have nothing to do with Abraham Lincoln or the "sneaking, lily-livered, pharisaical, humbug platform" on which he was elected.[59] For southerners, on the other hand, the Republican platform was a document full of menace and the election of Lincoln an act of aggression. "The tea has been thrown overboard," said the Charleston *Mercury.* "The revolution of 1860 has been initiated."[60] Such rhetoric was not entirely misplaced. The Republican victory did signify a revolutionary shift of political power, but in what respect, if any, did it amount to a constitutional revolution?

Imagine a prophet telling the members of the Constitutional Convention that the sixteenth president of the United States would be a man committed to the following principles: (1) Slavery was a great wrong that ought to be treated in such a way as to encourage its ultimate extinction. (2) The federal government had no legal power to interfere with slavery in the states where it already existed. (3) Congress did have the power to abolish slavery in the national capital but should do so only with the consent of its population and with compensation to the slave owners. (4) Congress also had the power to prohibit slavery in the federal territories and should do so in order to prevent further expansion of the institution. (5) As long as slavery

17

continued to exist, Congress was under obligation to provide an effective fugitive-slave law.[61] How would George Washington and James Madison and the other delegates have reacted to such a prophecy? In a variety of ways, no doubt, but surely few of them would have regarded the Lincoln program as revolutionary even for their own age, let alone for a time in the distant future. The Republican party threatened southern security in 1860 because its purposes conflicted sharply with the proslavery gloss on the living Constitution. Those purposes were entirely compatible, however, with the Constitution as written in 1787.

Notes

1. Charleston *Courier,* Jan. 7, 1850; J. Thomas Scharf, *History of Maryland from the Earliest Period to the Present Day,* 3 vols. (Hatboro, Penn.: Tradition Press, 1967, facsimile of 1879 ed.), vol. 3, p. 240; Dred Scott v. John F. A. Sandford, 19 Howard 393 (1857), pp. 451–52.

2. Joel Tiffany, *A Treatise on the Unconstitutionality of American Slavery* (Cleveland: J. Calyer, 1849), p. 9.

3. Lysander Spooner, *The Unconstitutionality of Slavery,* enlarged edition (Boston: Bela Marsh, 1860), pp. 56–57. The first edition of this work was published in 1845.

4. Roy P. Basler et al., eds., *The Collected Works of Abraham Lincoln,* 9 vols. (New Brunswick, N.J.: Rutgers University Press, 1953–1955), vol. 3, pp. 11–12, 18, 114–15, 117–18, 178, 219, 274, 276, 306–8, 315–16, 322–23.

5. Philip S. Foner, ed., *The Life and Writings of Frederick Douglass,* 4 vols. (New York: International Publishers, 1950), vol. 2, pp. 51–54, 155–57, 467–80, 559–60.

6. For an early statement by Garrison on the subject, see his letter to the editor of the London *Patriot,* Aug. 6, 1833, in which he called the Constitution an "infamous bargain" and "the most bloody and heaven-daring arrangement ever made by men for the continuance and protection of a system of the most atrocious villainy ever exhibited on earth." Walter M. Merrill, ed., *The Letters of William Lloyd Garrison,* 6 vols. (Cambridge, Mass.: Harvard University Press, 1971–1981), vol. 1, p. 249.

7. Wendell Phillips, *Review of Lysander Spooner's Essay on the Unconstitutionality of Slavery* (Boston, 1847), p. 92.

8. Wendell Phillips, *The Constitution a Pro-Slavery Document, or Selections from the Madison Papers, etc.* (New York: American Anti-Slavery Society, 1844), p. 4; and see Aileen S. Kraditor, *Means and Ends in American Abolitionism: Garrison and His Critics on Strategy and Tactics, 1834–1850* (New York: Pantheon Books, 1969), pp. 207–12; Robert M. Cover, *Justice Accused: Antislavery and the Judicial Process* (New Haven, Conn.: Yale University Press, 1975), pp. 150–54; and William M. Wiecek, *The Sources of Antislavery Constitutionalism in America, 1760–1848* (Ithaca, N.Y.: Cornell University Press, 1977), pp. 239–46.

9. Phillips, *Constitution a Pro-Slavery Document*, p. 6.

10. Tiffany, *Unconstitutionality of Slavery*, pp. 59, 62–83.

11. Spooner, *Unconstitutionality of Slavery*, pp. 67–89.

12. Richard Hildreth, *Despotism in America: An Inquiry into the Nature, Results, and Legal Basis of the Slave-holding System in the United States* (New York: Negro Universities Press, 1968, reprint of 1854 edition), pp. 218, 243–44; Tiffany, *Unconstitutionality of Slavery*, pp. 84–114; Alvan Stewart, "A Constitutional Argument on the Subject of Slavery," in Jacobus tenBroek, *Equal under Law* (New York: Collier Books, 1965), pp. 281–95; G. W. F. Mellen, *An Argument on the Unconstitutionality of Slavery* (Boston: Saxton & Pierce, 1841), pp. 55–65, 77–79; William Goodell, *Slavery and Anti-Slavery: A History of the Great Struggle in Both Hemispheres, with a View of the Slavery Question in the United States* (New York: W. Harned, 1852), pp. 475–77; Spooner, *Unconstitutionality of Slavery*, pp. 21–54; William M. Wiecek, *The Guarantee Clause of the U.S. Constitution* (Ithaca, N.Y.: Cornell University Press, 1972), pp. 155–65; and Wiecek, *Antislavery Constitutionalism*, pp. 249–75.

13. Phillips, *Review of Spooner's Essay*, p. 4.

14. Phillips, *Constitution a Pro-Slavery Document*, pp. 5–6.

15. Wiecek, *Antislavery Constitutionalism*, p. 243.

16. Smith to John Greenleaf Whittier, July 18, 1844, published in *Liberator*, Aug. 31, 1844.

17. William Jay, *View of the Action of the Federal Government in Behalf of Slavery* (New York: American Anti-Slavery Society, 1839), pp. 21, 214–19; and Jay to Henry I. Bowditch, March 19, 1845, published in *Liberator*, April 11, 1845.

18. Jay did come to embrace the Garrisonian doctrine of disunionism after the annexation of Texas, but on the grounds that the Constitution had been irreparably damaged, not that it was inherently proslavery. See his letter to Bowditch cited in note 17.

19. Horace Mann, *Slavery: Letters and Speeches* (Boston: B. B. Mussey & Co., 1851), pp. 539–40.

20. Wiecek, *Antislavery Constitutionalism*, pp. 17–18, makes much the same point.

21. Merton L. Dillon, *The Abolitionists: The Growth of a Dissenting Minority* (DeKalb, Ill.: Northern Illinois University Press, 1974), p. 17. See also Staughton Lynd, *Class Conflict, Slavery, and the United States Constitution* (Indianapolis, Ind.: Bobbs Merrill, 1967), p. 183.

22. Vincent Harding, *There Is a River: The Black Struggle for Freedom in America* (New York: Harcourt Brace Jovanovich, 1981), p. 46. See also Donald L. Robinson, *Slavery in the Structure of American Politics, 1765–1820* (New York: Harcourt Brace Jovanovich, 1971), p. 247; John Hope Franklin, *From Slavery to Freedom*, 5th ed. (New York: Alfred A. Knopf, 1980), p. 96; and Christopher Collier and James Lincoln Collier, *Decision in Philadelphia: The Constitutional Convention of 1787* (New York: Random House, 1986), p. 177.

23. Jay, *View of the Federal Government*, p. 21.

24. During the Convention, James Madison said that there were five southern states, divided from the other eight by "the institution of slavery and its consequences." He thus classified Delaware as northern. Max Farrand, ed.,

19

The Records of the Federal Convention of 1787, 4 vols. (New Haven, Conn.: Yale University Press, 1911), vol. 2, p. 10.

25. Farrand, *Records,* vol. 1, p. 486; vol. 2, pp. 9–10; and Howard Albert Ohline, "Politics and Slavery: The Issue of Slavery in National Politics, 1787–1815" (Ph.D. diss., University of Missouri, Columbia, 1969), pp. 31–33.

26. Robinson, *Slavery in American Politics,* pp. 156–59.

27. Phillips, *Review of Spooner's Essay,* p. 33; William H. Pease and Jane H. Pease, eds., *The Antislavery Argument* (Indianapolis: Bobbs Merrill, 1965), p. 344; Wiecek, *Antislavery Constitutionalism,* p. 58; and Harding, *There Is a River,* p. 46.

28. It is true that the Virginia plan suggested apportionment according to free population as one possible arrangement, but that was in connection with a proposal for proportional representation in both houses. Virginia and the South as a whole would have benefited more from proportional representation in both houses, even if based on free population, than from proportional representation in just one house with the slaves taken wholly or partly into account. See the table in Robinson, *Slavery in American Politics,* p. 180.

29. Don E. Fehrenbacher, *The Dred Scott Case: Its Significance in American Law and Politics* (New York: Oxford University Press, 1978), pp. 22, 601.

30. Howard A. Ohline, "Republicanism and Slavery: Origins of the Three-Fifths Clause in the United States Constitution," *William and Mary Quarterly,* 3d series, vol. 28 (1971), pp. 570–71, 581–84.

31. Foner, *Life and Writings of Douglass,* vol. 2, p. 472.

32. In Article V: "Provided that no amendment which may be made prior to the year one thousand eight hundred and eight shall in any manner affect the first and fourth clauses in the ninth section of the first Article."

33. Farrand, *Records,* vol. 2, pp. 168–69, 400, 415–17; Ohline, "Politics and Slavery," pp. 55–64; and Robinson, *Slavery in American Politics,* pp. 216–28.

34. Rush to John Coakley Lettsom, Sept. 28, 1887, in John P. Kaminski, Gaspare J. Saladino, et al., eds., *Commentaries on the Constitution, Public and Private* (Madison: State Historical Society of Wisconsin, 1981), vol. 1, pp. 262–63. This is volume 13 of *The Documentary History of the Ratification of the Constitution.*

35. *Annals of Congress,* 9th Cong., 2d sess., cols. 486–87.

36. Antislavery advocates later argued that the word "migration" constituted an explicit acknowledgment of congressional power over the interstate movement of slaves, but southerners replied that the word referred to immigration of free persons. Historians have continued the debate. See, for example, Walter Berns, "The Constitution and the Migration of Slaves," *Yale Law Journal,* vol. 78 (1968), pp. 198–228; David Brion Davis, *The Problem of Slavery in the Age of Revolution, 1770–1823* (Ithaca, N.Y.: Cornell University Press, 1975), pp. 125–30. The southern argument, even if correct, did not demonstrate an absence of congressional power over the interstate slave trade (by virtue of the commerce clause) but only the absence of a specific recognition of that power in Article I, section 9.

37. Lynd, *Class Conflict,* pp. 185–213, argues that the Constitutional Con-

vention joined with the members of Congress (then meeting in New York) to fashion a sectional compromise on slavery "essentially similar to those of 1820 and 1850." The main features of this "Compromise of 1787" were the three-fifths clause of the Constitution, the antislavery clause of the Northwest Ordinance, and the fugitive-slave clauses in both documents. It is difficult to believe, however, that such an agreement could have been achieved without leaving more documentary traces. Lynd's best piece of evidence is a recollection by Madison, as recollected in turn by his one-time secretary in the 1850s. Significantly, it speaks only of the two fugitive-slave clauses and says nothing about the three-fifths compromise.

38. The other two clauses in section 2 are the privileges-and-immunities clause and the flight-from-justice clause. Neither was implemented with federal enforcement legislation, although Congress in 1793 did designate the state governors as the officers responsible for the return of fugitives from justice.

39. Farrand, *Records,* vol. 2, pp. 601, 628.

40. Phillips, *Constitution a Pro-Slavery Document,* p. 4.

41. *Liberator,* Aug. 31, 1844.

42. Fehrenbacher, *Dred Scott Case,* pp. 83–84, 107–8, 150–51.

43. W. E. B. Du Bois, *The Suppression of the African Slave Trade to the United States of America, 1638–1870* (New York: Longmans Green, 1896), pp. 80–81, 94–108.

44. Ibid., pp. 108–17, 123–30, 158–67, 178–87; Hugh G. Soulsby, *The Right of Search and the Slave Trade in Anglo-American Relations, 1814–1862* (Baltimore: Johns Hopkins University Press, 1933).

45. Fehrenbacher, *Dred Scott Case,* pp. 181–87, 367–84.

46. *Annals of Congress,* 1st Cong., 2d sess., cols. 997–1001, 1678–80.

47. *U.S. Statutes at Large,* vol. 2, pp. 103–5.

48. See, for example, the remarks of John C. Calhoun in the Senate on March 9, 1836, in *Congressional Globe,* 24th Cong., 1st sess., Appendix, p. 225. For the petitions and gag rule controversy generally, see Mary Tremain, *Slavery in the District of Columbia: The Policy of Congress and the Struggle for Abolition* (New York: G. P. Putnam's Sons, 1892), pp. 65–90; and Henry H. Simms, *Emotion at High Tide: Abolition as a Controversial Factor* (Richmond, Va.: William Byrd Press, 1960), pp. 93–119, 144–70. An excellent contemporary analysis by an abolitionist is in Theodore Dwight Weld, *The Power of Congress over the District of Columbia* (New York: American Anti-Slavery Society, 1838).

49. *Congressional Globe,* 25th Cong., 2d sess., p. 36.

50. Andrew Stevenson to Lord Palmerston, July 29, 1836, Stevenson Papers, Manuscript Division, Library of Congress.

51. William R. Manning, *Early Diplomatic Relations between the United States and Mexico* (Baltimore: Johns Hopkins University Press, 1916), pp. 229–31, 240–46, 250–51; William R. Manning, *Diplomatic Correspondence of the United States: Canadian Relations, 1784–1860,* 3 vols. (Washington, D.C.: Carnegie Endowment for International Peace, 1940–1943), vol. 2, pp. 100–101, 110, 132–33, 135, 181, 634, 771–72.

52. *Register of Debates in Congress,* 19th Cong., 1st sess., col. 330; and Rayford W. Logan, *The Diplomatic Relations of the United States with Haiti, 1776–1891* (Chapel Hill: University of North Carolina Press, 1941), pp. 32–292.

53. For example, a report of the secretary of war in 1842 revealed that the Army Engineer department was hiring the labor of 545 slaves. Lesser numbers were being employed by the Quartermaster, Commissary, and Ordnance departments. *House Documents,* 27th Cong., 1st sess., no. 286 (Serial 405). See Ernest F. Dibble, "Slave Rentals to the Military: Pensacola and the Gulf Coast," *Civil War History,* vol. 23 (1977), pp. 101–13.

54. The Seminole Wars in Florida were about slave catching as well as Indian removal. See Kenneth Wiggins Porter, *The Negro on the American Frontier* (New York: Arno Press, 1971), pp. 235–36, 251, 262, 277–78, 282–83; and Joshua R. Giddings, *The Exiles of Florida* (Columbus, Ohio: Follett, Foster & Co., 1858), pp. 35–45, 78–81, 158–62.

55. W. Sherman Savage, *The Controversy over the Distribution of Abolition Literature, 1830–1860* (Washington, D.C.: Association for the Study of Negro Life and History, 1938).

56. Taney, in his Dred Scott opinion, declared: "The right of property in a slave is distinctly and expressly affirmed in the Constitution. . . . The only power conferred [on Congress] is the power coupled with the duty of guarding and protecting the owner in his rights." Dred Scott v. Sandford, pp. 451–52. For the relevant cases, see William M. Wiecek, "Slavery and Abolition before the United States Supreme Court, 1820–1860," *Journal of American History,* vol. 65 (1978–1979), pp. 34–59.

57. *U.S. Statutes at Large,* vol. 1, pp. 302–5. The law also dealt with the extradition of fugitives from justice and was originally introduced for that purpose. A provision extending legal protection to an alleged fugitive who had been resident for some time in a free state was struck from the bill before its final passage. See Thomas D. Morris, *Free Men All: The Personal Liberty Laws of the North, 1780–1861* (Baltimore: Johns Hopkins University Press, 1974), pp. 20–21.

58. Prigg v. Pennsylvania, 16 Peters 539, pp. 621–24.

59. Bertram Wyatt-Brown, *Lewis Tappan and the Evangelical War against Slavery* (New York: Atheneum, 1971), p. 337.

60. Charleston *Mercury,* Nov. 8, 1861, quoted in Charles Edward Cauthen, *South Carolina Goes to War, 1860–1865* (Chapel Hill: University of North Carolina Press, 1950), p. 30.

61. Basler et al., *Collected Works of Lincoln,* vol. 3, pp. 40, 41–42, 116–17, 254, 312–13, 317, 327, 460, 539.

2

"The Blessings of Liberty": Slavery in the American Constitutional Order

William M. Wiecek

Sir Lewis Namier once cautioned us about the risks of ahistoricism that we run when we "imagine the past and remember the future."[1] His warning is especially apt as we observe the bicentennial of the Constitution. We have an understandable tendency to project our cherished values back into the eighteenth century and to impute our own moral vision to the framers. This is particularly true of questions involving slavery and race. Slavery is an institution so abhorrent to us that we cannot imagine decent people—much less our constitutional forebears—embracing it. So we naturally want to believe that slavery was incompatible with the constitutional order that they established and that we revere. We persuade ourselves that the Declaration of Independence embodied the "real" values of the American governmental order and that slavery somehow crept unbidden into the Constitution eleven years later. It subsequently required a civil war to oust the usurper. Our values instruct us that human freedom is the norm and slavery an inexplicable diversion. Hence we hopefully ransack the past to find tendencies toward emancipation.

These assumptions are radically wrong. Any spuriously liberal past we create in that way will be little more than Napoleon's *fable convenue*. The following pages propound five alternatives to replace our imagined past.

First: Slavery has been universal in human experience and was an intrinsic component of the framers' social order.

Second: The framers' generation considered slavery to be entwined with human progress.

Third: In 1787 nearly all white Americans considered black slaves a degraded, alien group that could not be incorporated into the body politic at that time and quite possibly might never be. Whites considered blacks, because of their race, to be legitimately and properly the subjects of discrimination, exclusion, and oppression.

Fourth: It follows that in 1787 slavery was wholly compatible with the American constitutional order; indeed, was an essential element of it. America was then a racist, slaveholding society, and its constitutional order conformed to that fundamental characteristic.

Fifth: "The framers' intent" is a misleading phrase. There were numerous framers and varying intents. But one coterie at Philadelphia, comprising the South Carolina and Georgia delegates, extorted acquiescence in its single-mindedly proslavery program from all the other framers.

Slavery in Human Experience

Slavery is one of the few institutions that are truly ubiquitous in human experience. Charles Pinckney exaggerated when he claimed at the Philadelphia convention that "in all ages one half of mankind have been slaves," but his instinct was fundamentally sound.[2] Although the principal employment of unfree labor has been in agriculture, characteristic only of settled societies, slavery was known among pastoral and nomadic peoples as well. It predated recorded history and has existed in hunter-gatherer societies into modern times. Slavery appeared in ancient Mesopotamia and Egypt; it existed among the Persians and Babylonians (references to it appear in Hammurabi's code); the peoples of the ancient Near East, including the Jews, employed it; it pervaded the social structure of the Greek city-states and Rome. It has adapted to all occupations: agriculture, domestic service, mining and quarrying, prostitution, military and naval service, protoindustrial urban skilled and semiskilled labor, teaching, and the highest levels of government. It had its origins in debt servitude, sale of oneself or one's family members, kidnapping, captivity in slave raids or warfare, and punishment for crime. (Indeed, the Thirteenth Amendment today permits slavery and involuntary servitude "as a punishment for crime whereof the party shall have been duly convicted.")[3]

In Europe slavery gradually evolved into less severe forms of unfreedom, such as serfdom and villeinage. But the Portuguese circum-African navigations in the fifteenth century opened Africa to five centuries of slave trade exploitation, as the British, Dutch, French, Spanish, and Americans rushed in. The Spanish and Portuguese enslaved native Americans, and the British eagerly imitated them for a time in the seventeenth century. In a mercantilist international economic order, export staples such as coffee, tobacco, sugar, rice, and later cotton created a voracious demand for unskilled and unfree labor to work the plantation economies of the mainland and island colonies.

Thus by the time the U.S. Constitution was drafted, slavery was in no way an aberrant institution in human experience. Whether or not Eric Williams was correct in assigning slavery a crucial role in the development of the Atlantic capitalist economies,[4] it was vital to some sectors of the American economy in 1787. In the long view, Orlando Patterson's judgment is unassailable:

> There is nothing notably peculiar about the institution of slavery. It has existed from before the dawn of human history right down to the twentieth century, in the most primitive of human societies and the most civilized. There is no region on earth that has not at some time harbored the institution.

From this conclusion, certain political consequences follow:

> Slavery is associated . . . with the emergence of several of the most profoundly cherished ideals and beliefs in the Western tradition. The idea of freedom and the concept of property were both intimately bound up with the rise of slavery, their very antithesis.

Hence, Patterson concludes, "slavery and freedom are intimately connected."[5]

Slavery's legal origins in the island and mainland colonies of British North America are shrouded in ambiguity and obscurity, making it impossible to assign a precise time or pattern to its inception here.[6] In the Chesapeake, law coalesced around custom to create slavery.[7] Blacks originally arrived in Virginia and Maryland in some sort of unfree status—servitude often, not always slavery. During the first generation laws began to recognize or reflect race distinctions and then to embody them in a structure of laws that regulated unfree status, identifying the most severe grade of unfreedom—slavery— with race. But before the law of slavery hardened into a code (by 1705 in Virginia and 1715 in Maryland), blacks, both slave and free, were able to make a reasonably decent life for themselves, buying themselves and their kin out of slavery, accumulating property, and resorting to the legal process to protect themselves and their property.

New York was a special case. When the English first seized New Netherlands from the Dutch in 1664, they found slavery established there, but in a form so mild that it was scarcely recognizable as the predecessor of the later severely repressive racial slavery characteristic of the English colonies. Under the Dutch regime black slaves could

25

own land, could intermarry with whites and other free persons, were embodied in the militia, were easily manumitted, and could move into the peculiar status of "half-freedom," a sort of part-time slavery under which the master granted the slave his freedom in return for some annual labor or cash payment.[8] The English promptly moved to displace this relatively benign system with the harsher regime characteristic of the English colonies.[9]

In the New England colonies and Carolina, by contrast, slavery was imposed almost from the outset, for Indians after the Pequot War (1637) in the former and by John Locke in the Fundamental Constitutions for the latter. But whether established immediately or incrementally, slavery was an integral part of the legal order of nearly every colony by the time of the American Revolution.[10]

The law of slavery in the British American colonies expanded as the institution itself grew throughout the eighteenth century.[11] In its fully matured state of development, attained by the middle of the eighteenth century, the law established four fundamental characteristics of American slavery:

• Slavery in British America was above all racial slavery, in which the people subjected to it were identified by race (Negro, Indian, mulatto, and mestizo). Religious status (that is, pagan versus baptized Christian) was irrelevant in the eighteenth century.
• Slave status was derived from the legal condition of the mother, not the father. In this matter the common law jurisdictions were forced to adopt the civil law rule, *partus sequitur ventrem*, "the [condition of the] offspring follows [that of] the womb."
• Slavery was a lifetime condition, which distinguished it from indentured servitude.
• The slave was reduced to a condition of property, a vendible commodity, a capitalized asset—a human being reduced to the condition of a thing. Eventually, after considerable experimentation, the colonies worked out a status known as "chattel personal," whereby the slave was in the eyes of the law an item of personalty (like a horse or a wagon) rather than of realty.

These four elements constitute only the bare bones of the legal condition of slavery, however. Most of the law of slavery, both before and after independence, consisted of a detailed regulation of the slaves' behavior. The colonies created an elaborate listing of slave criminal offenses, for which they sometimes imposed atrocious punishments, including dismemberment, branding, slitting, castration, and judicially prescribed torture (including, in a few instances, burning or starving to death). The standard punishment for petty offenses was a whipping, an almost universal indicium of the status of slavery. The statutes also regulated the behavior of whites and free blacks in innumerable ways, as by forbidding whites to marry or associate with blacks, by impressing whites into service as slave patrollers, by prohibiting trade with blacks, and so on. The law made no attempt, however, to use public force to compel blacks to work. For that the master was left to his own devices. The American law of slavery was almost entirely a body of race control; only indirectly did it strive to coerce labor.

We mislead ourselves when we view the law of slavery as an aberration in a corpus of Anglo-American law that was otherwise *in favorem libertatis*. The law of slavery was not isolated in its suppression of one class of people for the benefit of others. Slavery's sibling, indentured servitude, was regulated as extensively and almost as harshly as slavery, the principal differences being that most servants were white and all could look forward to freedom if they survived the period of their indenture. The sumptuary laws of the colonial period sought persistently and unsuccessfully to police the behavior of lower classes by limiting how much money they could earn and, more important, how they could spend it. A Virginia statute (modeled on earlier English legislation) achieved some benchmark of meanness and specificity when it prohibited persons in seven specified lower-class occupations—farmers, sailors, fishermen, craftsmen, laborers, apprentices, and servants—from enjoying themselves at "Bear-baiting, Bull-baiting, Bowling, Cards, Cock-fighting, Coits, Dice, Football, Nine-pins, [and] Tennis."[12] Such legislation should not surprise us. America was a stratified, class-ranked society, and its laws merely reflected its innate character. Slavery was different only in degree, not in kind.

Slavery and Progress

Slavery seems to us an utterly regressive system, morally abhorrent and economically inefficient.[13] David Brion Davis has recently reminded us, however, that until the nineteenth century slavery was linked with progress.

> Plantation slavery, far from being an aberration invented by lawless buccaneers and lazy New World adventurers, as nineteenth-century liberals often charged, was a creation of the most progressive peoples and forces in Europe—Italian merchants; Iberian explorers; Jewish inventors, traders, and cartographers; Dutch, German, and British investors and bankers.[14]

Arabs and other Muslims pioneered the idea that slavery was a suitable condition for racially inferior peoples, benefiting not only the master class (by exempting them from heavy and tedious labor) but the submerged class as well, by bringing them into the light of an advanced civilization and the true religion. Christians as well as Muslims believed that slavery was essential for economic development and the progress of their civilizations.

A peculiar combination of Enlightenment humanism, classical liberal economics, and evangelical Christianity reversed those assumptions in the nineteenth century and produced our modern antislavery moral consciousness. But the men who drafted and ratified the Constitution lived in the earlier world, where it was natural for most of them to assume that slavery was the handmaiden of progress.[15] The great constitutional struggles of the nineteenth century came about precisely because the Constitution of 1787 contained no implicit assumptions that slavery was incompatible with the progressive governmental order that the document created.

White Views of Blacks in 1787

None of the members of the Philadelphia convention or the delegates to the ratifying conventions had any desire to incorporate black slaves into the body politic. Slaves, by definition, were excluded from political capacity. As to free blacks (then a relatively tiny group in absolute numbers),[16] very few white Americans could even envision their being embodied in the American political order. John Jay explained to the English abolitionist Granville Sharp in 1788 that "the great majority" of Americans condoned slavery and "very few among them even doubted the propriety and rectitude of it."[17]

We condemn Chief Justice Roger B. Taney's statement in his *Dred Scott* opinion that blacks in 1787 "had for more than a century before been regarded as beings of an inferior order, and altogether unfit to associate with the white race, either in social or political relations; and so far inferior, that they had no rights which the white man was bound to respect."[18] But we forget that his statement was a fair description of the constitutional world of 1787 at both the federal and the state levels. Given the prevalent racism of the eighteenth century, we may no more expect the original Constitution to contain an implicit egalitarian promise than we may expect it to confer full political capacity on women.

It must be granted, though, that changes were afoot in the 1780s. The American Revolution had a profound effect on the constitutional status of slavery, albeit of an ambivalent sort.[19] The revolution and the ensuing War for Independence weakened slavery as an institution in several important ways. The ideological concepts of slavery and freedom presented an unavoidable challenge to white Americans: what consequences did freedom from British "slavery" (of the rhetorical kind) have for freedom of blacks from American slavery (of the real kind)? Did the Declaration of Independence apply to black slaves? Less abstractly, the revolution and war also created, for the first time, a visible (though small) segment of the population that was anomalous in that it was black but free. The prevailing identity of race and status—white:free, black:slave—was undermined.

The antislavery impact of the American Revolution coincided with the beginning of an organized abolition movement in the United States. Although scattered and atypical voices had condemned slavery in America ever since the Germantown (Pennsylvania) Protest of 1688, it was only during the War for Independence that benevolent persons organized the state antislavery and black welfare groups known collectively as the abolition societies. Though gradualist in assumptions, the abolition societies were legally and constitutionally oriented and thus began to shape the debate over slavery in constitutional terms. They drew attention, for example, to the problems of fugitive slaves and the strains on interstate relations that were caused by the handing over, or rendition, of such slaves. At the same time, as an offset to the good done by the abolition societies, the southern states began to tighten up their laws controlling slaves and inhibiting manumissions, premising the harsher new slavery regime on explicitly racist considerations.

Southerners were not deceived by their own rhetoric about liberty and equality of rights. The delegates to the 1776 convention that approved Virginia's Declaration of Rights, America's first bill of rights and the prototype for all subsequent state bills of rights, noticed that its Article I provided that "all men are by nature equally free and independent, and have certain inherent rights" and that these rights included "life and liberty."[20] Obviously, such a statement could not be taken literally or applied to black slaves. Edmund Pendleton provided a resolution of their dilemma when he suggested adding a phrase after the word "rights": "of which, when they enter into a state of society." This, Virginians agreed, exempted slaves from the body politic. Such a meaning might not be obvious to someone outside a slave society, but to Virginians and other slaveholders it made plain something that was axiomatic in the slave states: black slaves were simply not members of "society." They were an alien mass, in society but not of it.[21]

Slavery and the Constitutional Convention

With these trends going on apace in the states, the Constitutional Convention met in Philadelphia in 1787. Twentieth-century interpretations of the convention, following the broader lines of American historiography generally, assign slavery an inconspicuous and peripheral role at the convention.[22] According to this dominant interpretation, pioneered by Max Farrand in 1913 and canonical ever since,[23] the central dispute at Philadelphia involved the distribution of power between the so-called large states at the convention and the small, the former seeking representation (and therefore power) in the national government on the basis of population and the latter seeking to preserve the "one state–one vote" apportionment of political power under the Articles of Confederation. This crisis was supposedly resolved by the so-called Great Compromise, whereby each side got something of what it wanted through the differing modes of representation in the bicameral national legislature.

This traditional interpretation is fundamentally out of focus. James Madison understood this clearly, and perhaps if we had listened to his words more attentively, we would not have been beguiled into thinking that the Philadelphia convention had little to do with slavery. On June 30 Madison reviewed the splits among the states at the convention and observed:

> The States were divided into different interests not by their difference of size, but by other circumstances; the most material of which resulted partly from climate, but principally from the effects of their having or not having slaves. These two causes concurred in forming the great division of interests in the U. States. It did not lie between the large & small States: it lay between the Northern & Southern.[24]

During the next two weeks the convention deadlocked over the apportionment of political power in the Union. One reason for the seriousness of the deadlock was that the delegates persisted in arguing about the wrong issues, and on July 14 Madison impatiently reminded them again of what was really at stake:

> It seemed now to be pretty well understood that the real difference of interests lay, not between the large & small but between the N. & Southn. States. The institution of slavery & its consequences formed the line of discrimination.[25]

A carefully wrought compromise package resolved the first great division at Philadelphia. Bicameralism with representation by state in one house and by population in the other took care of the nominal problem, but the heart of the compromise was the "federal number" clause, by which apportionment of political power in the House of Representatives was based on the slave states'[26] being able to count three-fifths of their slaves as part of the population on which apportionment was based.[27] Had slaves been excluded entirely from representation, the slave states would have had 41 percent of the votes in the House; had they been wholly included, those states would have had 50 percent; and by the federal number, they got 47 percent.[28] Well might Charles Pinckney explain to his fellow delegates at the South Carolina ratifying convention that "considering all the circumstances, we have made the best terms for the security of [slavery] it was in our power to make. We would have made better if we could, but on the whole, I do not think them bad."[29]

Moreover, the federal number clause was a double concession to slave interests. Not only did it inflate the voting power of the slave-state bloc; it was also the basis for apportionment of direct taxes and thus guaranteed that any future levy based on direct taxation would include a built-in partial exemption for one species of property, slaves. So important was this latter concession that it was redundantly written into the Constitution twice.[30] The provision also served as a security against some future antislavery taxation based on a capitation (head tax) laid on all the slaves.

The orthodox interpretation of the Constitutional Convention sees only one great crisis there. In reality there were two, the second also centering on slavery. The Committee of Detail, sitting in late July and early August, inserted into the draft constitution a prohibition on any effort by Congress to abolish or tax the international slave trade. Virginia's Governor Edmund Randolph drafted the clause, probably at the behest of the South Carolina delegates. When the clause came to the floor, it provoked an explosion from northern delegates like Gouverneur Morris of Pennsylvania and Rufus King of Massachusetts, who condemned the immorality of the trade as well as the Carolinians' greed and obstinacy. This new confrontation threatened to undo the earlier compromise and dissolve the Union.

Alarmed members of the Connecticut delegation, Oliver Ellsworth and Roger Sherman, were instrumental in forging another compromise to resolve the second impasse. This package, more intricate than the first, consisted of an interrelated complex of balancing concessions. Congress would be empowered to stop the international slave trade but not for twenty years and even then could permit it for a longer period if it wished. (No mention was made of the domestic slave trade. Later defenders of slavery insisted, with reason, that the explicit grant of power to Congress over the high-seas trade was an implicit denial of its power over the internal trade.) Imported slaves might be taxed but only up to a ceiling of $10 a head. All direct taxes had to be apportioned; navigation acts needed only a majority vote, rather than two-thirds, for passage (this was the quid pro quo to the New England carrying states for the slave trade concession to the Deep South); Congress and the states were both forbidden to lay export taxes; and the slave trade clause was made unamendable.[31]

Even these two major concessions did not sate the Carolinians' demands for the security of slavery. Near the close of the convention, on August 28, Pierce Butler and Charles Cotesworth Pinckney demanded a provision for the return of runaway slaves, and it was incorporated into the Constitution the next day.[32] The phrasing of the clause, like every other reference to slavery in the Constitution, afforded some spurious comfort to later generations of Americans embarrassed by the proslavery spirit of the Constitution. It referred not to "slaves" but to a "Person held to Service or Labour," thus resorting to an awkward euphemism. Why this reluctance to call things by their proper name? Luther Martin, a Maryland delegate, explained that his colleagues' sense of delicacy prompted them to avoid "expressions which might be odious in the ears of Americans, although they were willing to admit into their system those things which the expressions signified."[33]

So permeated was the Constitution with slavery that no less than nine of its clauses directly protected or referred to it. In addition to the three well-known clauses (three-fifths, slave trade, and fugitive slave), the Constitution embodied two clauses that redundantly required apportionment of direct taxes on the federal-number basis (the purpose being to prohibit Congress from levying an unapportioned capitation on slaves as an indirect means of encouraging their emancipation); two clauses empowering Congress to suppress domestic insurrections, which in the minds of the delegates included slave uprisings; a clause making two provisions (slave trade and apportionment of direct taxes) unamendable, the latter providing a perpetual security against some possible future antislavery impulse; and two clauses forbidding the federal government and the states from taxing exports, the idea being to prohibit an indirect tax on slavery by the taxation of the products of slave labor.[34]

The Framers' Intent

Slavery questions did not figure prominently in the ratification debates or in their best-known product, the *Federalist* papers. When slavery issues did surface, they were used opportunistically on both sides. Hence we can learn little about the framers' intent from these sources, and what we do glean is inferential. Expectably, the slave trade provision came under heavy attack in the states north of Virginia, while delegates from the slave states either extolled it or defended it with regrets, as James Iredell did in North Carolina: "Our situation makes it necessary to bear the evil as it is."[35] A similar tone of resigned apology and rationalization marked Madison's comments in *The Federalist*, although he went beyond other southern spokesmen in warning darkly of black political power and insurrections:

> an unhappy species of population abounding in some of the States, who during the calm of regular government are sunk below the level of men; but who in the tempestuous scenes of civil violence may emerge into the human character, and give a superiority of strength to any party with which they may associate themselves.[36]

All the framers, however, from the free and slave states alike, agreed that nothing in the Constitution contemplated the aboliton of slavery, particularly by federal action. In the Virginia convention, to cite one example, Patrick Henry, an opponent of ratification, used any stick available to beat the dog of the Constitution, and he conjured up the specter of a national emancipation. Madison indignantly spurned the idea: "There is no power to warrant it. . . . I believe such an idea never entered into any American breast." Edmund Randolph seconded him: "The southern states, even South-Carolina herself, conceived [slaves] to be secure by these words [that is, the slave trade clause]. . . . There was not a member of the Virginia delegation who had the smallest suspicion of the abolition of slavery."[37]

The Philadelphia convention did not labor in a vacuum. Its decisions concerning slavery must be considered in connection with actions taken concurrently by the Confederation Congress meeting in New York City. We do not know whether the two bodies actively coordinated their efforts in the summer of 1787 to accomplish a settlement of all slavery questions then before the nascent nation. What is important, however, is the combined effect of the Constitution and the Northwest Ordinance, enacted by Congress in the summer of 1787, on the future of slavery in the new nation. The two great constitutive charters comprehensively resolved every constitutional question of the era that involved slavery. Slavery was excluded from the Northwest Territory but enjoyed tacit permission to spread into the greater expanses of lands south of the Ohio River, which most Americans of the time expected to outstrip the Northwest Territory in population and wealth.[38] The Northwest Ordinance also contained a fugitive slave clause that partially offset the exclusion of slavery.

William Freehling has argued that although the bequest of the framers with respect to slavery was mixed, in the long term they ensured the destruction of the peculiar institution as a consequence of four policies or attitudes that they inaugurated: (1) they began the gradual abolition of slavery in the northern states; (2) they excluded slavery from the Northwest Territory; (3) in 1807 they closed off the international slave trade; and (4) they articulated and passed on an attitude that slavery was an evil and followed that precept by manumitting a few slaves. Although he freely concedes the proslavery character of the Constitution—"the Constitution perpetually protected an institution the Fathers liked to call temporary"—Freehling argues that on balance the antislavery legacy of the founders' generation doomed slavery eventually.[39] This is a generous estimate but a valid one. Yet it should not obscure the fact that the framers' generation also embedded slavery so firmly in the constitutional order that it required nothing less than a revolution in attitudes, followed by the slaughter of some six hundred thousand Americans, to eradicate it.

The charters of 1787 left slavery almost entirely a matter to be controlled by the states, not the federal government.[40] This meant that, viewed realistically, slavery in America was to be a perpetual institution. In states where slave monoculture was vibrant, there was no hope of eliminating slavery short of the millennium. And even in those other states south of Pennsylvania where its economic significance was beginning to dwindle, it could not be abolished because, as Thomas Jefferson laconically put it, "the public mind would not yet bear the proposition."[41]

Nor did prospects improve over time; if anything, they deteriorated. A generation after American independence, Jefferson resignedly conceded: "I have long since given up the expectation of any early provision for the extinguishment of slavery among us."[42] The only terms in which Virginians could conceive of black liberation were fantastic, as when Governor James Monroe remarked wistfully after Gabriel Prosser's rebellion in Richmond (1800): "It would certainly be a very fortunate attainment, if we could make [blacks] instrumental to their own emancipation, by a process gradual and certain, on principles consistent with humanity, without expense or inconvenience to ourselves."[43]

The Abolitionists and Responses to Them

Thus in the late eighteenth century it was not slavery but emancipation that was the exception and aberration. That was to change in the next half-century, however, and the process of change had already

begun by 1787. In constitutional terms, the foremost accomplishment
,of the era was the Pennsylvania Gradual Abolition Act of 1780. It freed
all *postnati* but held them in servitude until age twenty-eight. The
statute required registration of all slaves in the state, freeing those not
so registered, and reversed the presumption that a black was a
slave.[44] Rhode Island and Connecticut promptly followed suit; New
York and New Jersey delayed emancipation until the early nineteenth
century. The Quock Walker cases in Massachusetts (1781–1783) were
the highlight of slavery's rapid legal disintegration in the Bay State.[45]

The activity of the abolition societies provided invaluable legal
and welfare services to free and fugitive blacks in the gradual-aboli-
tion states, as well as effective state and federal lobbying until the War
of 1812. After a decade and a half of dormancy following the war, the
rejuvenated antislavery movement placed the issues of slavery and
abolition permanently on the national agenda.

The novelty and audacity of such ideas and ventures stunned
American society. Antebellum Americans responded to the abolitionists' innovations along five constitutional paths, three antislavery
and two proslavery. Each of us will find one more persuasive than the
others as a matter of morality and policy. But in their time each was a
legitimate response to the changing legal status of slavery.

One sect of abolitionists, whom I have elsewhere labeled Garrisonians[46] but will here call literalists, accepted the proslavery character
of the Constitution at face value. As their theological perceptions
intensified in the late 1830s, they demanded that all human institutions heed Jesus Christ's invitation: "Be ye therefore perfect, even as
your Father which is in Heaven is perfect" (Matthew 5:48). They
demanded no less of their constitutional order, and when they saw
how extensively it was implicated in slaveholding, they condemned it
and called on their fellow Americans to withdraw their allegiance
from it, individually and, as free states, collectively by secession.

It is easy to sympathize with the sense of frustration felt by the
followers of William Lloyd Garrison and even with their somewhat
paranoid vision of an omnipresent slavocratic conspiracy on its way to
an apocalyptic confrontation with God's elect. But practical consequences followed from the literalists' position, which they persistently evaded. As their opponents within the antislavery
movement never tired of reminding them, who would free the slaves
if decent people withdrew their participation from American political
life? Could the followers of Christ afford the luxury of disdaining the
instrumentalities of sinful humanity when nothing else was at hand to
effectuate emancipation? Was perfectionism not just self-indulgent
posturing? Garrisonians came up with ingenious and half-persuasive

rebuttals to these criticisms, but their responses came increasingly to seem sophistry, rationalization, and hypocrisy.

At the opposite end of the ideological spectrum from the literalists was a tiny but influential splinter of the antislavery movement referred to by the late Robert Cover as constitutional utopians.[47] They contended that the Constitution was actually an antislavery document that had acquired a proslavery gloss in the years since 1787. With a willful, not to say perverse, disingenuousness, they construed away all the proslavery clauses, while at the same time they seized on every conceivable phrase in the document that might be given an antislavery interpretation.

It was they, for example, who pioneered the idea that the due process clause of the Fifth Amendment outlawed slavery because of its guarantee that life, liberty, and property not be taken without due process of law. The upstate New York lawyer Alvan Stewart, the Boston attorney Lysander Spooner, and the lay activist Theodore Weld all pursued extravagant theories of federal power to abolish slavery in the states, demanding an end to the interstate slave trade under Congress's commerce clause powers, the destruction of slavery itself through the various Article I and Article II war powers, the abolition of slavery in the territories under Article IV powers, and refusal to admit new slave states, also under Article IV authority.

Granted that the utopians were prophetic zealots, what is remarkable about their views is that slavery was abolished precisely along the lines they suggested. A new social order replaced it that conformed to their vision of an egalitarian society where the rights of all would be protected by federal power derived from concepts of a universal due process of law, equal protection of the laws, national citizenship, and a guarantee of privileges and immunities secured to all people, both within a state and among the states. Their experience raises for us the question of the utility of prophetic zeal or, if Cover's judgment is to be accepted, utopianism. Is there a role for those who see a vision of a perfect social order and pursue it unrealistically and uncompromisingly?

The third antislavery response is in some ways the most fascinating and instructive. Its proponents pursued two separate paths. The first path led this abolitionist mainstream group into politics, and the second directed its lawyer members into innovative professional directions. In its origins the new antislavery movement of the 1830s eschewed partisan politics, but, like the defunct abolition societies, it lobbied for political goals. As the decade wore on, this strategy came to seem sterile and self-defeating, particularly to western abolitionists like the Ohio attorney Salmon P. Chase, who sensed the possibility of considerable impact in conventional political action. Repelled even-handedly both by Garrisonian perfectionism and by the utopians' demand for federal abolition, political action abolitionists organized the Liberty party in 1840 and ran the converted slaveholder James G. Birney for president. Their party creed at first consisted of one plank, summed up in their concept of "divorce": the absolute separation of the federal government and the free states from any involvement with slavery.

This program had numerous possibilities, such as prohibition of the interstate slave trade, but it realized its potential most effectively in 1846 when it hitched a ride on the coattails of the Wilmot Proviso, which would have excluded slavery from any territories acquired in the Mexican War. The proviso was unexpectedly popular, but this proved to be as much a short-term liability as a long-run blessing for the political action abolitionists. In the short term the Wilmot Proviso plank linked the antislavery movement to movements seeking to keep black people, not just slavery, out of the western territories. This link was affirmed in 1848, when the Liberty party submerged its separate existence in the Free Soil party and joined hands with racist, opportunist Democrats who detested blacks as much as they disliked southern domination of their national party. In the long run, however, the Wilmot Proviso program pointed the way to the more comprehensive antislavery program of Abraham Lincoln and the Republicans.

The legal action alternative of the antislavery mainstream is less well known. A group of young Massachusetts, Ohio, and New York abolitionists who were lawyers used their professional opportunities to challenge slavery in courts and legislatures. James C. Alvord persuaded the Massachusetts General Court to revive the writ of human replevin, a long-obsolete means of regaining custody of a person from someone detaining him, to be used in the defense of alleged fugitive slaves. Ellis Gray Loring served as counsel (together with the unlikely conservative Whig Rufus Choate) in the celebrated *Med* case of 1836,[48] which not only secured the freedom of a sojourner's slave but also reaffirmed the doctrine of Somerset's case in American law.[49] Loring was also of counsel, along with Theodore Sedgwick, Jr., Roger Sherman Baldwin, and the aged John Quincy Adams, in the *Amistad* litigation, which secured the freedom of a shipload of Africans seized in the international slave trade. Samuel E. Sewall led the defense efforts in the *Latimer* case of 1842, the first of the fugitive slave recapture attempts that challenged the conscience of lawyers and judges by confrontation with an unjust law.[50]

These abolitionist lawyers had the best of all worlds: they served their conscience, remained within the bounds of socially acceptable behavior, and provided a service to their cause for which they were best qualified: professional representation. Their example encouraged later lawyers and lay persons to attempt fugitive slave rescues in the 1850s and, through them, to challenge the Fugitive Slave Act of 1850 and slavery itself in the dramatic rescue cases of the decade: Jerry (Syracuse, New York, 1851), Christiana (Pennsylvania, 1851), Shadrach and Thomas Sims (Boston, 1851), Anthony Burns (Boston, 1854), and the Oberlin-Wellington Rescue (Ohio, 1858). They and their successors were responsible for the enactment of the personal liberty laws of nearly all the northern states, providing a repertoire of procedural devices to protect the liberty of captured blacks, including the right to jury trial, the writ of habeas corpus, and the services of states' attorneys.

Each of these antislavery responses, however, was a divergence from the letter and the spirit of the Constitution of 1787. Many Americans of the 1850s—perhaps a majority, although we can never know—stood by the old order: "the Constitution as it is, the Union as it was," in the words of wartime Democrats. Their attitudes varied but only within a narrow band along the ideological spectrum: slavery might be regrettable, but it was necessary; in any event it existed, and its abolition was unthinkable; blacks, slave or free, were an anomaly in the American social order; and slavery or some comparable form of degradation was their only conceivable lot.

Lemuel Shaw, the great chief justice of the Massachusetts Supreme Judicial Court, spoke for those Americans during the Missouri controversy in 1820: "Slavery, though a great and acknowledged evil, must be regarded, to a certain extent, as a necessary one, too deeply interwoven in the texture of society to be wholly or speedily eradicated." Therefore, he concluded, "The principles of self-defense and powerful considerations of national safety, constituting a case of political and moral necessity, require at least the continuance of this great evil."[51] This vast group of white Americans, North and South, found their voice in the Democratic party throughout the antebellum period, which hallowed their racist sentiments and transmuted them into a doggedly consistent proslavery policy that, they correctly maintained, constituted the only true exposition of the framers' Constitution.

Northern Democrats remained faithful throughout the antebellum period to a party creed and orientation first formed in the stress of the Missouri crises of 1819–1821. For forty years they consistently elevated the Union and the rights of the states as their highest values, subordinating all other considerations to them. Scholars disagree about the intensity and spontaneity of the Democrats'

Negrophobia and dedication to slavery. John McFaul sees their position as expediential: to Democrats the greatest possible evil was disunion and abolition the most serious threat to the stability of the Union. Hence their proslavery orientation derived not so much from hatred of blacks and love of slavery as from fears of a threat to the Union.[52] Others insist that Democrats were spontaneously, enthusiastically proslavery, racist, and hostile to abolitionists.[53] Democrats, in this view, would have joyously persecuted blacks, abolitionists, and other reformers even had they posed no threat to the Union.

We need not resolve this question of attitude and motivation here. What matters is that the northern Democrats cherished slavery as constitutionally protected. They sought to provide ironclad guarantees of its internal security in the states where it existed; to permit its expansion into all American territories; to support its penetration into the free states in the persons of sojourners' slaves and through fugitive recaptures; to suppress abolitionists by any means and to warp the Constitution in any way necessary to do so; to oppress free blacks; and—in striking contrast to their otherwise consistent states' rights credo—to expand the powers of the federal government and subordinate the states to achieve these ends. The northern Democrats were the group that remained closest to the original intentions, fears, hopes, and expectations of the framers.

Last, there were the political leaders of the slave states. The program of these men was articulated by John C. Calhoun from 1828 to his death in 1850 and after that by a generation of his intellectual progeny that included men like Jefferson Davis. They subsumed all the northern Democrats' attitudes but added to them the distinctive idea that slavery was universal in the American constitutional system except where it had been specifically abolished by positive law. They demanded that the free states revise their constitutional order by suppressing abolitionists, degrading free black citizens, and providing limitless participation in fugitive recaptures. The southern Democrats were the heirs of the Carolinians at Philadelphia in 1787.

Conclusion

Abraham Lincoln bespoke a northern consensus after 1858. Its central tenet was the exclusion of slavery from the territories. With that secured, Lincoln was prepared to grant the slave states any further security they demanded for slavery, including the original Thirteenth Amendment, which would have made slavery as perpetual as human institutions could make it. Just before his inauguration, he reiterated the Republican position on the territories, but "as to fugitive slaves, [slavery in the] District of Columbia, slave trade among the slave states, and whatever springs of necessity from the fact that the institution is amongst us, I care but little, so that what is done be comely, and not altogether outrageous."[54]

Lincoln's views have often been pilloried as racist; this misses the point. What was significant about his views was their innovative quality: the extent to which his constitutional beliefs and the northern consensus they embodied constituted a break from the American constitutional tradition that had stood unchallenged until the 1830s. In believing that slavery was a moral wrong, in seeking to put it "in the course of ultimate extinction," in insisting that it not spread further into any territories where it did not already exist, Lincoln and the Republican party sought to create a new constitutional order. They failed to accomplish that goal peacefully; eleven of the slave states chose independence and war to exempt themselves from the free-state vision. They too were innovators, first in their demand for federal protection of slavery in the territories before 1860 and then in the carefully wrought revisions of the slavery clauses in the Confederate national constitutions.

Why should we care one way or the other? Is this not just a pointless antiquarian exercise in retrospective judgment? No, it is not. For only by recognizing the extent to which the constitutional vision of Lincoln and the Republicans was a departure from the original Constitution can we understand the long struggles through the war, Reconstruction, and after to incorporate black Americans into the constitutional regime. Freedom, civil rights, and equality for them were not the delayed but inevitable realization of some immanent ideal in the Constitution. On the contrary: black freedom and equality were, and are, a revolutionary change in the original constitutional system, truly a new order of the ages not foreseen, anticipated, or desired by the framers.

Notes

1. Lewis B. Namier, "Symmetry and Repetition," in *Conflicts: Studies in Contemporary History* (London: Macmillan, 1942), p. 70.

2. Quoted in Madison's notes, August 22, in Max Farrand, ed., *The Records of the Federal Convention of 1787* (New Haven, Conn.: Yale University Press, 1911), vol. 2, p. 371.

3. Compare section 18 of Article I of the Constitution of the State of New Columbia (the state proposed to be created if the District of Columbia statehood constitutional amendment had been ratified), which declared in toto: "Slavery and involuntary servitude are prohibited." Period. Reprinted in

Philip G. Schrag, *Behind the Scenes: The Politics of a Constitutional Convention* (Washington, D.C.: Georgetown University Press, 1985), p. 263.

4. Eric Williams, *Capitalism and Slavery* (Chapel Hill: University of North Carolina Press, 1944).

5. Orlando Peterson, *Slavery and Social Death: A Comparative Study* (Cambridge, Mass.: Harvard University Press, 1982), pp. vii–ix. See also David Brion Davis, *The Problem of Slavery in Western Culture* (Ithaca, N.Y.: Cornell University Press, 1966).

6. Material in the following pages on slavery before the American Revolution is adapted from William M. Wiecek, "Law in the Morning of America" (Paper presented at the January 1986 meeting of the Association of American Law Schools), and from William M. Wiecek, "The Witch at the Christening: Slavery and the Constitution's Origins," in Leonard W. Levy and Dennis J. Mahoney, eds., *The Framing and Ratification of the Constitution* (New York: Macmillan, 1987), pp. 167–84.

7. On slavery's beginnings in the Chesapeake, see Jonathan L. Alpert, "The Origin of Slavery in the United States—the Maryland Precedent," *American Journal of Legal History,* vol. 14 (1970), pp. 189–221; A. Leon Higginbotham, Jr., *In the Matter of Color: Race and the American Legal Process* (New York: Oxford University Press, 1978), pp. 19–60; Winthrop D. Jordan, *White over Black: American Attitudes toward the Negro, 1550–1812* (Chapel Hill: University of North Carolina Press, 1968), pp. 71–82; and T. H. Breen and Stephen Innes, *"Myne Owne Ground": Race and Freedom on Virginia's Eastern Shore, 1640–1676* (New York: Oxford University Press, 1980), esp. pp. 72–114.

8. David Kobrin, *The Black Minority in Early New York* (Albany: n.p., 1971), pp. 11–13; and Edgar J. McManus, *A History of Negro Slavery in New York* (Syracuse, N.Y.: Syracuse University Press, 1966), pp. 1–22.

9. Pennsylvania, Rhode Island, the Jerseys, Delaware, and Georgia followed the Chesapeake–New York pattern of delayed imposition of complete slavery, whereby law gradually accumulated around custom and social reality.

10. On this legal order see Higginbotham, *In the Matter of Color,* passim; and William M. Wiecek, "The Statutory Law of Slavery and Race in the Thirteen Mainland Colonies of British America, *William and Mary Quarterly,* vol. 34 (1977), pp. 258–80. Slavery had only a nominal existence in New Hampshire and was not extensive in Connecticut.

11. This paragraph and the next summarize Wiecek, "Statutory Law." See also Higginbotham, *In the Matter of Color,* passim.

12. George Webb, *The Office and Authority of a Justice of the Peace* (Williamsburg, Va., 1736), p. 165.

13. On the economic efficiency point, however, compare Robert W. Fogel and Stanley L. Engerman, *Time on the Cross: The Economics of American Negro Slavery* (Boston: Little, Brown, 1974).

14. David Brion Davis, *Slavery and Human Progress* (New York: Oxford University Press, 1985), p. xvii.

15. Of the men at Philadelphia, Benjamin Franklin and Rufus King were

exceptions. Others, George Washington among them, may have had their doubts about slavery's association with progress, but they willingly subordinated those doubts in the interests of national union.

16. Less than one black in ten was free in 1790—roughly 60,000 in the thirteen states. Peter M. Bergman, *The Chronological History of the Negro in America* (New York: Harper and Row, 1969), p. 68. See also U.S. Bureau of the Census, *Negro Population in the United States, 1790–1915* (Washington, D.C., 1918), p. 57.

17. Jay to Sharp (1788), in Henry P. Johnston, ed., *The Correspondence and Public Papers of John Jay* (New York: Putnam's, 1890–1893), vol. 3, p. 342.

18. Dred Scott v. Sandford, 19 How. (60 U.S.) 393 (1857) at 407.

19. See, generally, Duncan J. MacLeod, *Slavery, Race, and the American Revolution* (Cambridge: Cambridge University Press, 1974).

20. The text of the Declaration of Rights is in William F. Swindler, ed., *Sources and Documents of United States Constitutions* (Dobbs Ferry, N.Y.: Oceana, 1979), vol. 10, pp. 48–50, at p. 49.

21. A. E. Dick Howard, *Commentaries on the Constitution of Virginia* (Charlottesville: University Press of Virginia, 1974), vol. 1, p. 62.

22. An excellent historiographic review of this subject is Staughton Lynd, "The Abolitionist Critique of the United States Constitution," in Martin Duberman, ed., *The Antislavery Vanguard: New Essays on the Abolitionists* (Princeton, N.J.: Princeton University Press, 1965), pp. 209–39.

23. Max Farrand, *The Framing of the Constitution of the United States* (New Haven, Conn.: Yale Univesity Press, 1913), pp. 105–10.

24. Farrand, *Records of the Federal Convention*, vol. 1, p. 486 (June 30).

25. Ibid., vol. 2, p. 10 (July 14).

26. Such usage is misleading here, because all the states were slave states in 1787, in the sense that slavery existed in each of them. I use the phrase "slave states" here to refer to Maryland, Virginia, North Carolina, South Carolina, and Georgia, where slavery was most entrenched politically and economically.

27. U.S. Constitution, Article I, section 2, clause 3.

28. Donald L. Robinson, *Slavery in the Structure of American Politics, 1765–1820* (New York: Harcourt Brace Jovanovich, 1971), p. 180. I have rounded off Robinson's figures.

29. Jonathan Elliot, comp., *Debates in the Several State Conventions on the Adoption of the Federal Constitution* (Philadelphia: Lippincott, 1901), vol. 4, p. 286.

30. U.S. Constitution, Art. I, sec. 2, cl. 3; and Art. I, sec. 9, cl. 4.

31. Art. I, sec. 9, cl. 1, 4, and 5; Art. I, sec. 10, cl. 2; and Art. V.

32. Art. IV, sec. 2, cl. 3.

33. Farrand, *Records of the Federal Convention*, vol. 3, p. 210; see the discussion of other authorities on this point in William M. Wiecek, *The Sources of Antislavery Constitutionalism in America, 1760–1848* (Ithaca, N.Y.: Cornell University Press, 1977), pp. 75–76.

34. Art. I, sec. 2, cl. 3; Art. I, sec. 9, cl. 1; Art. IV, sec. 2, cl. 3; Art. I, sec. 9,

cl. 4; Art. I, sec. 8, cl. 15; Art. IV, sec. 4, cl. 4; Art. V; Art. I, sec. 9, cl. 5; and Art. I, sec. 10, cl. 2.

35. James Iredell, "Answer to Mason's Objections," in Paul L. Ford, ed., *Pamphlets on the Constitution of the United States* . . . (Brooklyn, N.Y., 1888), p. 367.

36. Jacob E. Cooke, ed., *The Federalist* (Middletown, Conn.: Wesleyan University Press, 1961), p. 294 (Madison, no. 43).

37. Elliot, *Debates*, vol. 3, pp. 622, 698–99.

38. The relationship between the Philadelphia convention and the Confederation Congress was suggested in Staughton Lynd, "The Compromise of 1787" (1966), reprinted in Lynd, *Class Conflict, Slavery, and the United States Constitution* (Indianapolis, Ind.: Bobbs-Merrill, 1967), pp. 185–213.

39. William W. Freehling, "The Founding Fathers and Slavery," *American Historical Review*, vol. 77 (1972), pp. 81–93; quotation at p. 84.

40. The only exceptions to this general rule were Congress's explicit authority over the international slave trade after 1807 and its inferential authority over slavery in the territories and the admission of new states. The distortion of sectional political power embodied in the three-fifths clause also implicated the national government in slavery matters, but passively. The rendition of fugitive slaves was a matter of interstate comity in the beginning, rather than a recognized power of the federal government. See the discussion in Paul Finkelman, *An Imperfect Union: Slavery, Federalism, and Comity* (Chapel Hill: University of North Carolina Press, 1981), pp. 27–40.

41. Thomas Jefferson, "Autobiography," in Paul L. Ford, ed., *The Writings of Thomas Jefferson* (New York: Putnam's, 1892–1898), vol. 1, p. 68.

42. To William A. Burwell, January 28, 1805, ibid., vol. 8, p. 340.

43. Monroe to Jefferson, June 11, 1802, in Stanislaus M. Hamilton, ed., *The Writings of James Monroe* (New York: Putnam's Sons, 1898–1903), vol. 3, p. 353.

44. "An Act for the Gradual Abolition of Slavery," chap. 881, *Laws of the Commonwealth of Pennsylvania* (Philadelphia: Hall and Sellers, 1792–1801), vol. 1, pp. 838–42.

45. See John D. Cushing, "The Cushing Court and the Abolition of Slavery in Massachusetts: More Notes on the 'Quock Walker Case,' " *American Journal of Legal History*, vol. 5 (1961), pp. 118–44; and on gradual abolition generally, Arthur Zilversmit, *The First Emancipation: The Abolition of Slavery in the North* (Chicago: University of Chicago Press, 1967).

46. Wiecek, *Sources of Antislavery Constitutionalism*, chap. 10. For a sympathetic review of Garrisonian beliefs, see Aileen S. Kraditor, *Means and Ends in American Abolitionism: Garrison and His Critics on Strategy and Tactics, 1834–1850* (New York: Pantheon, 1969), pp. 197–217; and James B. Stewart, "The Aims and Impact of Garrisonian Abolitionism, 1840–1860," *Civil War History*, vol. 15 (1969), pp. 197–209.

47. Robert M. Cover, *Justice Accused: Antislavery and the Judicial Process* (New Haven, Conn.: Yale University Press, 1975), pp. 154–58.

48. Commonwealth v. Aves, 18 Pick. (35 Mass.) 193 (1836).

49. See the discussion in Leonard W. Levy, *The Law of the Commonwealth and*

Chief Justice Shaw: The Evolution of American Law, 1830–1860 (New York: Harper and Row, 1967; originally published 1957), chap. 5.

50. For a detailed evaluation of Sewall's role in *Latimer*, see William M. Wiecek, "*Latimer*: Lawyers, Abolitionists, and the Problem of Unjust Laws," in Lewis Perry and Michael Fellman, eds., *Antislavery Reconsidered: New Perspectives on the Abolitionists* (Baton Rouge: Louisiana State University Press, 1979), pp. 219–37.

51. [Lemuel Shaw], "Slavery and the Missouri Question," *North American Review,* vol. 10 (January 1820), pp. 137–68, at pp. 138, 143.

52. John McFaul, "Expediency vs. Morality: Jacksonian Politics and Slavery," *Journal of American History,* vol. 62 (1975), pp. 24–39.

53. Edward Pessen, *Jacksonian America: Society, Personality, Politics,* rev. ed. (Homewood, Ill.: Dorsey, 1978), pp. 301–3; Leonard L. Richards, "The Jacksonians and Slavery," in Perry and Fellman, *Antislavery Reconsidered,* pp. 99–118; and Harold M. Hyman and William M. Wiecek, *Equal Justice under Law: Constitutional Development, 1835–1875* (New York: Harper and Row, 1982), pp. 8–17.

54. Lincoln to William Seward, February 1, 1861, in Roy P. Basler, ed., *The Collected Works of Abraham Lincoln* (New Brunswick, N.J.: Rutgers University Press, 1953–1955), vol. 4, p. 183.

3

Slavery and the Moral Foundations of the American Republic

Herbert J. Storing

It is refreshing," said one of the dissenters in the case of *Dred Scott* v. *Sandford*, "to turn to the early incidents of our history and learn wisdom from the acts of the great men who have gone to their account."[1] It is a common opinion today, however, that, admirable as the American Founders may be in other respects, in their response to the institution of Negro slavery their example is one to be lived down rather than lived up to. A good expression of this opinion has recently come from the distinguished American historian John Hope Franklin. We need to face the fact, Franklin contends, that the Founders "betray[ed] the ideals to which they gave lip service." They failed to take an unequivocal stand against slavery. They regarded "human bondage and human dignity" as less important than "their own political and economic independence." They spoke "eloquently at one moment for the brotherhood of man and in the next moment den[ied] it to their black brothers." They "degrad[ed] the human spirit by equating five black men with three white men." The moral legacy of the Founders is shameful and harmful:

> Having created a tragically flawed revolutionary doctrine and a Constitution that did *not* bestow the blessings of liberty on its posterity, the Founding Fathers set the stage for every succeeding generation of American to apologize, compromise, and temporize on those principles of liberty that were supposed to be the very foundation of our system of government and way of life."[2]

This chapter first appeared in *The College* (St. John's College, Annapolis, Maryland), July 1976. It also appeared in Robert H. Horwitz, ed., *The Moral Foundations of the American Republic* (Charlottesville: University Press of Virginia, 1977).

This view of the American Founding—that the Founders excluded the Negroes from the "rights of man" expressed in the Declaration of Independence and sanctioned slavery and Negro inferiority in the Constitution—is a view that the radical Abolitionists, from whom John Hope Franklin descends, share with their proslavery antagonists. Indeed, one of the best, and surely most authoritative, expressions of this view came in the opinion of Chief Justice Taney in the famous Supreme Court case of *Dred Scott* v. *Sandford* in 1857, in which the Supreme Court, for the second time in its history, held an act of Congress unconstitutional and in which Taney tried to secure once and for all the place of slavery under the Constitution. I want to examine Taney's carefully worked-out reasoning, for there one can confront most clearly what is today the dominant opinion about the Founders and slavery.

Dred Scott was a slave owned by a Doctor Emerson, a surgeon in the U.S. Army. In 1834 Scott was taken by his master from Missouri to Rock Island, Illinois, where they lived for about two years, and from there to Fort Snelling in the federal "Louisiana territory," where they lived for another couple of years before returning to Missouri. On Emerson's death Scott tried to purchase his freedom from Mrs. Emerson. Failing in that, he sued in the Missouri courts for his freedom, on the ground that he had become free by virtue of his residence in a free state and a free territory. He won in the lower court, but the decision was reversed on appeal. The Supreme Court of Missouri, abandoning eight Missouri precedents and departing from the then almost universal adherence of Southern courts to the principle "once free, always free," held that, whatever his condition in Illinois and in federal territory, Scott was a slave upon his return to Missouri.

On Mrs. Emerson's remarriage, Scott became the property of her brother, John Sandford, a citizen of New York; and this enabled Scott to sue for his freedom in federal court under the provision of the Constitution that gives federal courts jurisdiction in cases between citizens of different states. He lost in the lower court and appealed to the Supreme Court, which in 1857 finally handed down its opinion—or rather its opinions, for all nine justices expressed their opinions, most at considerable length. I will be concerned here only with the opinion "of the court" given by Chief Justice Taney.

Taney held, in the first place, that because he was a Negro, Scott was not and could not be a citizen of the United States (whether he was free or not) and could therefore not sue in the federal courts on the grounds he had chosen. (I pass over Taney's dubious assumption that for a citizen of a state to be entitled to sue under the diversity clause he must establish citizenship of the United States.) Taney held, in the second place, that the federal act under which Scott claimed freedom, the Missouri Compromise Act of 1820 outlawing slavery in the northern part of the Louisiana Purchase, was unconstitutional: for Congress to prohibit slavery in federal territory was to deprive slave-owning citizens who might move into that territory of their property without due process of law.

These two holdings are the conclusions of two lines of argument, one concerning the status of Negroes and the other concerning the status of slavery, that provide my two themes. Taney emphasized throughout his opinion that he was merely giving effect to the Constitution. It was not his business to read into the Constitution the more favorable views toward the Negro that had emerged since the time of the Founding. Actually, as Lincoln correctly argued, opinion about Negroes had hardened rather than softened in the seventy years since the adoption of the Constitution.[3] But more important is the fact that Taney's reading of the Constitution and the views of the Founders was wrong, except perhaps in one very important respect.

Taney takes up first the question of Negro citizenship, then the question of Negro slavery; but it will be clearer if I reverse the order and look first at slavery. According to Taney, the Founders assumed the legitimacy of slavery; and back of that was a universal opinion of the inferiority of the Negro race.[4] Negroes "had for more than a century before been regarded as beings of an inferior order; and altogether unfit to associate with the white race, either in social or political relations; and so far inferior, that they had no rights which the white man was bound to respect; and that the negro might justly and lawfully be reduced to slavery for his benefit." "No one thought," Taney said, "of disputing" such opinions. Negroes "were never thought of or spoken of except as property."

Only on such a basis, it seemed to Taney, could the framers of the Declaration of Independence be absolved from utter hypocrisy. They *said* that "all men are created equal and are endowed by their Creator with certain unalienable rights." Yet they were, many of them, slaveholders; and they certainly did not destroy slavery. But there was no hypocrisy, because the writers of the Declaration "perfectly understood the meaning of the language they used, and how it would be understood by others; and they knew it would not, in any part of the civilized world, be supposed to embrace the negro race, which, by common consent, had been excluded from civilized governments and the family of nations, and doomed to slavery." The men of that age (that is, the white men) simply did not regard Negroes as included among the "all men" who are, according to the Declaration of Independence, "created equal"; and, Taney concluded, "no one misunderstood them."

This whole argument—and I repeat, it is identical to the common view today—is a gross calumny on the Founders. The truth is almost the exact opposite of Taney's account. The Founders understood quite clearly that Negroes, like men everywhere, were created equal and were endowed with unalienable rights. They did not say that all men were actually secured in the *exercise* of their rights or that they had the power to provide such security; but there was no doubt about the *rights*. Far from it being true that "negroes were never thought of except as property," not only Negroes but slaves were very frequently spoken of and treated as persons. All of the Constitutional provisions relating to slaves, for example, refer to them as persons. And while slaves were typically deprived of *civil* rights, they were regarded as persons under criminal law. As rational and, to some degree, morally responsible human beings, they were held capable of committing crimes, and they were protected by the law—in principle and surprisingly often in practice—against crimes committed against them. In the first three or four decades of our history, the injustice of slavery was very generally acknowledged, not merely in the North but in the South and particularly in Southern courts.

Since this is likely to be unfamiliar territory to most readers, let me give a couple of examples.

In 1820 the Superior Court in Mississippi was confronted with the question, there being no positive legislation covering the matter, whether the killing of a slave was murder under the common law.[5] The court held that it was; and this was the usual view of Southern courts that considered this question. The Mississippi judge began by emphasizing that "because individuals may have been deprived of many of their rights by society, it does not follow that they have been deprived of all their rights." The slave "is still a human being, and possesses all those rights, of which he is not deprived by the positive provisions of the law." Since the common law definition of murder is the taking away the life of a reasonable creature with malice aforethought and since a slave is a reasonable being, such a killing of a slave is murder.

Slavery is the creature, Southern as well as Northern judges said again and again, of positive law only; it has no support in natural law or in transcendent principles of justice. Yet slavery existed; it was lawful in the Southern states. Even when the judges were giving effect to the positive law of slavery (which they had a clear duty to do), they typically acknowledged the injustice of the institution.

In a Supreme Court case fifteen years before *Dred Scott*, *Prigg* v. *Pennsylvania* (1842), the Supreme Court upheld the constitutionality of the Fugitive Slave Act of 1793, which implemented the fugitive slave clause of the Constitution; the Court held that this federal power was exclusive, thereby invalidating state "personal liberty laws," which had been passed in a number of Northern states to try to give greater protection than the federal law provided to Negroes claimed as fugitive slaves.[6] The opinion was written by a strong antislavery man, Joseph Story, and many of Story's friends wondered how he could make such a decision. Story replied that his first obligation was to the law but that, in any case, he thought his opinion a great "triumph of freedom."[7] It was a triumph of freedom mainly because, while upholding the Fugitive Slave Law, Story took the opportunity to stress that slavery is a mere creature of positive law and has no support in natural law. "The state of slavery is deemed to be," in Story's words, "a mere municipal regulation, founded upon and limited to the range of the territorial laws." That means that the presumption is always against slavery, even while provisions of the positive law protecting slavery are being enforced.

The same view was common in the South. Indeed, contrary to Taney's claim that no one questioned the legitimacy of slavery, nothing was more common than Southern judges giving public utterance to the excruciating agony of trying to reconcile the law that protected slavery with the principle of justice that condemns it. One of the most interesting of these cases is an 1820 North Carolina case, *State* v. *Mann*, where the court held that a master cannot commit a legal battery upon his slave.[8] The court had held earlier that a white person could be punished for assault and battery against someone else's slave.[9] But the law cannot protect the slave, Judge Ruffin held, against his master, even in case of a wanton, cruel, senseless beating. Ruffin was offered by counsel the analogy of parent and child or master and apprentice, where the authority of the superior is limited and supervised by law. He reluctantly, but surely correctly, rejected the analogy on the ground that the end of these relations is the good and happiness of the child or the apprentice, whereas in U.S. slavery the end is nothing but the profit of the master. It is the wrongness of slavery that makes it impossible to limit it. "We cannot allow the right of the master to be brought into discussion in the courts of justice." To question that right is to deny it, and that cannot be the business of a judge in a slave state. "The slave, to remain a slave, must be made sensible that there is no appeal from his master. . . . I most freely confess sense of the harshness of this proposition; I feel it as deeply as any man can; and as a principle of moral right every person in his retirement must repudiate it. But in the actual condition of things it must be so. There is no remedy. . . . It constitutes the curse of slavery to both the bond and free portion of our population. But it is inherent in the relation of master and slave."

I should add that twenty years later, nevertheless, Ruffin upheld a conviction of murder in the case of an especially brutal, but probably not premeditated, killing by a master of his own slave.[10]

Another kind of case that was common in the Southern courts was like *Dred Scott;* it arose where a person who had been a slave but who had been taken to reside in a free state and then returned to a slave state sued in the courts of the latter for his freedom. As I have said, in such a case the Southern courts held (at least until the 1840s or 1850s) that such a person was free. Once the chains of slavery enforced by positive law are broken, they can never be restored.

A slave, Lydia, was taken in 1807 by her master from Missouri to free Indiana, where he registered her as his servant under Indiana's gradual emancipation law. He sold his right to her, but when her new master brought her back to Missouri, the court there upheld her claim to freedom.[11] The rights of her master had been destroyed in Indiana, "and we are not aware of any law of this state which can or does bring into operation the right of slavery when once destroyed." Can it be thought, the judge asked, that "the noxious atmosphere of this state, without any express law for the purpose, clamped upon her newly forged chains of slavery, after the old ones were destroyed? For the honor of our country, we cannot for a moment admit, that the bare treading of its soil, is thus dangerous, even to the degraded African."

The American Founders and their immediate descendants, North and South, not only believed in but emphasized the wrongness of slavery, at the same time that they wrestled with the fact of slavery and the enormous difficulty of getting rid of it. It was a fact; it seemed for the time being a necessity; but it was a curse—the curse of an unavoidable injustice.

It is true, as Taney said, that Negroes were thought to be inferior to whites; but it is not true that this was thought to justify slavery. In a famous section of his *Notes on the State of Virginia,* published in 1784, Thomas Jefferson reflected on Negroes and Negro slavery in terms which are today generally found offensive and which are in consequence usually distorted and misunderstood.[12] Proceeding in the spirit of the eighteenth-century student of natural history, and emphasizing the shameful lack of systematic study of this subject, Jefferson examined the differences between the races. He thought that the blacks "participate more of sensation than reflection." He judged them inferior to whites in physical beauty, in reason, and in imagination, though in many physical attributes and in what he called "endowments of the heart," or the "moral sense," they are equal. Jefferson did conclude that this inferiority was an obstacle to Negro emancipation; but the reason was not that it makes Negroes less entitled to liberty than whites or that their enslavement is in some way just—Jefferson emphatically and consistently held the contrary. He would have agreed fully with Lincoln's view that "in some respects [a Negro woman] certainly is not my equal, but in her natural right to eat the bread she earns with her own hands without asking leave of anyone else, she is my equal, and the equal of all others."[13] Negro inferiority hindered emancipation in Jefferson's view, not because it justified slavery, but because it increased the difficulty of knowing how to deal with Negroes, once freed. Before pursuing this, however, we need to return to Taney's defense of slavery in the Constitution.

Taney held that Congress cannot prohibit slavery in federal territory: "an Act of Congress which deprives a citizen of the United States of his liberty or property, merely because he came himself or brought his property into a particular Territory of the United States, and who had committed no offense against the laws, could hardly be dignified with the name of due process of law." Nor, Taney contended (and this is crucial and the point on which Taney abandoned both federal and state precedents) is there any difference between property in slaves and other property. In fact, he said, "the right of property in a slave is distinctly and expressly affirmed in the Constitution."[14] These words are striking: if one had to think of two adverbs that do *not* describe the way the Constitution acknowledged slavery, he could not do better than "distinctly and expressly."

No form of the word *slave* appears in the Consitution, and one would not know from the text alone that it was concerned with slavery at all. Today's beginning law students, I am told, are generally not aware that there are three provisions of the Consitution relating to slavery. This is testimony to the skill with which the framers wrote. Some concessions to slavery were thought to be necessary in order to secure the Union, with its promise of a broad and long-lasting foundation for freedom; the problem was to make the minimum concessions consistent with that end, to express them in language that would not sanction slavery, and so far as possible to avoid blotting a free Constitution with the stain of slavery. Frederick Douglass described it this way:

> I hold that the Federal Government was never, in its essence, anything but an anti-slavery government. Abolish slavery tomorrow, and not a sentence or syllable of the Consitution need be altered. It was purposely so framed as to give no claim, no sanction to the claim, of property in man. If in its origin slavery had any relation to the government, it was only as scaffolding to the magnificent structure, to be removed as soon as the building was completed.[15]

51

"Scaffolding" catches the intention exactly: support of slavery strong enough to allow the structure to be built, but unobtrusive enough to fade from view when the job was done.

Let us look at the provisions. Article I, sec. 2(3) provides, in a masterpiece of circumlocution:

> Representatives and direct Taxes shall be apportioned among the several States which may be included within this Union, according to their respective Numbers, which shall be determined by adding to the whole Number of free Persons, including those bound to Service for a Term of Years, and excluding Indians not taxed, three fifths of all other Persons.

"All other Persons" are slaves. Thus in counting population for purposes of determining the number of representatives and also apportioning land and poll taxes, five slaves count as three free persons. What this provision signifies in principle is extremely complex, and I will not exhaust the matter here.[16] The question came up in the Constitutional Convention in the course of a debate over whether numbers or wealth is the proper basis of representation. That issue was resolved, or avoided, by use of Madison's suggestion that numbers are in fact a good index to wealth. In the case of slaves, however, that is not so clear, partly because the productivity of slaves is thought to be lower than that of free men, so some kind of discount seemed appropriate. This line of reasoning is supported by recalling that the three-fifths rule originated under the Articles of Confederation as a way of apportioning population for purposes of laying requisitions on the states. Suggestions that the three-fifths rule implies a lack of full humanity in the slave, while not without some basis, are wide of the main point. The three-fifths clause is more a way of measuring wealth than of counting human beings represented in government; wealth can claim to be the basis for apportioning representation and is of course the basis for apportioning direct taxes. Given the limited importance of direct taxation, the provision was understood to be a bonus for the Southern slave states. That gives the common argument against the three-fifths clause an unusual twist. While it may be that the provision "degrades the human spirit by equating five black men [more correctly, five slaves] with three white men," it has to be noted that the Southerners would have been glad to count slaves on a one-for-one basis. The concession to slavery here was not in somehow paring the slave down to three-fifths but in counting him for as much as three-fifths of a free person.

Regarding the second constitutional provision relating to slavery, Justice Taney said, "the right to trade in [slave property], like an ordinary article of merchandise and property, was guaranteed to the citizens of the United States, in every State that might desire it, for twenty years."[17] Clearly this is a major concession to slavery. It protects not merely an existing slave population but the creation of new slaves. Practically, it allowed a substantial augmentation of the slave population and thus, of course, of the slave problem. Yet the concession is less than Taney suggests. Even on the basis of Taney's account, one might wonder why the slave trade is guaranteed only to those citizens "in every State that might desire it" rather than to all citizens; and one would surely ask why this guarantee was limited to twenty years. These qualifications suggest that there is something that is *not* ordinary about this particular article of merchandise and property. When we look at the clause itself, this suggestion is reenforced. The clause reads: "The Migration or Importation of such Persons as any of the States now existing shall think proper to admit, shall not be prohibited by the Congress prior to the year one thousand eight hundred and eight, but a tax or duty may be imposed on such Importation, not exceeding ten dollars for each Person" (Art. I, sec. 9[1]). We note that the form is not a guarantee of a right but a postponement of a power to prohibit. Moreover we see, what Taney neglects to point out, that the postponement of federal power to prohibit applies only to the states "now existing." We have here, apparently, a traditional or vested right or interest, which is to be preserved for a time but which Congress need not allow to spread to new states. The clause, fairly interpreted, gives a temporary respite to an illicit trade; the presumption was that Congress would, after twenty years, forbid this trade (as it would not and perhaps could not prohibit trade in ordinary articles of merchandise), and in fact Congress did so.

Finally, to quote Taney again, "the government in express terms is pledged to protect [slave property] in all future times, if the slave escapes from his owner."[18] Here is another major concession. It is a clear case of a new legal right of slavery—there was nothing like it under the Articles of Confederation. It amounts, moreover, to a kind of nationalization of slave property, in the sense that everyone in a free state has an obligation to assist in the enforcement, so far as fugitive slaves are concerned, of the institution of slavery. It is not surprising that this clause turned out to be the most intensely controversial of the three provisions dealing with slavery. Yet it was hardly noticed in the Northern ratification conventions. The fugitive slave clause in the Constitution, like its model in the Northwest Ordinance which outlawed slavery in the Northwest Territory, was the price of a broader freedom. And the price was grudgingly, at least narrowly, defined. Here are what Taney called "plain words—too plain to be misunderstood": "No Person held to Service or Labour in one State, under the Laws thereof, escaping into another, shall, in Consequence of any Law or Regulation therein, be discharged from such Service or Labour, but shall be delivered up on Claim of the Party to whom such Service or Labour may be due" (Art. IV, sec 2[3]). Whether or not these words are plain, they were carefully chosen.[19] The suggestion for such a provision was first made in the Constitutional Convention on August 28 by Pierce Butler and Charles Pinckney of South Carolina, who moved "to require fugitive slaves and servants to be delivered up like criminals." Following some discussion (in which, incidentally, Sherman equated "a slave or servant" and "a horse" for the purpose of limiting the slaveowner's claim), the motion was withdrawn, to be replaced the next day by the following version: "If any person *bound to service or labor* in any of the U——States shall escape into another State, he or she shall not be discharged from such service or labor, in consequence of any regulations subsisting in the State to which they escape, but shall be delivered up to the person *justly claiming* their service or labor," which was agreed to.[20] This was later revised by the Committee on Style to something close to the final version: "No person *legally held to service or labour* in one state, escaping into another, shall in consequence of regulations subsisting therein be discharged from such service or labour, but shall be delivered up on claim of the party to whom such service or labour *may be due.*" Thus the Committee on Style withdrew from the master the claim that he "justly claimed" the services of his slave, acknowledging only that the slave's labor "may be due." On September 15, the Committee on Style's description of a slave as a "person legally held to service or labour" (already probably a narrowing of the previous and morally more comprehensive decription, "bound to service or labour") was objected to by some who, in Madison's words, "thought the term (legal) equivocal, and favoring the idea that slavery was legal in a moral view." Thus "legally" was struck out and "under the laws thereof" inserted. Supposing that a concession to return fugitive slaves had to be made, it is hard to see how it could have been made in any way that would have given less sanction to the idea that property in slaves has the same moral status as other kinds of property.

The Founders did acknowledge slavery; they compromised with it. The effect was in the short run probably to strengthen it. Perhaps they could have done more to restrict it, though the words of a Missouri judge express what the Founders thought they were doing and, I think, probably the truth. "When the States assumed the rights of self-government, they found their citizens claiming a right of property in a miserable portion of the human race. Sound national policy required that the evil should be restricted as much as possible. What they could, they did."[21] "As those fathers marked it," Lincoln urged on the eve of the Civil War, "so let it be again marked, as an evil not to be extended, but to be tolerated and protected only because of and so far as its actual presence among us makes that toleration and protection a necessity."[22] Slavery was an evil to be tolerated, allowed to enter the Constitution only by the back door, grudgingly, unacknowledged, on the presumption that the house would be truly fit to live in only when it was gone, and that it would ultimately be gone.

In their accommodation to slavery, the Founders limited and confined it and carefully withheld any indication of moral approval, while they built a Union that they thought was the greatest instrument of human liberty ever made, that they thought would lead and that did in fact lead to the extinction of Negro slavery. It is common today to make harsh reference to the irony of ringing declarations of human rights coming from the pens of men who owned slaves. But I think that Professor Franklin is wrong when he says that "they simply would not or could not see how ridiculous their position was." They saw it all right, and they saw better than their critics how difficult it was to extricate themselves from that position in a reasonably equitable way. But they saw, too, a deeper irony: these masters knew that they were writing the texts in which their slaves would learn their rights.

Having, I hope, rescued the Founders from the common charge that they shamefully excluded Negroes from the principles of the Declaration of Independence, that they regarded their enslavement as just, and that in their Constitution they protected property in man like any other property, I must at least touch on a deeper question, where they do not come off so well. But at this deeper level the problem is not that they betrayed their principles, the common charge; the problem lies rather in the principles themselves. That very principle of individual liberty for which the Founders worked so brilliantly and successfully contains within itself an uncomfortably large opening toward slavery. The principle is the right of each individual to his life, his liberty, his pursuit of happiness as he sees fit. He is, to be sure, subject to constraints in the pursuit of his own interests because of the fact of other human beings with similar rights. But are these moral constraints or merely prudential ones? Locke says that under the law of nature each individual ought, as much as he can, "to preserve the rest of mankind" "when his own preservation comes not in competition."[23] Each individual is of course the judge of what his own preservation does require, and it would be a foolish man, an unnatural man, who would not, under conditions of extreme uncertainty, give himself every generous benefit of the doubt. Does this not tend to mean in practice that each individual has a right to pursue his own interests, as he sees fit and as he can? And is there not a strong tendency for that "as he can" to become conclusive? In civil society, indeed, each of us gives up the claim of sovereign judgment for the sake of the milder, surer benefits of a supreme judge. Even in that case there is a question whether the first principle does not remain that one may do what one can do. The Founders often described the problem of civil society as resulting from that tendency. In any case, regarding persons outside civil society, there is a strong implication that any duty I have to respect their rights is whatever residue is left after I have amply secured my own.

Now, in the case of American slavery, especially in the South at the time of the writing of the Constitution, there clearly was a conflict between the rights of the slaves and the self-preservation of the master. "[W]e have a wolf by the ears," Jefferson said, "and we can neither hold him, nor safely let him go. Justice is in one scale, and self preservation in the other."[24] Only an invincible naiveté can deny that Jefferson spoke truly. But the deeper issue, as I think Jefferson knew, is the tendency, under the principles of the Declaration of Independence itself, for justice to be reduced to self-preservation, for self-preservation to be defined as self-interest, and for self-interest to be defined as what is convenient and achievable. Thus the slave owner may resolve that it is necessary to keep his slaves in bondage for the compelling reason that if they were free they would kill him; but he may also decide, on the same basic principle, that he must keep them enslaved in order to protect his plantation, his children's patrimony, his flexibility of action, on which his preservation ultimately depends; and from that he may conclude that he is entitled to keep his slaves in bondage if he finds it convenient to do so. All of this presumes of course that he *can* keep his slaves in bondage. Nor does it in any way deny the right of the slave to resist his enslavement and to act the part of the master if he can. This whole chain of reasoning is a chilling clarification of the essential war that seems always to exist, at bottom, between man and man.

American Negro slavery, in this ironic and terrible sense, can be seen as a radicalization of the principle of individual liberty on which the American polity was founded. Jefferson wrote in his *Notes on the State of Virginia* of the demoralization of the masters caused by slavery and its threat to the whole institution of free government. Masters become tyrants and teach tyranny to their children (and, incidentally, to their slaves). Even more important, slavery, through its visible injustice, tends to destroy the moral foundation of civil society.

> And can the liberties of a nation be thought secure when we have removed their only firm basis, a conviction in the minds of the people that these liberties are of the gift of God? That they are not to be violated but with His wrath? Indeed I tremble for my country when I reflect that God is just; that his justice cannot sleep forever; that . . . an exchange of situation [between whites and blacks] is among possible events; that it may become probably [*sic*] by supernatural interference! The Almighty has no attribute which can take side with us in such a contest.[25]

I do not think that Jefferson was literally concerned with divine vengeance, but he was concerned with the underlying tension—so ruthlessly exposed in the institution of Negro slavery—between the doctrine of individual rights and the necessary moral ground of any government instituted to secure those rights.

Let me proceed, more briefly, to my second theme, Negro citizenship. Justice Taney was wrong in his claim that the Founding generation excluded Negroes from the principles of the Declaration of Independence. But he was not wrong in his claim that the Founders excluded Negroes from that "We the People" for whom and whose posterity the Constitution was made. Or rather, he was wrong in detail but right fundamentally.

Taney's reasonable contention was that citizens of the United States in 1787—the "People" by and for whom the Constitution was made—were all those people who were then citizens of the states. He went on to claim that Negroes were not then citizens of any states and are therefore forever excluded from U.S. citizenship. But it was easy to show, as Justice Curtis did, that free Negroes were citizens in many of the states; and Taney's argument excluding Negroes from U.S. citizenship collapses. In this matter Taney is simply wrong; but he had a better case at a deeper level. The way to this level is through the privileges and immunities clause, which was Taney's real concern here, even though it was not involved in the legal dispute. This clause provides that "the Citizens of each State shall be entitled to all Privileges and Immunities of Citizens in the several States." Taney said that the Southern states cannot be presumed to have agreed to a Constitution that would give any Northern state the power to make citizens of free blacks, who could then go to Southern states, claim there all of the privileges and immunities of citizens, and by their agitation and example disrupt the whole police system on which the maintenance of slavery, and the preservation of the white South, depended. The privileges and immunities clause was the knife by which Northern freedom cut into the South, as the fugitive slave clause was the knife by which Southern slavery cut into the North. And it could be said of the privileges and immunities clause that the South did agree, as the North agreed to the fugitive slave clause, even if it did not anticipate all the consequences; and that the bargain should be kept. But the deeper question is whether the Constitution was really meant to provide for a large-scale racially mixed polity. Here I think Taney was right, for although the answer is less clear than he says, it is nevertheless a fairly resounding no.

The position of most American statesmen from the time of the Declaration of Independence through the Civil War was well expressed by Jefferson in his autobiography: "Nothing is more certainly written in the book of fate, than that these two people are to be free; nor is it less certain that the two races, equally free, cannot live in the same government."[26] And in his *Notes on the State of Virginia* Jefferson gave perhaps the best explanation of this widely held view.[27] He gives an account of a scheme he had helped draft for reforming the laws of Virginia. Included in that plan was a provision for the emancipation of slaves, to be followed by their colonization to some suitable place, "sending them out with arms, implements of household and of the handicraft arts, seeds, pairs of the useful domestic animals etc., to declare them a free and independent people, and extend to them our alliance and protection, till they have acquired strength." At the same time, it was proposed that vessels be sent to other parts of the world for an equal number of white emigrants. Jefferson naturally anticipated the question, Why not leave the free blacks where they were and save the expense of resettling them and securing replacements? His answer can be collected under three heads. The first obstacle was the race prejudice of the whites—deep, aggressive, and invincible. Second was the blacks' sense of the injustice done to them, a sense sure to be kept alive by new injuries. Third were the natural differences between the races and particularly the actual and probably inherent inferiority of the blacks in certain respects that affect crucially the quality of civil society.

The first and second causes seemed to Jefferson and his generation to ensure that there would never be that sense of fellow feeling and mutual trust between the races that forms the indispensable social basis of civil society. The third (supposed Negro inferiority) expressed a concern not with the bare possibility but with the quality of civil life. Many of the advocates of Negro rights, Jefferson said, "while they wish to vindicate the liberty of human nature, are anxious also to preserve its dignity and beauty. Some of these, embarrassed by the question, 'What further is to be done with them?' join themselves in opposition with those who are actuated by sordid avarice only." Race prejudice, a tangled history of injustice, natural differences suggesting Negro inferiority—these are not promising materials for civil society.

These early American statesmen (including, by the way, many blacks) may have been wrong, as most of us would think today, in believing that a long-term biracial society was unfeasible and undesirable. They surely did not in fact provide any real alternative in their American Colonization Society and its minute settlement in Liberia. But we are likely to be too quick to assume that in trying to get rid of both slavery and Negroes they were being simply hypocritical or unprincipled. We have lost sight of the crucial difference between the two questions I am discussing: the question of freedom and the question of citizenship. To concede the Negro's right to freedom is not to concede his right to U.S. citizenship. And, on the other hand, to deny his right to U.S. citizenship is not to affirm that he is justly enslaved. There is nothing contradictory in arguing that while the Negroes have a human right to be free, they do not have a human right to be citizens of the United States. This distinction, which is today muddled inadvertently, was deliberately muddled by Stephen Douglas, and probably by Taney also. The former, Lincoln said in his magnificent speech on the *Dred Scott* decision, "finds the Republicans insisting that the Declaration of Independence includes ALL men, black as well as white; and forthwith he boldly denies that it includes negroes at all, and proceeds to argue gravely that all who contend it does, do so only because they want to vote, and eat, and sleep, and marry with negroes. He will have it that they cannot be consistent else. Now I protest against that counterfeit logic which concludes that, because I do not want a black woman for a *slave* I must necessarily want her for a *wife*. I need not have her for either, I can just leave her alone."[28]

Of course, the problem was that while an individual could "leave the Negro alone," the American polity could not. Unless there was to be a permanent class of underlings, Negro emancipation had to imply either political and social equality of the races in the United States or separation of the races into distinct polities. For Lincoln, as for nearly all American statesmen up to his time, only the latter seemed to hold any promise for the long-term viability and quality of the American polity. In advocating a policy of emancipation and colonization, the Founders may have been cold or unwise or inequitable, but they were not acting contrary to the principles of the Declaration of Independence. To put the point differently, American Negroes may have had a valid claim to U.S. citizenship (I think they did); but it was a claim depending on particular circumstances and history (and thus discussable on such grounds) quite distinct from their claim to freedom, which depended upon nothing but their humanity.

The American Founders would have done their work better, it is now generally thought, if they had seen the need for, and responded to, the challenge of a multiracial, heterogeneous, open society. Instead, they toyed with unrealistic schemes of colonization, temporized with racism and racial segregation, delayed justice for blacks unconscionably long, sanctioned second-class citizenship. They "set the stage," in John Hope Franklin's terms, "for every succeeding generation of Americans to apologize, compromise, and temporize on those principles of liberty that were supposed to be the very foundation of our system of government and way of life."[29]

What might one of the thoughtful Founders say in response to these charges and in the light of present-day circumstances in the United States?

First, I think he would be amazed at the degree to which blacks and whites have progressed in making a civil society together. I think he would frankly admit that he would never have expected anything like the degree of harmony, mutual trust and toleration, and opportunity for blacks that have been achieved in the United States at the bicentennial of our beginning. At the same time, on closer inspection, he might wonder whether even the elementary question of whether the races can live together in peace has yet been settled beyond doubt. Are the races so well bonded that long-term economic depression or large-scale war (fought perhaps mainly by black American soldiers against black or yellow enemies) could not still tear them apart?

Moreover, in defense of his "temporizing" with racism and segregation and injustice, our Founder might ask what else he could have done. What, he might slyly ask our generation, has been your most successful (perhaps your only successful) large-scale integration program? Surely the desegregation in the U.S. military forces. That example is interesting in two respects. First the success seems increasingly problematical, as festering racial antagonism and the worrisome prospect of an all-black army, or infantry, suggest. Second, to the extent that it is a success, why was that possible? Because an army is an army. But a political democracy is not an army. It rests on and is severely limited by opinion, which cannot be commanded. Prejudice—arbitrary liking and trust and, of course, also disliking and mistrust—is inherent in political life, and its role is greater as the polity is more democratic. To criticize a Jefferson or a Lincoln for yielding to, even sharing in, white prejudice is equivalent to demanding either that he get out of politics altogether—and leave it to the *merely* prejudiced—or that he become a despot.

Regarding the quality of civil life, as distinct from its bare possibility, our Founder might say much. He might point to the extraordinary vulgarity and triviality of American popular culture, to the difficulty that America has in generating any high culture of its own, to the superficiality of social bonds and community values. And he might ask whether these oft-observed and deplored characteristics of American civil life are not connected with its attempt to be all things to all men, with its attempt to embrace the most extreme heterogeneity, so that it can be nothing much to any of them.

Finally, however, I think our Founder might be intrigued, if not altogether persuaded, by the prospect of a free society consisting not merely of a huge aggregation of individuals but of diverse ethnic and religious and other groups. He would be interested in the possibility of a civil society, viable yet capable of exploring and exemplifying diverse significant human possibilties. He would see the point, I think (especially if he had read his Tocqueville), of criticisms by Negroes like W. E. B. Du Bois of the Declaration of Independence itself for a radical individualism that cuts each man off from his fellows and from God. While he would be skeptical, I think he would be interested in exploring the world into which Du Bois offers a window, a world that is built (perhaps more than Du Bois realized) on our Founders' principles and institutions, but that is nevertheless quite different from anything they imagined.

> If . . . there is substantial agreement in laws, language and religion; if there is a satisfactory adjustment of economic life, then there is no reason why, in the same country and on the same street, two or three great national ideals might not thrive and develop, that men of different races might not strive together for their race ideals as well, perhaps even better, than in isolation. Here, it seems to me, is the reading of the riddle that puzzles so many of us. We are Americans, not only by birth and by citizenship, but by our political ideals, our language, our religion. Farther than that, our Americanism does not go. At that point, we are Negroes, members of a vast historic race that from the very dawn of creation has slept, but half awakening in the dark forests of its African fatherland. We are the first fruits of this new nation, the harbinger of that black to-morrow which is yet destined to soften the whiteness of the Teutonic to-day. We are that people whose subtle sense of song has given America its only American music, its only American fairy tales, its

only touch of pathos and humor amid its mad money-getting plutocracy. As such, it is our duty to conserve our physical powers, our intellectual endowments, our spiritual ideals; as a race we must strive by race organization, by race solidarity, by race unity to the realization of that broader humanity which freely recognizes differences in men, but sternly deprecates inequality in their opportunities of development.[30]

Reflecting on thoughts like these and on present circumstances in the United States, our Founder might concede that the huge problem of racial heterogeneity, which his generation saw but could not master, may show the way to deal with another problem, which they did not see so clearly, the political and moral defects of mere individualism. He would surely point out that the foundation of this new polity is the old one; and he might wryly observe that his own principle of racial separation is, after all, an essential element in the new polity of racial and ethnic diversity. But I think he would concede, finally, that while in his heart of hearts he had thought that he and his generation had finished in its essentials the task of making the American polity, there is after all work still to be done.

Notes

1. Scott v. Sandford 19 How 393, 545 (1857) (Justice McLean).
2. John Hope Franklin, "The Moral Legacy of the Founding Fathers," *University of Chicago Magazine* (Summer 1975), pp. 10–13.
3. Abraham Lincoln, "The Dred Scott Decision," Speech at Springfield, June 26, 1857, in *Abraham Lincoln: His Speeches and Writings*, ed. Roy P. Basler (New York: World Publishing Co., 1946), p. 359.
4. Scott v. Sandford 19 How 407–10 (1857).
5. State v. Jones 1 Miss 83 (1820).
6. Prigg v. Pennsylvania 16 Pet 539, 611 (1842); cf. Taney's different view, 628.
7. William W. Story, ed., *Life and Letters of Joseph Story* (Boston: Charles C. Little and James Brown, 1851), vol. 2, pp. 390ff.
8. State v. Mann 13 N.C. 263 (1829).
9. State v. Hale 9 N.C. 582 (1823).
10. State v. Hoover 4 Dev & Bat (N.C.) 365 (1839).
11. Rankin v. Lydia 2 AK Marshall (Ky.) 470 (1820).
12. Thomas Jefferson, "Notes on the State of Virginia," Query 14, in Adrienne Koch and William Peden, eds., *The Life and Selected Writings of Thomas Jefferson* (New York: Modern Library, 1944).
13. Lincoln, "The Dred Scott Decision," p. 360.
14. Scott v. Sandford 19 How 450–51 (1857).
15. Frederick Douglass, "Address for the Promotion of Colored Enlistments," July 6, 1863, in *The Life and Writings of Frederick Douglass*, ed. Philip S. Foner (New York: International Publishers, 1950), vol. 3, p. 365.

16. See Donald L. Robinson, *Slavery in the Structure of American Politics, 1765–1820* (New York: Harcourt Brace Jovanovich, 1971), chaps. 4, 5.

17. Scott v. Sandford 19 How 451 (1857).

18. Scott v. Sandford 19 How 451–54 (1857).

19. The following deliberations are reported in Max Farrand, ed., *The Records of the Federal Convention of 1787*, 4 vols. (New Haven: Yale University Press, 1911–37), vol. 2, pp. 443, 453–54, 601–2, 628.

20. The emphases here and throughout this paragraph are mine.

21. Winny v. Whitesides 1 Mo Rep 472 (1824).

22. Abraham Lincoln, "Address at Cooper Institute," New York, February 27, 1860, in *Speeches and Writings*, p. 526.

23. John Locke, *Two Treatises of Government*, bk. 2, chap. 2, sec. 6.

24. Thomas Jefferson to John Holmes, April 22, 1820, in Jefferson, *Selected Writings*, p. 698.

25. Jefferson, "Notes on the State of Virginia," Query 18, pp. 278–79.

26. Thomas Jefferson, "Autobiography," in *Selected Writings*, p. 51.

27. Jefferson, "Notes on the State of Virginia," Query 14, pp. 255–62.

28. Lincoln, "The Dred Scott Decision," p. 360.

29. Franklin, "The Moral Legacy," p. 13.

30. W. E. B. Du Bois, "The Conservation of the Races," Washington, 1897, in Herbert J. Storing, ed., *What Country Have I? Political Writings by Black Americans* (New York: St. Martin's Press, 1970), pp. 82–83.

4

A New Birth of Freedom: Fulfillment or Derailment?

W. B. Allen

In the Constitutional Convention of 1787 James Madison was the first to introduce the question of slavery, apparently gratuitously.[1] We say gratuitously at first because the delegates to the convention clearly were mindful of how sensitive a question it was and how destructive it could be in the context of the major task before them. Upon closer review, however, we discover that Madison's use of the issue of slavery was in fact far from gratuitous; he recurred to it in what seemed to him an emergency: the necessity to dislodge the "small state–large state" voting formations if the convention were to progress at all.[2]

Thus the power of the issue of slavery in American politics was revealed in the context of the convention. It went to the heart of the question of the kind of people the Americans conceived themselves to be.

In the pages that follow I review the constitutional questions from the eras of the founding and the Civil War as a means of posing anew the question of where the United States Constitution stands today on the question of race, in the aftermath of the seminal Supreme Court case *Brown* v. *Board of Education* (1954). I argue that contemporary views about the status of the Constitution in those earlier eras, above all the notion that the Constitution was compatible, and the founders content, with the existence of slavery, are confused and mistaken.

Constitutional Issues from the Era of the Founding

The argument that the Constitution depended on slavery is by now a familiar one. It begins by concluding, from a negative, that because

---

The final section of this essay, on *Brown* v. *Board of Education*, is adapted from a lecture delivered in the Baker-McKenzie Foundation Lectures on Ethics and Law at Loyola University School of Law (Chicago), April 10, 1985.

the Constitution did not abolish slavery, it therefore *preserved* slavery. Then it calculates, from the positive provisions touching on slavery, that the Constitution *encouraged* slavery. On the strength of that prima facie demonstration, the various acts and deeds of individual founders are interpreted as if they were in the main consciously entertained with an eye to the putative result. What follows from this is generally a fairly disingenuous debate about the extent of culpability of the various founders.[3]

Alternatively, one might take the Constitution at face value and inquire how far it sustains or discourages any of a vast range of social and political practices both at the time of the founding and since. Against the view that the framers regarded slavery as "compatible" with the "progressive" regime they created, as William Wiecek asserts elsewhere in this volume, we have Madison's direct testimony. Madison is far the best example, because in some respects he is the worst case.[4] To avoid the danger of false imputation, I quote at length:

> In proportion as slavery prevails in a State, the Government, however democratic in name, must be aristocratic in fact. The power lies in the hands of property, not of numbers. All the antient popular governments, were for this reason aristocracies. The majorities were slaves. Of the residue a part were in the Country and did not attend the assemblies, a part were poor and tho in the City, could not spare the time to attend. The power was exercised for the most part by the rich and easy. Aristotle . . . defines a Citizen or member of the Sovereignty to be one who is sufficiently free from all private cares, to devote himself exclusively to the service of his Country. . . . *The Southern States of America, are on the same principle aristocracies.* In Virginia the aristocratic character *is increased* by the rule of suffrage, which requiring a freehold in land excludes nearly half the free inhabitants, and must exclude a greater proportion, as the population increases. *At present the slaves and non-freeholders amount to nearly ¾ of the State. The Power is therefore in about ¼.*[5] Were the slaves freed and the right of suffrage extended to all, the operation of the Government might be very different. The slavery of the *Southern States,* throws the power much more into the hands of property than in the northern States. Hence the people of property, in the former are much more contented with their establishd. Governments, than the people of property in the latter.[6]

This subtle political analysis conveys far more than evidence of a more sensitive understanding than is often assumed by scholars. It suggests the specific way in which the Constitution had a liberalizing tendency, apart from constitutional provisions. To be precise, to the

65

extent that Virginia ceased to be an independent nation and came to be integrated in a national republic, a republic verging dramatically less toward aristocracy than Virginia, Virginia itself would come to participate more in republicanism without effecting so much as a single change in its domestic institutions. The dynamics of democracy, more than any direct provisions of the Constitution, were the source of the antislavery implications of the founding. In that way the political accomplishment of the Constitution of 1787 was to deepen the influence and authority of the Declaration of Independence.

On the score of the Declaration also we may assess the special relation in which the founders stood to slavery. That slavery was considered a "necessary evil" neither derives from the era of the Missouri Compromise nor was alien to the Constitutional Convention. But over and beyond those familiar examples, we find extensive discussion of this theme throughout revolutionary America, from Georgia to New Hampshire. The pieties of revolutionary fever ought not to be taken as decisive, however. What counts far more is the official representations of the state governments to the Continental Congress, of which that from New Jersey in June 1778 is the most instructive. In it we behold in a single view the moral ambition and practical limitations of the American scene regarding slavery.

The Legislative Council and General Assembly of New Jersey had several reservations about the Articles of Confederation. None were voiced more stridently, however, than their concern over a provision in the ninth article. That article "provides, that the Requisitions for Land-Forces to be furnished by the Several States, shall be proportioned to the Number of *white* inhabitants in each."[7] New Jersey found an objection to this provision in the Declaration's affirmation that "we hold these truths to be self-evident, that all Men are created equal." A necessary deduction, they held, is that "the Inhabitants of every Society, be the Colour of their Complexion what may, are bound to promote the Interest thereof, according to their respective Abilities." Accordingly, blacks and whites alike should be accounted for in assessing obligations of self-defense. To the New Jersey legislators any problem created by this principle were "special local" problems. If due proportionality would send virtually all white southern males to the field of battle, leaving slaves in the fields and homes, the southern states would need to reconsider their institutions; for "admitting Necessity or Expediency to justify the Refusal of Liberty in certain Circumstances, to persons of a particular Colour; we think it unequal to reckon Nothing upon such in this Case."[8]

The New Jersey patriots did not affect to impose abolition of slavery on the South. They did, however, recognize and declare that a

due regard for liberty and equality might impose abolition on the
South. For on any other account free white northerners would have to
subsidize southern liberty at the cost of their own blood. Slavery in a
free republic not only created inequalities between blacks and whites;
it also created inequalities with respect to the obligations of citizenship between slaveholding and nonslaveholding whites—inequalities on both scales held to be incompatible with the Declaration
of Independence.[9]

Three events reveal as clearly as may be the nature of the slavery
option under the Constitution of 1787. The first was Madison's resort
to slavery at the Philadelphia convention to break up the logjam over
representation occasioned by the small state–large state division.
Robert Yates of New York tells us that Madison did this on June 29.
His purpose was unmistakable: "The great danger to our general
government *is the great southern and northern interests of the continent,
being opposed to each other. Look to the votes in congress, and most of them
stand divided by the geography of the country,* not according to size."[10]
The emphasis that Yates gave to this passage reflects very well the
shock that must have been occasioned by the conscious attempt to
make slavery an issue in the convention, which had been sitting for
over a month without once broaching the issue as such (though
invoking the Confederation Congress's "three-fifths clause" at least
ten times). Madison apparently repeated his argument the following
day, when the small state–large state controversy had reached such an
extreme as to call forth from Gunning Bedford of Delaware a threat to
take a "foreign power by the hand."

Not long after, however, the convention turned; the controversy
over size was supplanted by the controversy over slavery, especially
as signified in the representation question. The previously uncon-
troversial three-fifths provision became sufficiently controversial to
require, ultimately, a compromise. I submit, in other words, that
Madison resorted to the inherent division over slavery as a device to
overcome the division on the score of representation, placing a strain
thereby on the coalition that had previously sustained the dispute.
The implication of his move is that slavery was a threat to the consensus needed to build the Union.

The second event of the founding era that indicates the nature of
the slavery option occurred after adoption of the Constitution, in the
First Congress. The first major debate over constitutional interpretation in the Congress took place in the House of Representatives on
May 13, 1789. The subject was slavery, and it carried with it all the
ambiguous assumptions that freighted the several compromise provisions on the subject in the Constitution. Remember that the slave

trade clause (Article I, section 9), by which Congress could not prohibit slavery until 1808 but could impose an import tax on slaves, produced contrary interpretations even at the time, ranging from the more familiar southern claims that "we got all that we could" on behalf of slavery to the lesser known but extraordinary claim by James Wilson:

> I will tell you what was done, and it gives me high pleasure, that so much was done. . . . By this article after the year 1808, the congress will have the power to prohibit such importation, notwithstanding the disposition of any state to the contrary. I consider this as laying the foundation for banishing slavery out of this country; and though the period is more distant than I could wish, yet it will produce the same kind of gradual change which was pursued in Pennsylvania.[11]

The debate in the House of Representatives shows how far the hopeful interpretation prevailed over the shameful interpretation.

It was Madison who was most prepared to discuss the matter and most reluctant to yield to counsels of caution on a matter that others feared could abort the Union. His comments in this debate illuminate his resort to slavery to move the convention toward a Constitution almost two years earlier, for in this case it is the *existence* of the Union that weighs heavily in his reflections and promises the opportunity to act on the question.

> I cannot concur with gentlemen who think the present an improper time or place to enter into a discussion of the proposed motion. . . . There may be some inconsistency in combining the ideas which gentlemen have expressed, that is, considering the human race as a species of property; but the evil does not arise from adopting the clause now proposed; it is from the importation to which it relates. Our object in enumerating persons on paper with merchandise, is to prevent the practice of treating them as such. . . .
>
> The dictates of humanity, the principles of the people, the national safety and happiness, and prudent policy, require it of us. . . . I conceive the Constitution, in this particular, was formed in order that the Government, whilst it was restrained from laying a total prohibition, might be able to give some testimony of the sense of America with respect to the African trade. . . .
>
> It is to be hoped, that by expressing a national disapprobation of this trade, we may destroy it, and save ourselves from reproaches, and our posterity the imbecility ever attendant on a country filled with slaves. . . . If there is any one point

in which it is clearly the policy of this nation, so far as we constitutionally can, to vary the practice obtaining under some of the state governments, it is this.

To Madison, it appears, the slavery option was such that it could and should be subject to calculated disincentives. An analysis of the vote on this measure, in a house of fifty-nine representatives, ten of whom were present in the Constitutional Convention, reveals a preponderant disposition to treat slavery as an option to be discouraged but nevertheless a matter sufficiently sensitive to make that difficult.

The third event of the founding era that contributes to an understanding of the slavery option is the manner in which, when the constitutional prohibition had expired, the international slave trade was prohibited. The president and his secretary of state initiated the process in 1807 with apparent pleasure. They encountered a difficulty, however, that no one had anticipated. It centered on the question of what to do with any contraband (that is, ships and slave cargo) that might be apprehended. Thomas Jefferson's original proposal envisioned a traditional disposal in the interest of the government. But other parties, especially Quakers, pointed to the grand paradox that would involve the United States in selling Africans as a means of denying that privilege to American citizens in the name of the rights of humanity. Madison's speech of 1789—we treat persons as property in law to be able to prevent their being treated as property in practice—resonated loudly. It quickly became clear that Jefferson's proposal involved a mere oversight. Yet it was immensely difficult to discern what else might be done.

The counterproposal, that the Africans be freed rather than sold, touched off a heated debate; but that debate, above all in the House of Representatives, produced the first compromise on slavery admitting the existence of irreconcilable differences between North and South. Here, for the first time, there was an explicit threat of civil war over the institution of slavery and an accommodation that recognized that "easterners" must not be asked to turn their backs on the founding and principles of humanity or "southerners" to participate in a condemnation of their way of life. Therefore, the northern proposal, effectively to free the cargo within the United States and even within the slave states, was amended, first, to free them only in the North (that is to indenture them for a term of years at a stipulated wage) and, ultimately, to remand them to such provisions as the states might make, with the tacit understanding that they were not to be dealt with as property.

It is interesting to speculate about what might have eventuated had Jefferson and Madison reflected initially on the impropriety of proposing legislation to handle the Africans as contraband.[12] They might well have discovered the key whereby to unlock the door to the interstate commerce power as a device for regulating slavery. Not only did they not envision such a debate in 1807, but, more important, no one else did. Not even the Quakers, whose sharp-sightedness prevented a moral catastrophe, applied their principles in this way. It seemed in 1807 that no one at all, whether defender of slavery or abolitionist, looked at the "migration" language of Article I, section 9, as a probable means of resolving this difficulty.

This lends powerful credence to Madison's 1819 claim that the language of the migration portion of the slave trade clause did not apply to slaves, although it may have applied to free blacks.[13] His further remark, to the effect that any attempt so to construe it would have caused a brouhaha, helps explain the absence of recourse to it in 1807. The mild debate in 1807 produced threats of secession and war. Accordingly, Madison simply maintained that public opinion would not have abided such a turn, pointing to the one theme he consistently enunciated throughout his career, namely, the necessity of consent, not only to institute the government but to institute the fundamental change envisioned. This Madison explained repeatedly, as he did to Robert Evans in 1819.[14] For Madison the key to this progressive regime was consent, the index of which was public opinion. Whatever was to be accomplished had to be accomplished by that medium. So fervently did he believe this that he not only subordinated abolition to it but, as he expressly recounted, predicated all his labors to form the Democratic-Republican party on that premise.

While public opinion in 1807 countenanced the prohibition of the slave trade, it did not countenance federal abolition of slavery. In the end, for Madison, the theory of republicanism is not a theory about institutional relations; it is a theory about the dependence of power on opinion. The "changes" in his views all take place at the surface because, like planets, ideas about constitutionality wander about a fixed sun.[15]

In these three events, therefore, we may see a mosaic that captures all the dimensions of the role of slavery and race in American politics. The question regarding that role must be considered against the backdrop of the principles of the regime, because actions touching on slavery and race bear heavy implications for those principles, and vice versa. This results not so much from any cultural or traditional pattern as from the conscious choices with which Americans wrestled at every turn in our nation's history, up to and including the decisions of the present generation.

It is especially obvious in the 1807 struggle over the prohibition of the slave trade: from the moment that slavery was in any degree limited, the problem of how to handle the question of race arose to replace it. The answer to that question rests not only on the fact that the consciously chosen principles of the regime entail equality and liberty for all human beings but, far more important, on the question whether they require an open, heterogeneous society. The decisions made in the aftermath of the Civil War, in the form of the postwar amendments and civil rights legislation, indicate a positive response to this question. But how far was that true at the time of the founding?

While it is inaccurate to assert that no one before the last half of the nineteenth century imagined an interracial society founded on the principles of the Declaration of Independence, that question is of minimal concern here: first, because it is subordinate to the question whether the Declaration was understood to include all human beings without regard to the practical social implications of that principle; and second, because the status of slavery *and* race under the Constitution or regime—and how to legislate in regard to it—is and has been a single question. Madison's concern to avoid the "imbecility" of a country filled with slaves does not require the corollary of turning slaves into free citizens of the republic. As the 1807 slave trade debate reveals, however, that is the very question that arises the moment the freedom of the African is conceded. Hence the debate was in fact a debate about whether and how to integrate Africans within the United States. That Americans posed the same kind of question then as now points the way to an understanding of the dilemma we now face.

We have available to guide us in addressing the social question about racial equality both a practical account, from the official posture of the founding, and a theoretical account, at the center of *The Federalist*, No. 43.

First let us consider the practical account. All have heard it said that the Declaration excludes women, because it reads "all men are created equal." It excludes blacks because, when they wrote "men," they meant "white Anglo-Saxon Protestant males." It excludes Indians, and so on. The list goes on and on. But what is the truth, apart from this story we hear? And how should we uncover it?

I suggest that we return to the language that Jefferson used when drafting the Declaration of Independence. Allow him to speak for himself; he would point out that he used the term "men" three times in the document. "All men are created equal" was only the first; thereafter he wrote that "governments are instituted among men" and founded in the consent of the governed. To the question whether he regarded women as ungoverned, he might respond with an air of

71

incredulity. Surely women too were to be governed. Besides, when Jefferson liberalized the criminal code of Virginia, he included a provision specifically to deal with loose or ungoverned women. Women were surely to be governed and thus included in the language that "governments are instituted among men."

The third time Jefferson used the term "men" he reproved the king of England for obstructing the elimination of the slave trade in the colonies. There he wrote, "He has waged cruel war against human nature itself, violating its most sacred rights of life and liberty. . . . Determined to keep open a market where MEN should be bought and sold . . ." This was the only time he emphasized the word, printing it in bold capitals. Ask him whether, when he did this, he meant "white Anglo-Saxon Protestant males." Would he not return with the question, "Are you ignorant who the slaves were among us?" or, "Do you think me so dense as not to know?" Surely he knew intimately that they were not only black but male and female. Thus Jefferson would finally declare that the language of the Declaration is plain; it speaks to all humankind. None are excluded. When the Declaration affirms the proposition that "all men are created equal," meaning that no human being is by nature the ruler of any other, it means all human beings.

A pedantic objection to this discussion would remind us that the delegates to the convention did not accept Jefferson's language about the slave trade. From that truth they would erroneously conclude that the sense of the language was entirely deleted from the Declaration. We have seen that this was not so in the example of New Jersey, and there is a final, definitive example that the Declaration was taken after its adoption precisely in the sense in which it was originally formulated.

For a long time almost everyone in America has misunderstood the language in the Constitution that is referred to as the three-fifths clause. The general account is that the framers regarded black people as only three-fifths of human beings. That shows them as bigots and their opinion of black people as low indeed. Again, the palpable surface of the documents reveals the truth. Consider what they did in fact mean; then judge how well the framers confronted their moral dilemmas.

In April 1783 (not 1787) in the Confederation Congress the earliest form of the three-fifths compromise emerged after six weeks of debate. An eighth article was proposed for the Articles of Confederation, apportioning expenses for the Confederation on the basis of land values as surveyed. There the discussion opened, only to reveal how difficult it was to assess land values and, in the rude conditions of those times, to produce accurate surveys. Thus they resorted to numbers instead, speaking of population as a rough approximation of wealth. Taking the numbers of people in the respective states, they hit upon the following language:

> Expenses shall be supplied by the several states in proportion to the whole number of *white and other free inhabitants, of every age, sex, and condition,* including those bound to servitude for a term of years, and three fifths of all other persons not comprehended in the foregoing description, except Indians not paying taxes in each state.

What, then, does three-fifths apply to? Slaves, carefully and legally defined. But reread the opening clause, delimiting "the whole number of white and other free inhabitants." To whom does that apply? Surely not whites only or only males, since "every age, sex, and condition" is further appended. Clearly, they aimed at every free human being, white and nonwhite. The only significant free non-whites in the United States in 1783 were American blacks (another 10,000 of whom were emancipated between 1776 and 1787). In America in 1783, for example, there were no Asians. Thus the legislators included American blacks among the free inhabitants; the three-fifths clause applied not to blacks generically but rather to those in the peculiar legal relation of slavery. Three-fifths of the number of slaves were counted, not in terms of their humanity but with respect to their legal status.

The Confederation Congress fully affirmed the humanity of American blacks through the language of "white and other free inhabitants." When this same language was taken up again in 1787 in the Constitutional Convention, was that recognition of humanity withdrawn? Here is the provision:

> Representatives and direct taxes shall be apportioned among the several States which may be included within this Union, according to the respective numbers, which shall be determined by adding to the *whole Number of free persons,* including those bound to Service for a Term of Years, and excluding Indians not taxed, three-fifths of all other Persons.

The distance of four years has brought changes. But what are they? On the surface the changes are primarily editorial, introducing economy and exactness of language. As any composition teacher would point out, the first thing to notice is the elimination of redundancy. Why should it be necessary to say the "whole number of white and other free inhabitants, of every age, sex, and condition," when the "whole number of free persons" says the same thing? Further, "adding . . . three fifths of all other persons" is less awkward than the inclusion clause of 1783. Finally, the substitution of "Service" for "servitude" continues the liberal impulse of 1776. Thus the language of 1787 includes women and blacks; it does not exclude them.

The theoretical account from *Federalist* No. 43 requires a more involved explanation. There Madison spelled out how the principles of the Declaration of Independence might work in an imperfect world. The discussion concerns a defense of the Constitution's guarantee to all the states of "a republican form of government" and, further, the federal government's commitment to defend the states against domestic violence. The "superintending government" must have authority to purify a "confederacy founded on republican principles" of serious "aristocratic or monarchical" pretensions, and that rests on the ability to preserve the specific form of the republican regime:

> The more intimate the nature of such a union may be (the less distinct its confederal elements), the greater interest have the members in the political institutions of each other; and the greater right to insist that the forms of government under which the compact was entered into should be *substantially* maintained.[16]

It *could* arise that a majority have not the right to alter the government to the extent that a particular people with a genuine public good may be said to exist or intended to exist. The *illegitimate* majority may tyrannize a minority and may derogate from the public good non-tyrannically.[17]

What this might mean Madison makes clear by introducing a distinction between a "majority of citizens" and a "majority of persons."[18] A minority of citizens bringing some other persons—slaves, perhaps?—to their side could constitute a majority of persons while nothing would have changed in the republican nature of the regime itself. Insofar as any particular regime leaves any human beings outside the status of citizen, a possibility exists, at once theoretical and practical, that a minority of citizens may unite with other persons to bring greater force to bear on the regime.

Nothing can show more clearly than this that the founders did include *all men* when they recognized that "all men are created equal." In those terms—and according to Publius it is the Declaration we are expounding—a majority of men are at any time within their rights in forming a regime. They may not be able to claim the right from any given regime, precisely because every given regime ideally originated in a like appeal to natural right. The difficulty that is created is not the confusion of rights. That can be resolved. It is rather the possibility that recognition of the *natural majority* undermines the entire significance of citizenship.[19]

Madison rescued the fair damsels of republican state, county, and district governments, not by means of justice but by means of the superior and disinterested force of a federal government able to intervene and suppress insurrection. "It may be doubtful on which side justice lies," but the federal government can quench the flame of violence. "Happy would it be if such a remedy for its infirmities could be enjoyed by all free governments; if a project equally effectual could be established for the universal peace of mankind."

Short of such "universal peace"—the logical result of modern natural rights—every solution is provisional. Madison could not avoid following his prayer with the natural question, earlier left unanswered:

> Should it be asked what is to be the redress for an insurrection pervading all the States, and comprising a superiority of the entire force, though not a constitutional right? The answer must be that such a case, as it would be without the compass of human remedies, so it is fortunately not within the compass of human probability.

Is the answer sufficient? It must be seen as radically insufficient save on one of two grounds. Either the slaves were such as indeed to make it beyond the "compass of human probability" for a natural majority, including them, to arise within the United States, or by some process the potential for such a natural majority would be diminished by encompassing all persons within the meaning of citizenship and *at the same time* exercising a sufficiently salutary influence on the opinions of the citizens as to ensure a preponderant allegiance to the Constitution.

This dilemma made slavery the kind of option that had to be discouraged, and it was understood as such fully as much by slavery's defenders as by its enemies. The elder Charles Pinckney reflected this understanding in the South Carolina ratifying convention when, challenged to account for the absence of a bill of rights in the Constitution, he responded that, inasmuch as such documents characteristically begin with a clause to the effect that "all men are created equal," it seemed to the delegates of the South that they would make such a declaration with decidedly ill grace. As fate would have it, however, that doctrine was already so far inwrought in the soul of the regime that by the time of the Constitution it had become impossible to hide it.

This review of the constitutional questions from the era of the founding enables us to pose anew the question of where the U.S. Constitution stands today, in the aftermath of *Brown* v. *Board of Education*. We should have to stretch our imaginations beyond their limits, however, to jump entirely beyond the development of these issues as they arose in the Civil War. To understand the meaning of equality as it has developed in the course of American politics, we may consider the drama acted out in the fifth joint debate between Abraham Lincoln and Stephen A. Douglas. That debate was an important one in a series that effectively secured for Lincoln the Republican nomination and the presidency in 1860. It thereby secured to us that very Constitution we now consider and, further, preserved to our memories the influence of those great Virginians Washington, Madison, John Marshall, and Jefferson. Without them we would not have our Constitution; without the Union their memories would have gone to secessionist Virginia.

The Issues at the Time of the Civil War

The fifth joint debate between Douglas and Lincoln on October 7, 1858, at Freeport, Illinois, may have seemed at the time only a way station on the journey to Alton, where the seventh and final debate in the series was held, but clearly it was more than that. This most important of the debates demonstrated precisely how principles of just constitutionalism come to inform popular deliberation in American politics, without which there would be no defense possible for that politics. The issue at stake was, of course, the status of slavery in America, but the *form* that the issue assumed is what concerns us. For it is clear that the abstract principle of the injustice of slavery was of far less importance than whether the Constitution were friendly or hostile to it.

The debate over the founding intention was fairly and fully carried out in the era immediately before the Civil War. Lincoln and Douglas, above all, resorted to the Constitution "as our fathers made it." They produced evidences, comprehensive if not complete, on the one side and the other. Accordingly, every new argument along those lines bears the obligation to respond to the arguments they formulated. The fact that this obligation is seldom honored makes a strong prima facie case that no one has succeeded in marshaling a stronger case on behalf of either the one or the other.

The questions I now propose—what rights and limitations did slavery have under the Constitution, and how far were they beneficial or harmful to slavery?—constitute the genuine issue that was in dispute between Lincoln and Douglas, although their exchange tended sometimes to obscure it. A brief review of their exchange reveals the point at which we find in the founding the strongest grounds for answering these questions. Such a review should begin with the Freeport debate, in which Lincoln propounded to Douglas the famous "third interrogatory": "If the Supreme Court of the United States shall decide that the states cannot exclude slavery from their limits, are you in favor of acquiescing in, adhering to and following such a decision, as a rule of political action?"

Lincoln recognized how extraordinary this proposition was, how far-reaching its threat to the rule of law. To his mind, though, "this slavery question . . . endangered our republican institutions." Accordingly, he appealed to the necessary foundations of our constitutional polity, forcing Douglas to join him in extensive and painstaking constitutional analyses before the tribunal of the people. We have in these two able counselors the presentation of briefs unexcelled by any yet produced before the bar of the Supreme Court.

The implications of this process are borne out best in Douglas's 1859 *Harper's Magazine* article, in which he finally met Lincoln's challenge. It was Douglas's most comprehensive response to the third interrogatory and its correlative, "Are you in favor of acquiring additional territory in disregard of how it may affect us upon the slavery question?" What characterizes the *Harper's* essay above all is that it is a lengthy, laborious search for historical precedent to sustain the constitutional interpretation that local self-government entailed the right to regulate all domestic practices, including the ownership of slaves. Douglas plumbed the records of revolutionary history to sustain his point, though noticeably omitting (as Lincoln later pointed out) any mention of the antislavery provision contained in the Northwest Ordinance of 1787 originally passed by the final Confederation Congress and readopted by Congress in 1789 under the new Constitution.

Douglas's argument was ingenious. He sought the principles of the U.S. Constitution outside and before the Declaration of Independence, locating them in what he called the colonists' defense of the "unalienable right of local self-government." Unlike Chief Justice Roger B. Taney's oxymoronic attempt in the *Dred Scott* case to interpret the idea that "all men are created equal" as if "men" meant "Anglo-Saxon immigrants" (which Lincoln easily embarrassed by reminding continental emigrants that their liberties were endangered thereby), Douglas's attempt had the clear virtue of selecting a principle that demonstrably included the recognition of slavery among the domestic practices subject to local regulation. Further, because the colonists sought for a long time to win from the mother country the absolute right to control the introduction of slaves into the colonies as well as to regulate the practice of slavery, Douglas could maintain that this was one of the privileges for which they had "shed their blood." Hence they would not have surrendered it to a new national government without express language to that effect. Avoiding the contentions that blacks were not "men"—an argument with which he otherwise agreed—he simply concluded that slavery lay within the ordinary powers of the governments established through the Revolution. The constitutional status of slavery, moreover, was that unless it were expressly prohibited, it had to be permitted.

Douglas argued that there never was a direct constitutional decision on the merits of slavery. If there were not a direct decision originally, if slavery existed as it were from time immemorial, there would be a precedent to avoid a direct decision now. Had there been a direct decision before, even in *favor* of slavery, that would give color to a direct decision now, a constitutional decision *against* slavery. In some ways Douglas understood the South's necessities better than the southerners. He wished slavery to have a constitutional status somewhat akin to that of the family. The family has no express constitutional recognition; yet who would deny that it had constitutional protection? Further, local regulation of marriages and other family matters exists even in the absence of express constitutional recognition of the family. Unfortunately for Douglas, the analogy breaks down when we begin to discuss the "unalienable right of local self-government" to permit or prohibit practices of immemorial usage; an option is precisely not a matter of universal custom. The family could never be an option, as slavery had been an option.

This is the point at which Lincoln hammered: slavery had been an option, and then only in the sense of an exception to principles otherwise established. Lincoln rooted the concept of self-government in the meaning of that "abstract truth," "all men are created equal." The fact that this irreducible principle was not given its full scope alone preserved the option of slavery; to that extent it constituted a qualification of the founders' achievement. What they did not achieve in practice, however, the founders dedicated themselves to in principle.

On the basis of this interpretation, Lincoln challenged Douglas for a seat in government and demanded insistently that the Declaration of Independence and the Missouri Compromise be considered together *the* statement of national policy toward slavery. For Lincoln the slaves were *men* of a given legal status. Hence it was necessary to affirm the existence of slave law as an exception to America's primary conception of the relation between men and law. Slavery, though an option, had to be publicly acknowledged as an exception, not only to equality but to the consent of the governed. The failure to do so was seen as a threat to fundamental law and hence a threat to *free* men. In other words, *Lincoln insisted that free men be understood as free in relation to their rights as men and not by virtue of their accidental juxtaposition with slaves.* Lincoln and Douglas agreed, therefore, that slavery had been an option at the founding. They disagreed about the nature of the option.

The Question of Race

The ambiguities that surrounded the question of what kind of option slavery was were swiftly transmitted to the question of race once the war had ended and slavery was gone. The process was dramatic and dynamic. The issue over which the Civil War started—whether there was a right to expand slavery into the territories—ceased to be the central issue from the moment war began. Thereafter the issue became slavery itself, above all the problem of the character of the regime. And then there was race, achieving its most ambiguous form by 1896 in the famous *Plessy* v. *Ferguson* decision enunciating the "separate but equal" doctrine.[20] From that vantage point we may stand midstream, reaching back to the founding and also forward to our own time, to trace an evolution of the status of slavery under the Constitution to our present-day concerns with race and the meaning of equality.

The American people resolved the dilemma that Tocqueville took as the ultimate source of their destruction, and in the most unlikely way. By doing so, however, they raised Tocqueville's question of the "three races in America" to the level of a regime question, rather than leaving it a mere question of cultural differences. Transformed into the question of the two races in America, it became the decisive vehicle for the interpretation and development of the principles of the regime into the twentieth century. The test of whether a nation "so conceived could long endure" has frequently been approached but never actually resolved. Just as the nation existed for nearly a century before coming to terms with the paradox of slavery in a regime founded on the basis of the Declaration of Independence, so today the nation has continued for more than a century without coming finally to terms with the question of race.

Brown v. *Board of Education* offered the Supreme Court occasion for such a resolution, but they failed to achieve it.[21] The reasons for that failure reveal that the question of race and slavery retains the same power for good and evil that was revealed in Madison's parliamentary exploitation of the issue in the Constitutional Convention. The Court in *Brown* explicitly spoke of overturning the decision in *Plessy*. Just as emphatically ever since, many scholars and commentators have insisted that in *Brown* it did no such thing. The difference turns on the fact that *Brown* did not specifically adopt the opinion of Justice John M. Harlan's dissent in *Plessy*, the famous dissent that gave us the expression "Our Constitution is color-blind, and neither knows nor tolerates classes among citizens." Accordingly, "today the *Brown* decision is considered the progenitor of a host of color-conscious and group-specific policies."[22]

The decision in *Brown v. Board of Education* was handed down in 1954. At that time I had turned ten years of age and was completing my fourth-grade year at Peck Elementary School, in Fernandina Beach, Florida. Peck was a black segregated school, with elementary and secondary schools housed in a single facility; it was segregated from grade one through grade twelve. About that time my parents were conferring with my teacher, Mr. Simpson. At length they all concurred that I should not be skipped ahead of my class, in spite of working significantly beyond grade level. The principle of their decision was that intellectual growth was one thing, maturation another, and the latter had its own laws. They deliberated seriously and for a good long time before reaching their decision. Of these two decisions, that rendered in *Brown* and that rendered by my custodians, the latter had by far the more profound influence on my own development and the life I now live. We must consider *Brown*, of which so much was expected, to learn why this was so.

The debate over whether *Brown* succeeded or failed is misplaced and tendentious. Turning as it does on results generalizable over classes, the debate obscures if not everts all consideration of the choices faced and made by individuals. By raising the question of my own success or failure as a question that might trace its answer to lines independent of *Brown*, I mean to suggest that there are other grounds, principled grounds—constitutional, historical, and ethical grounds— on which to consider the case and the conditions of its implementation. Here I follow the spirit of Mary Beard:

> For the consideration of the nation as community there is required both a looking backward and a looking all around at the present. Americans have not been accustomed to thinking of their United States in its entirety as an expression of civilization and culture. Instead they have been inclined for the most part to live from day to day, taking advantage of the extraordinary opportunities for personal advancement as

they have lavishly presented themselves, or waging a lone fight against disadvantages.[23]

I am not interested in *Brown* v. *Board of Education* as a model of jurisprudence. The jury is in on that; it was not. I am interested in it from the simple perspective of its important position in a line of events contributing to the continuing elaboration of the principles of American life, above all that all men are created equal.

It is characteristic of American life that we regularly re-pose for ourselves the question of the meaning of that principle (knowingly or not). We do so as scholars. We do so as citizens. Thoughtful people, like Lincoln, have amply demonstrated that certain political junctures impose on us the necessity to reconsider our fundamental principles. At such moments the cast of our situation is such that we risk losing them altogether and can preserve them only at the cost of self-conscious exertion. Is there inherent in the very principles by which we live a need to risk losing them by virtue of the endeavors they impose on us? Cannot our guiding principles acquire and preserve an enduring authority over our souls and our children's souls through the traditional reliance on example and ritual? I believe the answer to these questions is yes, and the explanation entails a brief inquiry into the life lived in accord with equality and consent.

Legitimate governments derive their just powers solely from the consent of the governed. That is the world of the Declaration. In almost all antecedents to this theory men consent rather to the fact of government than to its forms and powers. What we confront in the Declaration is the identical question that animated Machiavelli's dialogue with the ancients: Who has just title to rule? The answer in the Declaration is that the least shall rule (insofar as the many means the least); that is, there were no longer any reservations recognizing the priority of the best. This statement makes the answer simpler than it is in fact. The Declaration is not an anathema against the best. But the principle of equality in the Declaration was a direct response to the earlier recognition of distinctions in men respecting titles to rule. From such principles it emerged clearly that the form or structure of government was the secondary element of republicanism. With the vision of a polity in which no adventitious titles would determine who should rule, republicanism had emerged as more than a device to prosecute peace between warring classes. It was a way of life in which those distinctions would lose fundamental political significance.

Considering the consent that equality entails and enquiring how that consent may be exercised, we are forced to investigate the character of the consenting person. Not only is it of primary importance to preserve the right of consent for men in general, but men in general must exercise it to vindicate the principles. Yet is it not manifest that only men in a certain condition and of a certain character (namely, free agents subject to rational and moral persuasion) can in fact exercise the power of consent? All concur that neither those in the condition of slaves (whether enslaved to men or to passions) nor those of a slavish character can exercise the power of consent. At the heart of the ethical question, then, lies the question of character.[24]

The character of the free, consenting citizen must generally reflect the disposition to weigh social and political actions in the light of the principles that guide us. Certainly, at least, it must be the aim of law to encourage such habits of soul. Let us not fail to notice, however, that such law may also encourage, however mildly, a skepticism about the principles by which we govern ourselves. Individuals who must judge not only whether laws accord with equality and consent but also whether equality and consent provide for what is good will sometimes judge falsely. While they have the powerful influence of tradition and prior demonstration to guide them, those forces are insufficient in themselves to determine individual judgment in every case. Accordingly, our laws contain an openness to good-willed abandonment of the principles that guide us. We should candidly confront the prospect that men, fully intending to reaffirm the sufficiency of equality and consent, may actually wander beyond the reach of these limits of safety.

In that light, let us ask about *Brown* v. *Board of Education,* Does it measure up to the task outlined by Lincoln? Politically I believe the answer is yes. The political task in *Brown,* capping a long series of halting steps in this direction, was to reaffirm the commitment of this nation and its citizens to the principle of equality. That is precisely the task that the Court accepted and carried out to the extent of its powers. Indeed, I consider it fair to say that the Court bears great responsibility and deserves praise for the eventual passage of the 1964 Civil Rights Act, in which this process culminated. One may even say that the colloquial judgment of the Court's work adequately states the case on behalf of the Court. It has become fashionable to fasten on the ambiguous phrase "with all deliberate speed" to diminish the Court's achievement by suggesting that it was too willing to allow recalcitrant states to go slow in dismantling segregated school systems. While it is true that by the time schools were integrated in Fernandina Beach I had already left to attend a private college in the West, by 1968 I could return to teach in the single high school attended by all pupils.

Politically, then, the change we have all witnessed is no illusion, whether sufficient or no. And that it is a return to fundamental principle, we have the retroactive testimony of James Wilson to confirm:

> With regard to an individual, everyone knows how much his fortunes and his character, his infelicity or his happiness depend on his education. What education is to the individual, the laws are to the community. "Good laws," says my lord Bacon, whose sentences are discourses, "make a whole nation to be as a well ordered college." With what earnestness should every nation—with what peculiar earnestness should that nation, which boasts of liberty as the principle of her Constitution—with what peculiar earnestness should she endeavor, that her laws . . . should be improved to a degree of perfection as high as human policy and human virtue can carry them![25]

In one area only do I conceive it possible to raise a political objection to the *Brown* decision. The problem stems from the Court's shrinking from the declaration that the Constitution is colorblind. The Court did so, I am convinced, because it had accepted the perspective of the *Carolene* footnote, in 1938, that "prejudice against discrete and insular minorities may be a special condition, which tends to curtail the operation of those political processes ordinarily to be relied upon to protect minorities, and may call for a correspondingly more searching judicial inquiry."[26] The *Carolene* Court strongly implied that enhanced judicial scrutiny not only remedied but supplanted the defect of recourse to ordinary political processes. The *Brown* Court, accordingly, undertook its political mission voluntarily hobbled, already inclined to forgo reliance on ordinary political processes to achieve the objective.

What were those ordinary political processes? In general this must be regarded as a reference to the ordinary processes of elections, lobbying, and general participation in the formation of public opinion. In this context, however, the proper expression would be rule by the majority. The Court saw itself as the protector of minority rights against majority intransigence, in a case in which it did not conceive it possible that the minority could be incorporated directly into the political process and in which it did not conceive of any other possible protection for minorities.

This is the famous problem set forth in Madison's tenth *Federalist* paper, in which he held that "if a faction consists of less than a majority, relief is supplied by the republican principle," namely, majority rule. When a faction is a majority, however, Madison acknowledged a peculiar difficulty, in that the republican form worked against an easy solution. He affirmed, however, that the end, "the great object in view," has to be both to "secure the public good and private rights" and "at the same time to preserve the spirit and the form of popular government." Too often Madison is read as offering nothing more than "interest group liberalism" as the solution to this great difficulty. Not only is that an inadequate reading of the limited remedy offered in *Federalist* No. 10; it also neglects the fully developed response that Madison offered in *Federalist* No. 51. That is where we find the authoritative account of the relation between the ordinary political processes under the Constitution and the preservation of minority rights. We can see there that the Court failed utterly, both in 1938 and in 1954, to comprehend how far it was obligated to rely on ordinary political processes properly to achieve its political mission.

Madison argued that the most important test of the American system would always be its ability to guarantee the freedom of minorities *without* special provisions for their protection. On that basis the optimal condition of freedom would be that degree that would allow the majority to govern without permitting it to abuse the rights of others. Every special protection for minorities, then, would be a further barrier to majority rule. Unfortunately, however, it would amount to establishing a "will independent of the society" to enforce it. Madison ruled that out as incompatible with republicanism and as the reestablishment of the aristocratic principle. He defended the specific constitutional design, the process, as accomplishing all that was necessary and all that was desirable to achieve the end. For a process to bear that much weight calls for conscious attachment on the part of the people. And that is what was provided: to avoid the evil of majority faction while relying on majority rule, through the citizens' conscious attachment to republican principles and processes.

The founders relied on this conclusion as the active principle of the regime: the people's determination to work through certain well-designed and well-established processes would provide safety not only for liberty but for the pursuit of "justice and the general good." This is the purpose of the defense of the separation of powers and representation; not so much wisdom and the adaptability of the representatives (which *were* important) as the stability and decency of democratic opinion would be ensured thereby. The constitutional debate over separation of powers and checks and balances, at its best, would be a debate about how far the people's continuing justice and happiness might be impaired in departures from the design.

I am aware that there is an objection to this interpretation of the ordinary political processes from which the Court had departed in

84

adjudicating questions of civil rights. As it is usually stated, any proposal to allow fundamental guarantees of civil rights to be enforced by the majority (not intending to eliminate private litigation) would merely be a return to rule by whites in the interest of whites, or males in the interest of males, or heterosexuals in the interest of heterosexuals, *ad infinitum*.[27] But the belief that minorities are "protected" by laws rather than by the opinions of the poeple is based on a fundamental misunderstanding. The assumption is that every special protection of a minority exists in opposition to the preponderant sentiment of the community. If that were strictly true, however, such laws and programs would not remain in force.

I conclude, therefore, that the *Brown* Court failed to restore confidence in ordinary political processes. That failure stemmed from an error in judgment, founded in ignorance of the connection between the principle by which we govern ourselves and our ordinary political processes, between equality and consent. Thus the Court achieved its objective of reaffirming our commitment to equality, without recognizing that a commitment to consent required fully as much to be reaffirmed. Ironically, then, it preserved the *Plessy* principle: "When the government, therefore, has secured to each of its citizens equal rights before the law and equal opportunities for improvement and progress, it has accomplished the end for which it is organized." In that principle the government usurps the role of the governing citizens, who govern through consent. By leaving intact those *Plessy* powers (assumed to inhere in state legislatures, but actually opposed to consent) at the same time as it failed to rely on ordinary political processes, *Brown* succeeded in renewing our commitment to our guiding principle while depriving us of the correct means of implementing it.

"Self-government" refers not only to the processes of popular government but also, and especially, to the fact that every self needs governing. That is the light in which the dependence of consent upon character becomes interesting. Here we confront different kinds of challenges, having far more to do with the actual post-*Brown* environment. It is here that the debate over the success or failure of *Brown* becomes most important. And it is here that the question of the ethics of its implementation becomes central: just what options are available to establish the priority of the principle that all men are created equal?

We have already noted that *Brown* spoke of, without accomplishing, the overturning of *Plessy* v. *Ferguson*, with the result that "today the *Brown* decision is considered the progenitor of a host of color-conscious and group-specific policies." The problem centers on the Court's refusal to adopt the Harlan dissent. Why is the Harlan opinion significant? We are inclined to imagine that its importance has been inflated by the tendency of partisans to appeal to it, even though it was a lone dissent and, as Justice Harry A. Blackmun argued in *Bakke,* never accepted as law by the Court.[28] Perhaps, though, there is a principle beyond the decisions of the Supreme Court.

The idea that there exists a higher or last resort beyond the Court is reflected in the history of Harlan's opinion. The frequent recurrence to it suggests that it speaks to an understanding of the rule by which we govern ourselves at once deeper and more difficult to eradicate than passing Court opinions might conceive. Even in court records themselves we find this phenomenon borne out. Harlan's dissent is perhaps the most frequently and widely cited dissenting opinion in the history of constitutional adjudication before American courts. From 1947 to 1978 (before the *Bakke* decision), there were sixty-four Harlan dissent citations, twenty-seven of them in school cases. This phenomenon suggests that Harlan's opinion speaks more directly to our expectations of the rule of equality than any of the long line of majority opinions touching on the question of race in America.

In effect, the constant recurrence to the Harlan dissent demonstrates that Lincoln succeeded in preventing Douglas from "blowing out the moral lights around us," from "penetrating the human soul, and eradicating the light of reason and love." But Lincoln's defense of popular deliberation as a higher constitutional authority than the Supreme Court has failed to make an impression on the Court itself. For it has yet to accept Lincoln's faith in the sufficiency of the consent of the governed. The reason, perhaps, is that the Court has not understood the connection between equality and consent in such a way as to lead it to prefer only those measures of implementation that reinforce the consent of the governed. While it cannot be doubted that every justice would prefer a situation in which the ethical authority of our guiding principle governed individual souls, it is fair to say that few justices have ever been confident that that was possible. Thus, in spite of *Brown,* we struggle still with the question about the just means of implementing standards of equality and fairness in American life.

Over the years we have searched so diligently for "discrete and insular minorities" that what began as a supposedly necessary suspension of the operation of ordinary political processes has turned into the ordinary, nay, traditional procedure for our generation. The needs of "discrete and insular minorities" have turned into the demands of special interests, and our lawmakers seem to have lost all capacity to legislate in the common interest. Looking at the university, George Anastaplo has aptly characterized the problem:

One proper concern of the law, as of the community whose instrument the law is, must continue to be the education of the public. But no system of education can mean much if it is not guided by men who have some rough idea of what is good—of what would be an improvement, of what would be deterioration. This means, for example, that the delusive character of certain programs (such as most of those devoted to so-called black studies and those that make much of "black English") should be recognized.[29]

Inasmuch as the task suggested by Anastaplo could only be undertaken by persons who took seriously the work described above—to entrust to free, consenting citizens the goal of weighing social and political actions in the light of the principles that guide us—it follows that the explanation for the difficulties we have encountered in implementing the principle so well established in *Brown* stems in large measure from that decision's neglect of the means that ought to have accompanied its goal.

While there exists a sufficient scholarly history of the development of those interpretations that have occasioned our difficulties, the case can be adequately documented from the contemporary judicial record.[30] Accordingly, I will rest here with a single example, again making Harlan's dissent the mediating focus of concern.

Thirty years ago, presenting the plaintiff's cause in *Brown*, the present Justice Thurgood Marshall said, "I think so far as our argument on the constitutional debate is concerned . . . the state is deprived of any power to make any racial classification in any governmental field."[31] His exchange with the justices at the bench placed a definitive gloss on the statement in the NAACP brief concerning the idea that "our Constitution is color-blind": "It is the dissenting opinion of Justice Harlan, rather than the majority opinion in *Plessy v. Ferguson*, that is in keeping with the scope and meaning of the Fourteenth Amendment." How changed, then, some would say of the justice's opinion in *Bakke*, twenty-four years later. No, I would say, there is no inconsistency between Mr. Marshall of counsel and Mr. Justice Marshall. But unlike those who labor to interpret away the manifest contradictions in his language, urging divergent contexts and other exculpations, I insist that Marshall is consistent despite the contradictions in his language (not unlike Madison of the previous century).

Here is what he wrote in *Bakke:*

We must remember, however, that the principle that the "Constitution is color-blind" appeared only in the opinion of the lone dissenter. . . . It is because of a legacy of unequal

> treatment that we now must permit the institutions of this society to give considerations to race in making decisions about who will hold the positions of influence, affluence and prestige in America.

Note well that, in addition to justifying race-conscious legislation, Marshall incidentally justifies the right of government—not the people—to decide "who gets what," "who will hold positions of influence, affluence and prestige." That is to say that Marshall adopted the *Plessy* principle of the plenitude of state power. This violation of the people's right of self-government is the real injury that inheres in the opinion. Once the right of self-government is surrendered, it matters little whether the masters who emerge base their judgments on race or on the positions of the stars. Liberty is lost and with it every occasion for ethical conduct.

I find Marshall's consistency in his good intention to bring about a constitutional result, namely, "meaningful equality," respecting which he has not deviated one whit. But this is precisely where the problem surfaces. For not all the good intentions and high-sounding language one may muster can supply the soundness on which ethical judgment rests. The contradictions in Marshall's language do not indict him a hypocrite; but they prove that he failed, first and last, to comprehend the precise means required to relieve our nation's distress. And in that he was less seriously in error than the *Brown* majority, for he at least voiced the correct argument. In reviewing *Brown* and the decisions leading up to it, he concluded in 1978, "Those decisions . . . did not . . . move Negroes from a position of legal inferiority to one of equality." He perceived, in other words, that something had gone wrong in the implementation of *Brown*. There we agree, although I cannot subscribe to his pessimistic account. As I have tried to show, what went wrong was already present in the *Brown* decision's unanimous neglect of the need to rely on ordinary political processes to produce results in accord with the rule by which we govern ourselves.

The necessity I speak of here lies in our need to maintain in ourselves the character befitting a people who govern themselves through the principle of consent. The demonstration that we *can* govern ourselves cannot be the result of governmental regulations. The question of race obscures this truth; nevertheless, *Brown* has kept alive for us in this era the importance of reflecting on the requirements of equality and consent. Because of that we are able to raise anew the claims of virtue within our polity. Further, it is no small achievement that we have already erected a powerful consensus in favor of equality. We would all be justified in taking the optimistic view that a full understanding of equality and consent remains a distinct possibility. We have matured beyond the illusion that political integration is the prior condition of peace within our society. We can now see that social integration is the necessary support of political integration, as Aristotle argued more than two thousand years ago. We can also see that the necessary means to nurture and sustain that social integration are intimately connected with our appreciation of the principles and promises of the American Constitution. With a proper regard for the ethical imperatives of equality and consent, we can ensure that the victories we have already gained will eventuate in the fulfillment of that new birth of freedom to which, in 1863, Lincoln gave witness of his people's resolve.

At the time of the founding, confusion about the requirements of the Constitution could be attributed to the inherent tensions of an imperfect world, even as the salutary influence of the Declaration and Constitution worked to produce an improvement in human political life. Given the achievements of past eras, confusion about the requirements of the Constitution in our own time is less readily explicable. For the first time the practical conditions for the rule of the regime's guiding principle are wholly consistent with private and public efforts to justify the experiment in self-government.

Notes

1. Earlier in the Constitutional Convention, on May 30, Madison steered the delegates away from a discussion of slavery, stating that "the words 'or to the number of free inhabitants' [in the article on representation in the Virginia plan] might occasion debates which would divert the Committee [of the whole] from the general question whether the principle of representation should be changed." On his motion the words were struck.

2. Gordon Lloyd described the politics of the convention thus:

> [Madison] reminded the delegates that the real division to be faced in America lay between north and south and not between large and small states. . . . [He] deliberately chose to push the issue of slavery to the forefront in order to make sure that North Carolina, South Carolina, and Georgia joined the three large states in voting down the five small states from the north. The ⅗ths clause was a genuine offer, to the small southern states, so that they would think large.

Lloyd's comments appear in a paper delivered at the American Political Science Association Annual Meeting of 1985, commenting on the paper of John Alvis, "The Slavery Provisions of the U.S. Constitution: Means for Emancipation." The analysis below differs somewhat from Lloyd's, but the essential remains: Madison's awareness of the status of slavery at the founding may be distinguished from his principles, in themselves abolitionist.

3. William Wiecek's " 'The Blessings of Liberty': Slavery in the American

Constitutional Order" follows that path in setting out "five principles," which include the claim that "slavery was wholly compatible with the American constitutional order; indeed, was an essential component of it." In this conclusion he seems to confuse an "essential" element (intrinsic to the meaning or purpose of a whole) with a "necessary" element (that part or condition of a whole without which the whole itself cannot be realized). I will show below the degree to which this view does not state the views of the founders in general and, therefore, does not sustain Wiecek's conclusion that "the Constitution of 1787 contained no implicit assumptions that slavery was incompatible with the progressive governmental order that the document created."

4. Cf. Walter Berns's definitive analysis of the constitutional provision touching on slavery in "The Constitution and the Migration of Slaves," *Yale Law Journal*, vol. 78 (1968). Madison seemed to stray through his career from the position of abolitionist in principle if not in practice to the position of a defender of slaveholding interests (p. 209). The problem, according to Berns, arose from Madison's shrinking from employing the interstate commerce power under the Constitution in relation to Article I, section 9, which affirmed a congressional authority, after 1807, over not only the "importation" but also the "migration" of slaves within the United States. Such a power could well have been employed to force the practical abolition of slavery. What follows in this essay presents what I take to be the only credible response to Berns's well-defended argument.

5. Cf. *Federalist* No. 43, Madison's discussion of the "natural majority," and the discussion of that principle below.

6. James Madison, "Notes for the National Gazette Essays," *The Papers of James Madison*, ed. Robert A. Rutland et al. (Charlottesville: University Press of Virginia, 1983), vol. 14, pp. 160–61. Madison's outline is incorrectly taken, I believe, as "notes for his *National Gazette* essays." It appears rather to be a tentative approach to a comprehensive treatise on political principles. In that light it also confutes the thesis of Gordon Wood to the effect that the framers adopted a "democratic" language to defend their "aristocratic" institutions. Cf. Gordon Wood, *The Creation of the American Republic, 1776–1787* (New York: W. W. Norton and Co., 1972), esp. pp. 492–98.

7. Merrill Jensen, ed., *The Documentary History of the Ratification of the Constitution*, vol. 1, *Constitutional Documents and Records, 1776–1787* (Madison: State Historical Society of Wisconsin, 1976), p. 116.

8. Ibid.

9. As General Charles Pinckney recognized in the South Carolina ratification debate. See below.

10. Max Farrand, *The Records of the Federal Convention of 1787* (New Haven, Conn: Yale University Press, 1966 [1911]), vol. 1, p. 476. Emphasis in original.

11. Pennsylvania state ratifying convention, December 3, 1787.

12. See the *Annals of Congress*, 9th Congress.

13. Letter to Robert Walsh, November 27, 1819, printed in Farrand, *Records*, vol. 3, p. 436.

14. Letter to Robert Evans, June 15, 1819, in *The Writings of James Madison*,

ed. Gaillard Hunt (New York: G. P. Putnam's Sons, 1908), vol. 8, pp. 439–41.

15. See especially Madison's account of his "different" opinions on the constitutionality of a national bank, in the letter to President James Monroe, December 27, 1817. *Writings*, vol. 3, pp. 55–56.

16. Alexander Hamilton, James Madison, and John Jay, *The Federalist*, ed. Jacob E. Cooke (Middletown, Conn.: Wesleyan University Press, 1961), pp. 288–98.

17. On February 19, 1787, Madison urged Congress not to renounce its intention to support Massachusetts in quelling Shays's Rebellion, in spite of legitimate doubts about the authority of the Confederation. This clear case of exercising a power "not expressly delegated" conflicted with the Articles and, worse, brought the Confederation into conflict "with the principles of Republican govts. which as they rest on the sense of the majority, necessarily suppose power and right always to be on the same side." [*Journals of the Continental Congress*, xxxiii, p. 721.] Madison nevertheless found reason to support federal opposition to a possible Shays's majority in Massachusetts. A sense of the federal good seems to prevail over manifest power and right in Massachusetts. Madison went to the Constitutional Convention three months later having already affirmed the priority of democratic nationalism over majority rule in any one of the states. *Federalist* No. 51 should be reread in this light.

18. Note that the term "persons" not only is used of slaves in the Constitution but also is used by Madison to refer to slaves throughout his May 13, 1789, speech.

19. Compare with the opinion of Chief Justice Roger B. Taney in Dred Scott v. Sandford, 19 How. 393, 404 (1857).

20. 163 U.S. 537. Contrast the language of Mr. Justice Brown (announcing the majority's doctrine of "separate but equal") with that of Justice John M. Harlan (insisting that the "Constitution is color-blind"). The terms by which Brown and Harlan referred to American blacks convey a sense of their own attitudes. Three terms appear: black, negro, and colored. Brown did not once resort to "black," used "negro" but twice, and employed "colored" some thirty times. Harlan, by contrast, did not use "negro," used the prevalent "colored" fifteen times, and used "black" twenty-one times.

21. 347 U.S. 483.

22. Diane Ravitch, "The Ambiguous Legacy of *Brown v. Board of Education*, " *New Perspectives*, vol. 16, no. 1, p. 6.

23. Mary Ritter Beard, "A Changing Political Economy As It Affects Women," American Association of University Women, Washington, D.C., 1934, p. 55.

24. We may define character as the patterned representation of the content of the soul. A good judge is not called such by virtue of a single good judgment but by virtue of repeated and consistent good judgment. One who indifferently judged well or ill would not be called a good judge. So, too, a generous man; to be known as such his actions must be generous in general and not sometimes generous, sometimes miserly. Accordingly, the character

for which one is known is produced by the dispositions or habits of soul that determine one's actions in a consistent manner over time. The character itself is a sign of the soul's content.

25. A Charge Delivered to the Grand Jury in the Circuit Court of the United States, for the District of Virginia, May 1791.

26. 304 U.S. 144, 152, n.4.

27. Of course, the foregoing sections of this paper have already demonstrated how far this view is a mischaracterization of the American past.

28. Regents of the University of California v. Allan Bakke, 438 U.S. 265 (1978).

29. George Anastaplo, "Race, Law, and Civilization," in *Human Being and Citizen: Essays on Virtue, Freedom, and the Common Good* (Chicago: Swallow Press/Ohio University Press, 1975), chap. 15.

30. I discuss the historical question in detail in my essay "In Search of Freedom: Slavery and the Principles of the American Founding," *American Journal of Jurisprudence*, vol. 18 (1983), pp. 249–71.

31. The best treatment of the development of Marshall's views and the decision in *Brown* and its repercussions, is Raymond Wolters, *The Burden of Brown* (Knoxville: University of Tennessee Press, 1984). Marshall's briefs and oral comments at trial are preserved in the record of the case, and his written dissent in *Bakke* is published with the case.

5
Equality and the Constitution: A Study in the Transformation of a Concept

Kenneth M. Holland

"In running over the pages of our history," Alexis de Tocqueville writes in his introduction to *Democracy in America*, "we shall scarcely find a single great event of the last seven hundred years that has not promoted equality of condition." Although Tocqueville was describing the demise of the aristocratic privileges associated with European feudalism, the history of constitutional development in the United States is also a story of equality's advance. During the founding period and the nineteenth century, equality had two essential and complementary meanings: equality of rights and equality of opportunity. During the last half of the present century, however, the concept has undergone a major transformation. Equality has come to signify equality of result. Originally, the largely unlimited freedom to acquire and dispose of property was believed to be perfectly compatible with equality among men. Today, this degree of liberty in the marketplace is morally suspect because it generates unacceptable gradations in men's situations. Originally, equality demanded a minimal role for government; today, more and more regulatory power flows into government hands in the name of achieving a more equal society. Opponents of this change, such as Robert Nisbet, regard the following words of Tocqueville as prophetic:

> The foremost or indeed the sole condition required in order to succeed in centralizing the supreme power in a democratic community is to love equality or to get men to believe you love it. Thus, the science of despotism, which was once so complex, has been simplified and reduced, as it were, to a single principle.[1]

The tension between freedom and the "new equality" is the greatest domestic issue of our time. There are ample justification and need to

93

examine the stages of this transformation. The only reference in the Constitution to equality of persons occurs in the Fourteenth Amendment.[2] It is, therefore, appropriate to commence the analysis of the meaning of the concept with the Reconstruction Amendments.

The Reconstruction Amendments and the Concept of Equality

The Reconstruction Amendments embody the traditional conception of equality, that is, equality of rights and equality of opportunity. They extended the size of the group enjoying equality without qualitatively changing its content. In December 1865, the Constitution was amended for the thirteenth time. This amendment reads:

> *Section 1.* Neither slavery nor involuntary servitude, except as a punishment for crime whereof the party shall have been duly convicted, shall exist within the United States, or any place subject to their jurisdiction.
> *Section 2.* Congress shall have power to enforce this article by appropriate legislation.

As is clear from the debates in Congress preceding its proposal, the Thirteenth Amendment had two purposes: to abolish slavery and to eliminate the relics of slavery. The Supreme Court accepted this broad view of the amendment's objective in the *Civil Rights Cases* (1883):

> The 13th Amendment may be regarded as nullifying all state laws which establish or uphold slavery. But it has a reflex character also, establishing and decreeing universal civil and political freedom throughout the United States; and it is assumed that the power vested in Congress to enforce the article by appropriate legislation, clothes Congress with power to pass all laws necessary and proper for abolishing all badges and incidents of slavery in the United States.[3]

The amendment, therefore, was aimed at "all badges and incidents of slavery" as well as slavery itself. The Court enumerated the most visible of these "burdens and disabilities": right of the master to the compulsory service of the slave; restraint of the slave's movements; incapacity to hold property, to make contracts, to sue, to be a witness against a white person; and punishments for crimes more severe than those imposed on free men. By "decreeing universal civil and political freedom" the amendment and the Civil Rights Act of 1866, passed under the authority of section two of the amendment, secured to former slaves "those fundamental rights which are the essence of civil freedom, namely: the same right to make and enforce contracts, to sue, be parties, give evidence, and to inherit, purchase, lease, sell and convey property, as is enjoyed by white citizens."[4]

The Court erroneously held that the Thirteenth Amendment did not reach private acts of racial discrimination, precipitating a dissent by Justice Harlan, whose view of the scope of the Thirteenth Amendment was subsequently adopted by the Court's majority.[5] Justice Harlan elaborated this view in two dissents, one in the *Civil Rights Cases* and the other in *Plessy* v. *Ferguson* (1896). Harlan agreed with the 1883 majority that the object of the Thirteenth Amendment was "the eradication, not simply of the institution, but of its badges and incidents."[6] American slavery, he pointed out, differed in kind from ancient Greek and Roman slavery. The latter enslaved whites; the former placed in bondage only African Negroes. Therefore, racial discrimination in the United States, said Harlan, is a relic of slavery, forbidden by the Thirteenth Amendment: "The arbitrary separation of citizens, on the basis of race . . . is a badge of servitude wholly inconsistent with the civil freedom and the equality before the law established by the Constitution. It cannot be justified upon any legal grounds."[7] The Thirteenth Amendment consequently "removed the race line from our governmental systems,"[8] with the result that "our Constitution is color-blind, and neither knows nor tolerates classes among citizens."[9]

By itself, the Thirteenth Amendment prohibited all forms of racial discrimination practiced by governments or by individuals and corporations providing public services. If the amendment reached this far, then why did Congress propose the Fourteenth Amendment, and is it not in fact redundant? Section 1 of the Fourteenth Amendment contains four important clauses:

1. All persons born . . . in the United States . . . are citizens of the United States and of the State wherein they reside.
2. No State shall make or enforce any law which shall abridge the privileges or immunities of citizens of the United States;
3. nor shall any State deprive any person of life, liberty, or property, without due process of law;
4. nor deny to any person within its jurisdiction the equal protection of the laws.

The Fourteenth Amendment came into being because of problems the federal government experienced in enforcing the Thirteenth Amendment's ban on race discrimination. The Fourteenth Amendment does not materially add to the substance of its predecessor. Justice Harlan explained clearly the relationship of the two amendments:

The 13th Amendment does not permit the withholding or the deprivation of any right necessarily inhering in freedom. It not only struck down the institution of slavery as previously existing in the United States, but it prevents the imposition of any burdens or disabilities that constitute badges of slavery or servitude. It decreed universal civil freedom in this country. This court has so adjudged. But that amendment having been found inadequate to the protection of the rights of those who had been in slavery, it was followed by the 14th Amendment.[10]

What was the enforcement problem associated with the Thirteenth Amendment? Justice Harlan answered:

Between the adoption of the 13th Amendment and the proposal by Congress of the 14th Amendment, on June 16, 1866, the statute-books of several of the States . . . had become loaded down with enactments which, under the guise of Apprentice, Vagrant and Contract Regulations, sought to keep the colored race in a condition, practically, of servitude [and thus were violations of the Thirteenth Amendment]. It was openly announced that whatever might be the rights which persons of that race had, as freemen, under the guaranties of the National Constitution, they could not become citizens of a State, with the privileges belonging to citizens, except by the consent of such State; consequently, that their civil rights, as citizens of the State, depended entirely upon state legislation. To meet this new peril to the black race, that the purposes of the Nation might not be doubted or defeated, and by way of further enlargement of the power of Congress, the 14th Amendment was proposed for adoption.[11]

The key clause of the Fourteenth Amendment, then, is the one that states that "all persons born or naturalized in the United States . . . are citizens . . . of the state wherein they reside." This clause made clear that the "universal civil freedom" established by the Thirteenth Amendment could not be annulled by the states on the pretext that their black residents were not citizens. Blacks received an explicit "exemption from race discrimination in respect of any civil right belonging to citizens of the white race in the same State."[12]

The goals of the Fourteenth Amendment are identical to those of the Thirteenth. The amendments are, in fact, largely redundant. Raoul Berger has shown that the purpose of the Fourteenth Amendment was "to embody and protect" the Civil Rights Act of 1866, authorized by the Thirteenth Amendment, which had been ratified in 1865.[13] The Civil Rights Acts of 1866 and 1875 do not need the support of the Fourteenth Amendment, said Justice Harlan, because "discrimination practiced by corporations and individuals in the exercise of their public or quasi public functions is a badge of servitude, the imposition of which Congress may prevent under its power, by appropriate legislation, to enforce the 13th Amendment."[14] Further statements support the conclusion of superfluity: "The 13th Amendment *alone* obliterated the race line, so far as all rights fundamental in a state of freedom are concerned."[15]

After listing several examples of racially discriminatory state laws passed in 1865 and 1866, Harlan asked:

> Can there be any doubt that all such enactments might have been reached by direct legislation upon the part of Congress under its express power to enforce the Thirteenth Amendment? Would any court have hesitated to declare that such legislation imposed badges of servitude in conflict with the civil freedom ordained by that Amendment? That it would have been also in conflict with the 14th Amendment, because inconsistent with the fundamental rights of American citizenship, does not prove that it would have been consistent with the 13th Amendment.[16]

The Fourteenth Amendment made explicit what the Thirteenth implied and eliminated a pretext used by some of the states in a vain effort to avoid the intent of the Thirteenth Amendment's framers.

The drafters of the Fourteenth Amendment regarded the privileges and immunities clause as much more important than the due process and equal protection clauses in guaranteeing legal equality for freed Negroes. Note that each provision has a different audience. The privileges and immunities clause is directed at legislators. It prohibits racially discriminatory statutes. The due process clause is aimed at prosecutors and judges who might be tempted to take legal action against blacks who had not received notice of the offense with which they were charged and who had not been given an opportunity to present their case in open court prior to sentencing or judgment. The equal protection clause addresses police officers and other law enforcement officials who might consider tolerating white assaults on blacks while arresting blacks who assaulted or threatened whites. Congress has taken precisely this view of the addressee of the equal protection prohibition. A statute empowering the president to employ the federal armed forces to suppress civil disturbances provides that whenever insurrection, civil violence, unlawful combinations, or conspiracies in any state so oppose, obstruct, or hinder the execution of the laws of the state, and of the United States, as to deprive any person of rights, privileges, and immunities named in the Constitution and secured by laws, and the *authorities* of the state are unable to or fail to or refuse to provide such protection, it will be deemed a denial by that state of the equal protection of the laws.[17] The due process and equal protection provisions, read literally, do not primarily restrict legislatures, but rather those charged with carrying out the law. The Supreme Court's erroneous emasculation of the privileges and immunities clause in the *Slaughter-House Cases* (1873) facilitated the emergence of the doctrine of "substantive due process" in the 1880s and the doctrine of "substantive equal protection" in the 1960s. The Court has employed both doctrines in a rather disreputable way to strike down legislation thought to be inconsistent with the judges' notions of justice and equality.

The Fifteenth Amendment proclaims that "the right of citizens of the United States to vote shall not be denied or abridged by the United States or by any State on account of race, color, or previous condition of servitude." Taken together the three Reconstruction Amendments clarify the status of Negroes born in the United States: (1) the Thirteenth emphasizes the applicability of the statement in the Declaration of Independence that "all men are created equal" to blacks by recognizing their humanity and their equal possession of natural rights; (2) the Fourteenth Amendment acknowledges the membership of blacks in the American republic as full and equal citizens, entitled to the same privileges and immunities as white citizens; the Fourteenth Amendment emphasizes that blacks possess civil rights while continuing to deny them to unnaturalized aliens; and (3) white and black women were regarded as citizens, but they were not permitted to participate in the deliberative and judicial functions of the polity; the Fifteenth Amendment placed black males on an equal footing with white males by acknowledging their right to vote; it extended to blacks political rights.

The conception of equality implicit in these amendments is that blacks enjoy the same legal rights as whites and that blacks possess the same opportunity to acquire property and accumulate wealth as whites. The particular civil rights mentioned by the Fourteenth Amendment's framers—the rights "to make and enforce contracts, to sue, be parties, give evidence, and to inherit, purchase, lease, sell and convey property"—are bulwarks of a free market economy and certain to produce wide gradations in individual wealth: in other words, certain to produce a society marked by poverty as well as by comfort and luxury. In Justice Harlan's words, the equality of the Reconstruction Amendments required merely that the laws be "color-blind."

The limited notion of equality imbedded in these amendments must not obscure the radical change they were intended to work in the composition of the American body politic. The Fourteenth and Fifteenth Amendments proved that the fears expressed by the South, by Chief Justice Roger Taney in *Dred Scott* v. *Sandford* (1857), and by Stephen Douglas in the Lincoln-Douglas debates were well founded. Douglas, for instance, argued that if Negro slaves were emancipated it would be impossible to deny them full social and political equality. Taney came to believe that the continuation of Negro slavery, although an injustice, was preferable to the admission of millions of blacks to membership in what he regarded as a country founded by whites for whites only.[18] Motivating the seceding South was not only fear of losing the right to own property in slaves but the haunting questions, What is to be done with the blacks? and Is the North going to make them citizens? Lincoln attempted to draw the line between opposing slavery, which he regarded as a moral question, and advocating Negro citizenship, which he regarded as a policy issue. Thus he asked freed slaves to leave the country and, like Jefferson, Adams, and Clay before him, supported efforts to colonize blacks to Africa and the Caribbean while resisting, to the point of war, the extension of slavery into the territories of the United States. His opposition to the extension of slavery into the territories in fact was an effort to erect not only free states but white states in the west. Lincoln's attempt at line drawing failed, and in the 1860s, following his death, the Constitution brought into being a racially mixed political community, something he did not desire. He thus stated in an 1858 speech:

> I will say, then, that I am not, nor ever have been, in favor of bringing about in any way the social and political equality of the white and black races: that I am not, nor ever have been, in favor of making voters or jurors of negroes, nor of qualifying them to hold office, nor to intermarry with white people.[19]

Prior to the Civil War, the Constitution tolerated four categories of people born in the United States: (1) those possessing natural rights to life, liberty, and the pursuit of happiness but deprived of the opportunity to exercise them (slaves); (2) those enjoying natural rights but denied membership in the political community (free Negroes); (3) members of the sovereign people who enjoy the rights of citizenship but not the franchise (white women); and (4) those citizens who possess full civil and political rights (propertied white men). The Reconstruction Amendments abolished the first and second category of native-born residents. The extension of the suffrage to women by the Nineteenth Amendment in 1920 eliminated the third category of natives.

To establish whether the conception of equality in the Reconstruction Amendments is consistent or inconsistent with that implicit in the 1787 Constitution requires an examination of the relationship between that document and the Declaration of Independence.

Pre-Reconstruction Meanings of Equality

The Declaration of Independence. The Declaration of Independence furnished the principles of free and legitimate government. The Constitution structured a democratic republic in keeping with those principles. The declaration begins, "When, in the course of human events, it becomes necessary for *one people* to dissolve the political bands which have connected them with *another* . . ."[20] Jefferson here alludes to the conventional quality of politics, which contrasts with the natural basis of civil society stressed in the succeeding paragraph. Although "all men are created equal," they are justified in forming sovereign political communities, admitting those they believe will contribute to the greater safety or prosperity of the society and excluding those they believe will render the community less happy or secure. Religious, ethnic, linguistic, or racial differences can be legitimately regarded as threats to peace or prosperity, for each community is the final judge of what makes an applicant for membership fit or unfit. Accordingly, in *Notes on the State of Virginia* Jefferson defends the decision to exclude Negroes from the American polity on the grounds that blacks are less beautiful, less intelligent, and less moral than whites.[21] He applauds the founders for their commitment to keeping the community as beautiful as possible by limiting membership to Europeans. The division of the world into sovereign nation-states, each seeking racial or religious homogeneity, appears to be compatible with human nature and with justice, according to the opening lines of the declaration.

"We hold these truths to be self-evident, that all men are created equal, that they are endowed by their Creator with certain unalienable rights, that among these are life, liberty and the pursuit of happiness": Chief Justice Taney in *Dred Scott* contended that because blacks were excluded from membership in the American polity in 1776, the phrase "all men are created equal" was meant to include only whites. This restriction, however, is clearly not Jefferson's intention. There is no contradiction between saying that blacks are equal to whites in their humanity, in their capacity to form a political community and to exercise civil and political rights, on the one hand, and declaring that whites are justified in reserving their particular civil society for men like themselves, on the other hand. Jefferson's support for the colonization movement underscores his belief in the capacity of freed slaves and other Negroes to perform these tasks. Moreover, Jefferson certainly intended his words to be a moral condemnation of slavery. That the institution of human bondage was a violation of the inalienable rights of men is a teaching that shines through all his writings, including his initial draft of the declaration. Jefferson and Washington were able to own slaves while damning slavery because there was no adequate place in Virginia society for emancipated slaves, who were largely deprived of the means of livelihood.

The key point about the declaration's treatment of equality is that equality is presented as a fact, as a truth of nature: "all men *are* created equal." Equality is not something government achieves; it is a given that government must acknowledge if it is to be legitimate. Even the convention of slavery cannot deprive men of their natural equality. The primary purpose of this clause is to refute the doctrine of the divine right of kings, under which European monarchs based their right to rule on their supposed inheritance as lineal descendants of Adam, to whom the book of Genesis says God gave dominion over the earth. It also refutes the teaching of Shintoism in Japan that the emperor's right to rule is derived from his divinity as well as Plato's teaching of natural right, according to which philosophers are entitled to govern by reason of their wisdom. The following sentence in the second paragraph makes this point clear: "That to secure these rights, governments are instituted among men, deriving their just powers from the consent of the governed." No one can rule others without their consent, no matter how wise, how divine, or how direct his link to Adam. The fact that all men are created equal means that no man can rule others either as a god ruling men (as claimed by the divine right theory) or as a man ruling beasts (as claimed by the "positive good" apologists for slavery).

The declaration's conception of equality means that government comes into being by means of a social contract, with each member having an equal vote in selecting the sovereign, which must be done, as Thomas Hobbes explains, by majority vote. In the words of the declaration, the community of equals can consent to any "form, as to them shall seem most likely to effect their safety and happiness." That they can consent to be ruled by a king or by a body of aristocrats is made clear by Jefferson's need to prove that King George is an illegitimate ruler not because he is a monarch, as Tom Paine argued, but because he is a tyrant. Only "a prince, whose character is . . . marked by every act which may define a tyrant, is unfit to be the ruler of a free people," says Jefferson in the conclusion.

The teaching of the declaration is that monarchy is in theory compatible with both equality and liberty and that even democracy is an enemy of freedom if it becomes a tyranny of the majority. The Constitution, however, rejected monarchy in favor of a limited democracy and established equality of opportunity to hold office and to compete in the marketplace. The triumph of opportunity over feudal principles is evident in Article I, sections 9 and 10, which provide that "No title of Nobility shall be granted by the United States" and "no State shall . . . grant any Title of Nobility." Jefferson's corpus suggests that the natural rights to "life, liberty and the pursuit of happiness" are identical to John Locke's rights to life, liberty, and property.

"To secure these rights, governments are instituted among men" means that government must protect persons and property against the depredations of one's fellow citizens and must defend the nation-state against foreign aggression. The declaration's understanding of equality, in other words, is consistent with the minimal state. Jefferson's fear of despotism and the centralization of power led him to the extreme point of advocating a revolution every twenty-five years, for the tree of liberty, he believed, must be watered periodically with the blood of patriots and tyrants.

The 1787 Constitution. Given the central position occupied by human equality in contemporary politics, it is surprising to many that the purview of the Constitution omits any reference to it. Given the relationship between the declaration and the Constitution, however, such a reference, except with regard to slavery, would have been out of place. The declaration stated the self-evident truth that all men are created equal. No government could make men less or more equal than "the laws of nature and of nature's God" had made them. The purpose of the Constitution was to establish a government based on the consent of the governed, that is, on their equality, that would secure life, liberty, and property. The primary objects of the Constitution were security for individual liberty, provision for majority rule, and competent government.[22] To have made greater equality among whites a goal in 1787 would have obscured the teaching of the declaration and would have placed equality on the same plane as freedom and property, when in fact rights to freedom and property are derived from equality.

Although condemning slavery as a violation of natural rights, the framers considered inequality of wealth a sign of the health of the regime. James Madison makes this point clear in *Federalist* No. 10:

> The rights of property originate [from] the diversity in the faculties of men. . . . The protection of these faculties is the first object of government. From the protection of different

and unequal faculties of acquiring property, the possession of different degrees and kinds of property immediately results.

Madison's words echo those of Locke, who in the *Second Treatise on Government*—probably the single most influential work of political philosophy on the American founders—demonstrated how the inequality of possessions arose directly from the natural equality of men.

> It is plain that men have agreed to disproportionate and unequal possession of the earth, they having, by a tacit and voluntary *consent,* found out a way how a man may fairly possess more land than he himself can use the product of, by receiving in exchange for the overplus, gold and silver, which may be hoarded up without injury to anyone, these metals not spoiling or decaying in the hands of the possessor.[23]

The scarcity of the prepolitical state of nature is replaced by the abundance produced by able and industrious men who exchange for money the surplus they produce on the land they have enclosed. No one is cheated by the resulting inequality in wealth, as Robert Goldwin explains,[24] because even the poorest men, who share in the vastly increased wealth, are much more fortunate than they would be in a society without private property. Government comes into being because the possessions of the "industrious and rational"—the men upon whom the well-being of all depends—must be protected from the "fancy or covetousness of the quarrelsome and contentious."[25] Thus, Locke concludes, "the increase of lands, and the right employing of them, is *the* great art of government: and that prince, who . . . by established laws of liberty . . . secure[s] protection and encouragement to the honest industry of mankind [shall be deemed] wise and godlike."[26]

Note that Madison says the first object of government is the protection of the "*faculties* of acquiring property," not the protection of property itself, and that Locke cites as "the great art of government" security for the "industry of mankind," not security for the fruits of that industry. This is because the well-being of society depends upon labor, calculation, and invention. If government's duty were to protect property, then it could not tamper with the inheritances of the indolent, who themselves contribute nothing to the nation's wealth. From this point of view, laws that redistribute wealth are only suspect to the extent that they reduce the incentive of the talented to produce.

The foundation of private property (and thus economic inequality) is not only the public good, however, but also morality. The industrious deserve to enjoy the fruits of their labors. As Lincoln said in 1858: "Certainly the negro is not our equal in color—perhaps not in many other respects; still, in the *right* to put into his mouth the bread that his own hands have earned, he is the equal of every other man."[27] Each man, in other words, has an equal right to be treated justly, and a just society is necessarily unequal. It is not immoral for the naturally gifted to acquire more than the less fortunate. The less gifted benefit, and the more gifted deserve the extra they have produced.

The Supreme Court reiterated Locke's and Madison's teaching in *City of New York* v. *Miln*, 36 U.S. 102 (1837). New York had enacted legislation excluding the poor from entry into the state. The Court held that such an action was within the police power of the state, referring to "the moral pestilence of paupers," and reasoning that it was as reasonable for a state to exclude the poor as it was to exclude "convicts" or "infectious articles." The judges believed that poverty was due to the poor habits and uncontrolled passions of the individual. The assumption was that if men worked hard and were provident in a land of freedom and opportunity, they would be able to support themselves. The poor, by definition, lack industry. At the Constitutional Convention Charles Pinckney contended that "equality is . . . the leading feature of the U. States."[28] He makes clear that by equality he means equality of rights and opportunity:

> [In the United States] every freeman has a right to the same protection and security; and a very moderate share of property entitles them to the possession of all the honors and privileges the public can bestow: hence arises a greater equality, than is to be found among the people of any other country, and an equality which is more likely to continue—I say this equality is likely to continue, because in a new Country, possessing immense tracts of uncultivated lands, where every temptation is offered to emigration & where *industry must be rewarded with competency,* there will be few poor, and few dependent—Every member of the Society almost, will enjoy an equal power of arriving at the supreme offices.[29]

Pinckney noted that in the United States, in contrast to Britain, wealth tended to accumulate in the hands of the deserving. In America many poor men have had sons and grandsons, he said, who acquired fortunes, while the sons and grandsons of many rich men have squandered and lost their inheritance. This vast shifting of wealth over generations from family to family was a sign that there is equality of opportunity and that a free society is a just society.

Equality as a Goal. In the Gettysburg Address, Lincoln recalls the Declaration of Independence in these words: "Four score and seven years ago our fathers brought forth on this continent, a new nation, conceived in liberty, and dedicated to the proposition that all men are created equal." There is a subtle but important difference in the way Jefferson and Lincoln speak about the relationship between equality and government. While Jefferson says, "We hold these truths to be self-evident," Lincoln declares that the nation is "dedicated to the proposition that all men are created equal." To hold something means to have it; to be dedicated to something means that one does not yet have it but is devoted to obtaining it. Equality has now become a goal instead of a starting point. Lincoln has added greater equality, the amelioration of inequality, to the missions of government. For Jefferson, equality is a fact; for Lincoln, it is an aspiration that may not be achievable: "Now we are engaged in a great civil war, testing whether that nation, or any nation so conceived and so dedicated, can long endure." Lincoln emphasizes the break from the limited Jeffersonian understanding of equality by prophesying in the peroration "that this nation, under God, shall have a new birth of freedom."

Lincoln's understanding of equality, nevertheless, is entirely consistent with Jefferson's. The doctrine of equality of natural rights places upon government the obligation to abolish slavery; the doctrine of republican equality demands that government remove artificial barriers to equality of opportunity. Although Jefferson's declaration that all men are created equal was a moral condemnation of slavery, Jefferson failed in all his attempts to effect an end to the South's peculiar institution. Jefferson articulated the duty that the fact of human equality imposed upon the nation, but the task fell to Lincoln to lead the nation in the discharge of its moral obligation. Jefferson said it was wrong to rule a man without his consent; Lincoln acted to end such rule.

The theory of equality contained in the declaration, as we have seen, was indifferent with regard to forms of government—monarchy, aristocracy, and democracy are all equally acceptable, as long as they secure to each member of society his natural rights and receive his consent. The Constitution, however, establishes and guarantees a republican form of government and is incompatible with any vestige of aristocracy. The abolition of established churches, primogeniture, and entail, a struggle led by Jefferson in Virginia, constituted positive acts of the state governments to bring about equality of condition. The politics of the Jacksonian period were, as Tocqueville saw, marked by the preeminence of equality and by war against monopolies, such as the Charles River Bridge in Boston and the Bank of the United States. The dominant idea of the 1830s was that a man's wealth should be a reflection of his industry and not his parentage, connections, or luck in gambling halls or stock exchanges. Government's special role is to remove barriers to meritocracy. Lincoln, as a young Whig, entered politics during the Jacksonian era. That he understood equality in the same way Jefferson, Madison, and Pinckney understood it is evident from his message to Congress of July 4, 1861. The cause of the Union, he said, was to perpetuate in the world "that form and substance of government, whose *leading object* is, to elevate the condition of men— to lift artificial weights from all shoulders—to clear the paths of laudable pursuit for all—to afford all, an unfettered start, and a fair chance, in the race of life."[30] The "new birth of freedom" foreseen by Lincoln, then, had a dual meaning: the freedom of the emancipated slaves and the freedom of all Americans to compete in the marketplace, free of the impediments of privilege and monopoly. The most appropriate symbol of Lincoln's view of republican equality is the Statue of Liberty.

Although Jefferson and Lincoln understand equality in the same way, Lincoln puts this understanding to a different use. Slavery demonstrated that men could consent to enslave their fellow man, that a man could define the pursuit of happiness as appropriating the labor of another; the abolition movement revealed that men could abuse their liberty by engaging in mob violence and other forms of lawlessness. The theory of the declaration taught selfishness and provided an insufficient check on evil. Lincoln's solution was a civil religion; and, as the Gettysburg Address, rich in religious imagery, indicates, dedication to the proposition that all men are created equal was the central tenet of this American creed. As Harry Jaffa explains:

> Lincoln transforms a truth open to each man as man [the self-evident truth that all men are created equal] into something he shares in virtue of his partnership in the nation. The truth . . . in the Gettysburg Address also imposes an overriding obligation to maintain the integrity, moral and physical, of that community which is the bearer of the truth. The sacrifices . . . required by that truth . . . transform . . . that nation dedicated to it from a merely rational and secular one, calculated to "secure these rights"—i.e., the rights of individuals—into something whose value is beyond all calculation. . . . [The] union [has] ancestors and . . . posterity; it is organic and sacramental.[31]

Lincoln thus helped make equality of rights and opportunity an ideal worth dying for—an achievement that gave not only the Civil War meaning but also World War II, the Korean War, and the Vietnam War, each in its way a struggle against slavery.

Equality of Result

In the 1970s the understanding of equality held by many policy makers changed in a fundamental way, thus altering dramatically the relationship between equality and government. The policy of ameliorative racial preference and the controversy over the constitutional status of the welfare state illustrate the vivid contrast between contemporary conceptions of equality and those animating the Reconstruction Amendments and the Founding.

The Policy of Racial Preference. Benign discrimination is the practice of giving preferential treatment to racial minorities purely on the grounds of their race. It involves giving advantages to black, Asian, Hispanic, and other minority applicants in employment decisions and school admissions to compensate for the alleged effects of past invidious racial discrimination. Critics refer to benign discrimination as reverse discrimination, for it often leads to discrimination against some groups, most obviously whites. The critics argue, in part, that reverse discrimination is based on a false and dangerous conception of equality and is premised on an erroneous assumption that present inequality is due to past discrimination. Proponents argue that the Constitution prohibits only invidious racial discrimination and that justice requires the elimination of the effects of 300 years of black slavery and second-class citizenship.

The struggle against racial discrimination in the United States can be divided into three phases.[32] During the first stage, the United States followed a "colorblind" policy. No government official or private employer was permitted to discriminate on the basis of race. Racial identity was not acknowledged, and even racial record keeping was considered improper. Phase I began in 1954 with the Supreme Court decision in *Brown* v. *Board of Education,* declaring separation by law of the races in the public schools a violation of the equal protection clause of the Fourteenth Amendment, and culminated in the congressionally enacted Civil Rights Act of 1964 and the Voting Rights Act of 1965. Title VII of the Civil Rights Act prohibits discrimination in employment on the basis of race, color, religion, sex, or national origin. The Educational Amendments of 1972 extended Title VII to include faculty in institutions of higher education. Administration of Title VII is by the Equal Employment Opportunity Commission, which was given enforcement powers by Congress in 1972. Title VI of the act declares that "no person in the United States shall, on the ground of race, color, or national origin, be excluded from participation in, be denied the benefits of, or be subjected to discrimination under any program or activity receiving Federal financial assistance."

107

Passage of the Elementary and Secondary Education Act the following year (1965), providing massive federal financial aid to the nation's public schools, greatly facilitated enforcement of the 1954 ban on racial discrimination in educational institutions. Enforcement of Title VI is the responsibility of the Office for Civil Rights of the Department of Education.

In 1965 the United States gradually, almost imperceptibly, switched to a "color-conscious" phase, fostered by the use of the term "affirmative action" for the first time in section 706(g) of the Civil Rights Act of 1964. In Executive Order 11246, issued in 1965, President Lyndon Johnson required employers with federal contracts to "take affirmative action to ensure that applicants are employed and that employees are treated . . . without regard to their race, color, religion, or national origin." The affirmative action mandate was later extended to education, housing, military service, and other areas. These laws commanded that employers take positive steps, such as advertising in magazines and newspapers read by blacks, to recruit minorities, but there was no requirement that goals or quotas be met. In 1970, consistently with the abandonment of colorblindness as a standard, the U.S. Civil Service Commission began collecting racial employment data on state and local agencies that were recipients of federal grants. Few whites in the labor force felt that they suffered injury from such reaching out to minorities, and there was also no real intellectual challenge to this policy.

Phase III commenced in 1971 when the Department of Labor promulgated an interpretation of the Civil Rights Act and the executive order that mandated racial quotas. This regulation, known as Revised Order No. 4, sets forth in detail the required contents of "affirmative action plans" to be developed and maintained by institutions holding contracts with the federal government. The institutions must identify areas in which members of "protected groups" are "under-utilized." Among the protected classes are blacks, Hispanics, women, workers over fifty, the handicapped, members of religious minorities, and Vietnam War veterans. "Under-utilization" is defined as a disparity between the employment of members of a racial or ethnic group in a job and their "availability." Availability is the percentage of minorities with the required skills or the capacity to acquire them within the institution's recruiting area used to determine underutilization. The institution must set "specific goals and timetables" to eliminate any underutilization and to achieve "parity."

The Department of Labor has delegated responsibility for administering Executive Order 11246 and Revised Order No. 4 to the Office of Federal Contract Compliance Programs. Although still called "affirmative action," this third phase requires qualitatively more than directing employers to try harder. The government now requires that statistical goals be established for minorities. Although the regulations distinguish between "goals" ("numerical projections referring to the representation of minorities in job groups in which they have been under-utilized") and "quotas" ("court-ordered hiring and/or promotion ratios of minorities into positions from which they have been excluded"), the distinction has proved to be a semantic rather than a real one. Given the scarcity of jobs and the competition for them, any statistical goal that results in a preference for an equally or less-qualified black acts as a quota that excludes the equally or more-qualified white. What is a positive "goal" for one group is seen as a negative "quota" by its complement. Racial discrimination is always exclusive from the viewpoint of the nonprivileged race.

For all practical purposes, the Supreme Court endorsed the use of racial quotas in education in *Regents of the University of California* v. *Bakke* (1978). The Court attempted another semantic distinction similar to that between "goals" and "quotas" and that between "affirmative action" and "reverse discrimination." Justice Lewis Powell, who cast the controlling vote, said that professional schools may not employ explicit quotas but may regard race as a "plus" in admissions. Again, given the fact of scarcity, if race is considered a qualification in itself, then a person otherwise equally or better qualified can lose a position solely because of his race.

The debate over ameliorative racial preference involves two different views of equality. What proponents of benign discrimination usually mean by equality is equality of result. Equality is achieved only when the percentage of minorities in schools or occupations matches the percentage of the general population represented by those minority groups. Disproportions exist, it is said, because of past discrimination committed by the majority. To give advantage to minorities is then "ameliorative" or "compensatory." But the case for equality of condition need not rest on evidence of past acts of injustice by the majority. Some argue for government-induced quotas to achieve racial and ethnic balance on the ground that justice or the public interest demands such balance.

Opponents of reverse discrimination argue that such a formula of distributive justice could be enforced only by state tyranny, Tocqueville's centralized despotism crushing freedom in the name of sovereign equality. They invoke the traditional definition of equality as equality of opportunity or treatment. They reject "parity" as the criterion of equality and advocate nondiscrimination rather than racial preference. Their conception of equality requires only the removal of legal barriers to advancement, the elimination of de jure racial discrimination. Some advocates of equality of opportunity insist that employers are not free to hire and promote whomever they wish but must prefer those who can offer evidence of individual desert. Only a meritocracy is compatible with justice, which mandates that reward go to effort and talent. The factors of skin color or parental origin are thus irrelevant to the objectives of a just society: "The color of a person's skin and the country of his origin are immutable facts that bear no relation to ability, disadvantage, moral culpability or any other characteristics of constitutionally permissible interest to government."[33]

This conception of equality is too expansive, however, for other opponents of racial quotas, such as Nisbet. Nisbet says that the American people value security and freedom more highly than equality and that therefore employers should be free to hire and promote whomever they wish, even if that means acting on the basis of racial prejudice or rewarding the less deserving. The demands of equality are satisfied as long as the law permits all to compete in the marketplace and places no special burdens on one race or another. The Supreme Court expressed this view in the *Civil Rights Cases* when it held that Congress could not prohibit acts of private discrimination.

The difference between the conceptions of equality as equality of opportunity and equality as equality of result is illustrated by remarks made by President Johnson, who dedicated the nation to becoming a Great Society and attempted to link civil and economic rights, rights against government tyranny and rights to government-conferred benefits, with these words: "*Equal opportunity* is essential, but not enough. We seek not just legal equity but human ability, not just equality as a right and a theory but equality as a fact and *equality as a result*."[34] The two conceptions of equality mentioned by President Johnson, however, are mutually exclusive. Advocates of statistical goals attempt to conceal the dichotomy. Proponents often disingenuously describe "the laws and regulations that affect affirmative action programs [as] designed to provide equal opportunity for all employees . . . regardless of race" and at the same time refer to these laws and regulations as justifying racial preferences.[35] One of the chief government agencies responsible for the initial imposition of quotas euphemistically calls itself the Equal Employment Opportunity Commission.

Plato defined justice as desert, that is, giving like to like and unlike to unlike. Traditionally, the American legal system understands justice as procedural or formal equality. Rules must be objective, that is, they must have the same meaning for everyone. Where two similar individuals have committed the same civil or criminal acts, we expect that the outcome in their two cases will be the same. Like cases should be treated alike. Today's losers accept their losses as just because they know that if someday they are put in the position of the other party they can expect to be treated accordingly.[36]

Opponents contend that a policy of advancing disdvantaged minorities in admission to educational institutions and in employment violates the principle of formal equality because it trenches upon the right of whites to equal treatment. They point to the dissenting opinion of Justice Harlan in *Plessy* v. *Ferguson*. In *Plessy* the majority upheld the right of states to demand the separation of the races in railroad passenger cars on the ground that it promoted the public interest in racial harmony. The Court held that, as long as the facilities made available to black passengers were equal to those available to white passengers, the principle of equality of treatment was not violated. If blacks felt they were being treated as inferiors, that was due to a construction they placed upon the law, not one intended by lawmakers. Justice Harlan, however, citing the principle of formal equality, refused to sanction any form of racial discrimination:

> In respect of civil rights, common to all citizens, the constitution of the United States does not, I think, permit any public authority to know the race of those entitled to be protected in the enjoyment of such rights. . . . Our constitution is color-blind, and neither knows nor tolerates classes among citizens. In respect of civil rights, all citizens are equal before the law. The humblest is the peer of the most powerful. The law regards man as man, and takes no account of his surroundings or of his color when his civil rights as guaranteed by the supreme law of the land are involved.[37]

According to Harlan, then, the Fourteenth Amendment's prohibition that "no state shall deny to any person within its jurisdiction the equal protection of the laws" means that race is never a permissible basis for classifications in law. As the Supreme Court stated in *Strauder* v. *West Virginia* (1880), the Fourteenth Amendment declares "that the law in the states shall be the same for the black and the white; that all persons, whether colored or white, shall stand equal before the laws of the states." All races and all individuals are entitled to equal opportunity to compete for the good things offered by society. To distribute goods on the basis of race or ethnic origin is to deny others those benefits solely for the same reasons, which in law amounts to a denial of equal protection to the one while granting special privileges to the other. In the words of the Supreme Court in *Brown* v. *Board of Education*, "Such an opportunity [public education], where the state has undertaken to provide it, is a right which must be made available to all on equal terms."

Opponents of reverse discrimination argue that the principle of formal equality is embedded in the language of the Fourteenth Amendment and in the Civil Rights Act of 1964, as well as the Voting Rights Act of 1965 and the Fair Housing Act of 1968, all of which prohibit discrimination on the basis of race. They say that the right of an individual not to be given a disadvantage because of his race applies to members of the white race as well as the black race. To them the laws proscribing discrimination in employment, education, voting, and housing are colorblind. The concept of formal equality is consistent, they say, with the main thrust of liberalism in the United States—the primacy of individual rights. Under the principle of formal equality, individual rights are not subject to erosion in the light of empirical findings that blacks or Hispanics are not proportionally represented in all occupations and at all income levels. These disproportions, they say, are probably not the result of past discrimination and, in any case, can never justify violations of the rights of the individual.

Advocates of ameliorative racial preference contend that the Supreme Court has endorsed the notion that "equal protection" requires that the white majority make restitution to the victims of generations of racial discrimination. The effects of this history are obvious, they say. According to the 1970 census, for example, the median family income for blacks was $6,063, while the median family income for whites was $9,961. Forty-three percent of welfare recipients were black. The median years of school completed by adult blacks was 9.8, while for comparable whites it was 12.1. Blacks constituted 2 percent of the legal profession and 3 percent of the medical profession. Less than 1 percent of all doctorates earned in the United States were received by blacks. Racial preference is needed to attain statistical parity. A nation dedicated to the proposition that all men are created equal, they say, must not rest until that goal is reached.

Compensatory racial preference will affect a relatively small percentage of blacks, primarily university students and those entering the skilled-labor and managerial market. It can achieve only a modicum of redistribution of wealth. Some adherents of the concept of equality as equality of result, however, have attempted to extend its logic and advocate public policies that would have a far greater redistributive effect and would entail far more extensive intrusion upon the constitutional principles of individual freedom and majority rule.

112

The Constitution and the Welfare State

On December 10, 1948, the General Assembly of the United Nations adopted and proclaimed the Universal Declaration of Human Rights. Article 25 boldly states that "everyone has the right to a standard of living adequate for the health and well being of himself and his family, including food, clothing, housing and medical care and necessary social services." In a similar vein, Article 20 of the West German Constitution stipulates that "the Federal Republic of Germany is a democratic and *social* federal state." To the Germans, this provision means that the state is duty bound to protect each of its inhabitants from social insecurity and to work toward social justice, goals that are met by an array of welfare legislation ranging from sickness, accident, and old-age insurance to child support, rent subsidy, and employment. In the 1960s and 1970s Supreme Court Justice William O. Douglas expressed chagrin at the fact that unlike the German and other "modern" constitutions, the U.S. Constitution imposes no duty upon the state to provide the material conditions for a dignified life.[38] Douglas's embarrassment could be overcome by enactment of a constitutional amendment guaranteeing to every citizen adequate food, shelter, clothing, medical care, and education. In today's climate, however, a balanced budget amendment is far more likely to pass than a right-to-welfare amendment. If the welfare state is to have a constitutional foundation, the change will have to come by judicial fiat, by a reinterpretation of the document by the Supreme Court.

In the 1960s it appeared as if the liberals on the Warren Court, William Brennan, Thurgood Marshall, Earl Warren, and Douglas, were developing a concept of "equal protection" as a weapon to impose on government an affirmative obligation to redistribute wealth to ensure economic subsistence for everyone. The election of Richard Nixon in 1968 arrested this development, because he appointed several justices who rejected the liberals' thesis. The Burger and Rehnquist Courts have provided little constitutional ammunition for the war on poverty. Under their reading, not only is there no constitutional right to welfare, government is free to make regulations adversely affecting the poor and welfare recipients (if the legislature chooses to provide assistance to the needy) as long as they have a "reasonable" basis—a test that nearly all such regulations meet easily. Given the kind of appointments to the high court President Reagan has made and is likely to make, public assistance will remain a constitutional privilege rather than a right for the foreseeable future.

Politics, however, is an arena of change. The presidency and thus the judiciary will not remain indefinitely in conservative hands. The "modernization" of the Constitution could occur quickly, given the right change in the attitude of the majority of the Supreme Court, because scholars sensitive to Douglas's lament have worked diligently to prepare an interpretation of the text according to which the Constitution guarantees social welfare. These readings, both novel and ingenious, lie ready-made, awaiting sympathetic hands. The history of constitutional development teaches us, moreover, that the ascendant philosophies are the philosophies of reform rather than those that accept the status quo. The "almost" Constitution of the 1960s could very well become the actual Constitution of the twenty-first century. It is the purpose of this concluding section to describe briefly the major attempts to create a constitutional right to be free from poverty.

Proponents of constitutionalizing welfare have discovered government obligations to the poor in the First Amendment's guarantee of freedom of speech, in the Ninth Amendment, in the Fourteenth Amendment's guarantees of "due process" and "equal protection," in the Fifth and Fourteenth Amendments' protections for "property," and in the Fourth Amendment's prohibition against "unreasonable searches and seizures."

Welfare and the First Amendment. What exactly are the constitutional obligations of the state to the impoverished? To avoid the criticism that the contents of such a list are merely an expression of the advocate's preferences, proponents attempt to link new affirmative duties to explicit constitutional language. According to Justice Thurgood Marshall, "The determination of which interests are fundamental should be firmly rooted in the text of the Constitution. The task in every case should be to determine the extent to which constitutionally guaranteed rights are dependent on interests not mentioned in the Constitution."[39] The fact that the Court has held repeatedly that rights need not be named in the text to have constitutional status aids Marshall's reasoning. Fundamental rights, that is, rights that cannot be infringed by government except on a showing of compelling interest, now include the right to travel, the right to marry and to procreate, the right to vote in state elections, the right of association, and the right of privacy—none of which is explicitly mentioned in the Constitution but each of which is implied by rights specifically stated. Thus, Justice Brennan would elevate education to the status of a fundamental right because "it is inextricably linked to the right to participate in the electoral process and to the rights of free speech and association guaranteed by the First Amendment."[40] The present doctrine is that states may infringe even fundamental rights in certain circumstances. The more radical interpreters argue that because one cannot make effective use of the rights to speak and to vote if one is hungry, cold, or illiterate, the Constitution furnishes an *absolute* guarantee of food, shelter, clothing, and education.

The chief stumbling block to such an analysis is that the explicit and implicit rights involved here are of two different kinds. Freedom of speech on the one hand is a "negative right," an area of autonomy that the government cannot touch. It negates government intrusion. Housing, on the other hand, is a "positive right," a legal claim the individual can make on government, which it can only meet by positive disbursement of benefits. Failure to touch the individual is here a violation, not a virtue. Reformers attempt to solve this problem by proving that negative rights are meaningless in the absence of positive rights. If government is bound by the Constitution to secure rights to life and liberty, it is ipso facto bound to provide the material prerequisites of a minimally decent human life.

Justice Douglas attempted to bolster the implicit rights argument by pointing to the language of the Ninth Amendment: "The enumeration in the Constitution, of certain rights, shall not be construed to deny or disparage others retained by the people." Although the framers probably had in mind negative rights here, Douglas contended that the rights to education, to work, to recreation, and to pure air and pure water, which depend on government largesse, "may well be rights 'retained by the people' under the Ninth Amendment. May the people," he asked, "vote them down as well as up?"[41]

Justice and the Welfare State. Both the Fifth and the Fourteenth Amendments stipulate that no person shall "be deprived of life, liberty, or property, without due process of law." The preamble announces that one of the purposes of the Constitution is to "establish Justice." Several scholars have sought to persuade the Court that only the welfare state meets the constitutional standard of justice, of the treatment that is due. In an important article in the *Harvard Law Review* Professor Frank Michelman set out systematically to identify those "needs" or "wants" that are so "fundamental" as to call for a constitutional obligation to fulfill them when the individual cannot do so himself.[42] The claim to "minimum protection" means that persons are entitled to have certain wants satisfied by government. Everyone should be ensured against certain risks. Just wants are those that every person ranks higher on his list of priorities than any other and would be immediately satisfied if the individual had access to the means. To support the doctrine of just wants, Michelman invoked John Rawls's idea of "justice as fairness," elaborated in his influential 1971 book, *A Theory of Justice.*

To identify just institutions, Rawls employs two hypothetical devices, "the original position" and the "veil of ignorance." He asks the reader to imagine that he is present at the founding of a regime and is participating in the design of its constitution. He does not know his income, age, sex, race, physical condition, aptitudes, or intelligence, but he knows the frequency of sickness, blindness, poverty, and hunger. He also knows how grave is the failure to fulfill each of a variety of wants. The list of needs that someone in the original position under the veil of ignorance would demand absolute assurances for constitute the content of governmental duties to the individual.

Rawls's rationale for the welfare state is even more radical than this summary suggests. If someone is hypothetically ignorant of what particular place in society awaits him, would he not find all inequalities unacceptable? Does not justice, then, require strict equality in income and accumulation? Here Rawls introduces the "difference principle," inspired at least in part by Locke's justification for private property, according to which inequalities of income or wealth are unjust unless they are necessary to a system that assures the least well-off in the society a better situation than they could expect under an equal distribution of the net social product. Those inequalities are just that provide incentives and market allocations that make the economy more efficient and productive than it would be under strict equality. Inequality of affluence is more "fair" than equality of poverty. The key point about the Rawlsian conception of justice is that the justice of a political community is determined largely by how it treats its least-advantaged members.

Charles Reich believes that justice requires that the poor be compensated for their contribution to today's complex, industrial society that relies on the existence of a vast "reserve army" of the unemployed. The poor, *New York* v. *Miln* notwithstanding, he says, are no longer to blame for their poverty. Poverty is a consequence of economic forces like automation, competition, and changing technologies, beyond the control of individuals. The unemployed have a right to a minimal share in the commonwealth whose wealth they help generate by their existence as a pool of idle laborers whose presence keeps wages low. These reformers thus employ a syllogism: (1) the Constitution mandates that government meet the requirements of justice; (2) justice requires the welfare state; (3) therefore, the Constitution mandates the welfare state.

116

The New Property. In a well-known 1964 *Yale Law Review* article, cited by Justices Douglas, Brennan, and Marshall in a number of their opinions, Charles Reich described welfare benefits as a species of "new property" brought into being by modern industrial and bureaucratic society. Reich's primary intention was to elevate public assistance from the category of charity or largesse to a right that could not be lost without due process of law. As long as welfare was considered largesse, government could impose otherwise unconstitutional conditions, such as the right to conduct "midnight raids" on recipients' homes to see if all eligibility requirements were being complied with. Implicit in Reich's formulation was the view that the word "property" as used in the Constitution has no fixed meaning, a view shared by Michelman, who urges that it is the role of judges to "supply content" to the concept of property, a term that is undefined by the Constitution but can include a variety of interests and relations.

C. B. Macpherson saw in Rawls's "new property" approach the defect that it did not impose an absolute duty on the state to provide adequate housing and other benefits. All that Reich's argument requires is that if the state grants welfare, the grant becomes a property right of the recipient rather than charity. Agreeing that constitutional property protections encompass guaranteed jobs, public low-cost housing, education, and other "subsistence goods," Macpherson insists that because individual property means essentially the development and enjoyment of human capacities, the Constitution establishes these goods as "inalienable, non-exclusive rights."[43]

Welfare and the Right to Privacy. Albert Bendich rejects the attempt to ground the welfare state in the constitutional protections for property. First, property is not very secure against government intrusion, as the development of zoning and land use laws has demonstrated. Second, property is an economic right, while welfare benefits are, in Bendich's scheme, civil liberties. Under the contemporary Constitution, civil liberties, such as free speech and freedom from self-incrimination, are much more sacred than property rights. Bendich locates the right to welfare within the civil liberty of privacy.

Although the Constitution nowhere explicitly mentions privacy, the Supreme Court found a constitutional right to privacy within the "emanations and penumbras" of several amendments, including the Fourth Amendment's guarantee of freedom from unreasonable searches and seizures. The right to procure abortions, the Court ruled in *Roe* v. *Wade*, is contained within this constitutional privacy right. The Constitution, says Bendich, presumes that citizens have privacy.

Otherwise, why provide protections for it? The reality, however, is that millions of Americans lack privacy because they suffer from economic deprivation. Thus, he concludes that "if poverty is at war with the Constitution, the Constitution is equally at war with poverty." If everyone has a constitutional right to privacy, he also has a right to "the conditions which are indispensable to its regulation."[44]

Bendich's conception of privacy is broad. Privacy includes "the freedom and dignity of the individual, his right to determine his own destiny." Echoing Article 2 of the West German Constitution, Bendich asserts that "the constitutional guarantee of privacy has increasingly come to be thought of as protecting dignity and free development of personality." Important consequences flow from the inclusion of dignity within privacy, for Bendich indicates that persons in American society cannot achieve dignity without minimal income, minimal housing, or minimal education. The right to privacy requires, he says, "the welfare state to provide welfare."

A major obstacle to anchoring welfare entitlements in the implied constitutional right to privacy is that, in the words of Justice Louis Brandeis, privacy essentially means "the right to be let alone," by government as well as by one's fellow citizens. In other words, is privacy not a negative right? Bendich's response is that the negative rights of property and life do not mean that the government should leave one alone when he is being assaulted or his house is burning. In a similar way, government cannot ensure privacy by leaving alone the deprived. It must provide financial assistance. Negative rights, in other words, inexorably yield positive rights.

Equality and the Safety Net. Does justice demand that the state eliminate the most serious privations associated with poverty—lack of adequate food, housing, medical care, and education—or does it require that the gap between the rich and the poor be narrowed or even eliminated? Which is the real evil, poverty or inequality? Advocates of a constitutional basis for welfare split on this issue. Some identify the evil as *absolute* privation"; others abhor "*relative* deprivation." Rawls and Michelman adopt the more radical view of justice. They reject the policy of equal shares for everyone only because the least-advantaged would be better off in a system that allocates unequal shares. Every stratification in income and accumulated wealth must constantly be scrutinized to determine if it serves the needs of the least well-off. The "radicals" define equality as equality of result. The "traditional" reformers define equality as equality of opportunity. The familiar "safety net" image is more compatible with the latter conception of equality than the former.

118

Kenneth Karst and Harold Horowitz have attempted to anchor welfare entitlements in the Fourteenth Amendment's guarantee that no state shall "deny to any person within its jurisdiction the equal protection of the laws." Confronted with what appears to be a prohibition on discriminatory government action, Karst and Horowitz reinterpret the clause as a prohibition on government inaction. In their hands, the equal protection clause becomes the source of substantive rather than procedural rights. If the state tolerates private conduct that produces inequality, it has denied the poor "equal protection of the laws by treating unequals equally." They conclude that "to rectify these denials of equal protection the state may be required . . . to perform an 'affirmative duty.' "[45] Anatole France expressed a similar thought in his quip that the law in its majesty equally forbids the rich and the poor to sleep beneath bridges. The affirmative duty means, say Karst and Horowitz, that government is constitutionally obligated to fulfill "fundamental interests" or "just wants" for those who cannot afford them. Their view is consistent with the social safety net approach.

Equality as equality of opportunity, however, has its own radical implications. Justice Thurgood Marshall advocated classifying education as a fundamental interest because "every American [has] the right to an equal start in life." Education is necessary if children are "to reach their full potential as citizens," he said.[46] Even if schools were equally funded, Marshall's goal, students would not actually enjoy equal chances at fulfilling their potential. As Michelman and Rawls indicate, the single greatest barrier to realizing equal opportunity is not government neglect but the family. "Sesame Street," for example, has failed in its mission of improving the relative school performance of inner-city poor children because suburban middle-class children who watch the popular television program in large numbers and whose parents stress the value of learning have benefited more rapidly and more extensively. The show has actually increased the gap between lower- and middle-class children. The implication is that true equality of opportunity demands the abolition of the private family.

According to these scholars and judges, whatever provision is said to render the Constitution at war with poverty and inequality—that relating to free speech, equal protection, due process, privacy, or property—the result is a public obligation to provide a national welfare system. The system could take the form of payments in kind—food, housing, clothing, education, medical care, or legal assistance—or payments in cash, that is, a guaranteed minimum income or negative income tax. The key difference from the existing policy is that this redistribution of wealth would be mandated by the Constitution and removed from the discretion of legislators. These entitlements could be enforced in court if a legislature did not honor them. Precedents for judicial intrusion on the legislative taxing and spending powers have accumulated since the early 1970s, when federal district courts began to order states to expend millions of dollars to alleviate unconstitutional conditions in their prisons and mental hospitals. The stakes of this controversy are large indeed.

A major roadblock to the judicial discovery of a constitutional right to welfare is that such a right is inconsistent with the conception of equality embedded in both the letter and the genius of the Constitution. The views expressed in this novel doctrine are at war with the framers' understanding and with Lincoln's. That justice, in their opinion, does not mandate the welfare state is evident, for example, in *Federalist* No. 10, quoted above. Unlike Rawls, who believes that, because a person's intelligence or aptitude is not the product of free choice, it is immoral to reward the gifted and talented, Madison regards protection for the unequal faculties of acquiring property to be "the first object of government."

The reformers do not in fact dispute this reading of the framers' intent. What they dispute is that that intent is relevant to any discussion of what the Constitution means today. The Constitution, they say, is a living document with no fixed meaning. The words are empty vessels into which Supreme Court justices each generation pour new meaning. Changes in social conditions inevitably produce changes in constitutional meaning. "The economic shift from a laissez faire to a welfare state system," says Bendich, "requires appropriate changes in legal conceptions in order that the law may remain viable."[47]

The proponents of a policy of ameliorative racial preference and a constitutionally mandated safety net must, therefore, convince the federal judiciary of the truth of three propositions: (1) equality means more than equality under the law and equality of opportunity; (2) equality has higher value than freedom; and (3) the Constitution, in the words of Charles Evans Hughes, is whatever the judges say it is. On the outcome of this effort depends the nature of the Constitution of the twenty-first century.

Notes

1. *Democracy in America,* quoted in Robert Nisbet, *Twilight of Authority* (New York: Oxford University Press, 1975), p. 198.

2. Article V prohibits constitutional amendments that would deprive a state of its "equal Suffrage in the Senate" without its consent.

3. 109 U.S. 3, 20.

4. Ibid., p. 22.

5. Jones v. Alfred H. Mayer Co., 392 U.S. 409 (1968).

6. Civil Rights Cases, 109 U.S. 3, 35 (1883), J. Harlan, dissenting.

7. Plessy v. Ferguson, 163 U.S. 537, 561–562 (1896), J. Harlan, dissenting.

8. Ibid., pp. 555–56.

9. Ibid., p. 559.

10. Plessy v. Ferguson, 163 U.S. 537, 555 (1896), J. Harlan, dissenting.

11. Civil Rights Cases, 109 U.S. 3, 43–44 (1883), J. Harlan, dissenting.

12. Ibid., p. 48.

13. Raoul Berger, *Government by Judiciary: The Transformation of the Fourteenth Amendment* (Cambridge, Mass.: Harvard University Press, 1977), p. 20.

14. Civil Rights Cases, 109 U.S. 3, 43 (1883), J. Harlan, dissenting.

15. Ibid., p. 40 (emphasis added).

16. Ibid., p. 37.

17. 10 USC 333, 3500 (emphasis added).

18. Kenneth M. Holland, "Roger Taney," in Morton Frisch and Richard Stevens, eds., *American Political Thought*, 2d ed. (Itasca, Ill.: F. E. Peacock Publishers, 1983).

19. Quoted in Harry V. Jaffa, *Crisis of the House Divided: An Interpretation of the Lincoln-Douglas Debates* (Seattle: University of Washington Press, 1959), p. 365.

20. Emphasis added.

21. Query 14.

22. Martin Diamond, *The Founding of the Democratic Republic* (Itasca, Ill.: F. E. Peacock Publishers, 1981), pp. 10–12.

23. Section 50. Emphasis added.

24. Robert Goldwin, "John Locke," in Leo Strauss and Joseph Cropsey, eds., *History of Political Philosophy*, 2d ed. (Chicago: Rand McNally, 1972), pp. 460–70.

25. Section 34.

26. Section 42. Emphasis added.

27. *The Collected Works of Abraham Lincoln*, ed. Roy Basler (New Brunswick, N.J.: Rutgers University Press, 1953), vol. 2, p. 530.

28. Max Farrand, ed., *The Records of the Federal Convention of 1787* (New Haven: Yale University Press, 1966), vol. 1, pp. 400–401.

29. Ibid., p. 398. Emphasis added.

30. Ibid., vol. 4, p. 438.

31. Jaffa, *Crisis of the House Divided*, p. 227.

32. Nathan Glazer, *Ethnic Dilemmas, 1964–1982* (Cambridge, Mass.: Harvard University Press, 1983), pp. 159–62.

33. Fullilove v. Klutznick, 65 L.Ed. 2d 902, 954–955 (1980), J. Stewart, dissenting.

34. Quoted in Robert Pear, "Don't Count Economic Rights as Civil Rights, Some Argue," *New York Times*, September 18, 1983. Emphasis added.

35. Lois Vander Waerdt, *Affirmative Action in Higher Education: A Sourcebook* (New York: Garland Publishing Co., 1982), p. 5.

36. See Craig R. Ducat, *Modes of Constitutional Interpretation* (St. Paul, Minn.: West Publishing Co., 1978), pp. 47–55.

37. 163 U.S. 537, 554–555 (1896), J. Harlan, dissenting.

38. See Palmer v. Thompson, 403 U.S. 217, 233–234 (1971).

39. San Antonio Independent School District v. Rodriguez, 411 U.S. 1 (1973).

40. Ibid., p. 63.

41. Palmer v. Thompson, 403 U.S. 217, 233–234 (1971).

42. "On Protecting the Poor through the Fourteenth Amendment," *Harvard Law Review,* vol. 83 (1968), p. 7.

43. C. B. Macpherson, *Property: Mainstream and Critical Positions* (Toronto: University of Toronto Press, 1978), chaps. 1 and 12.

44. Albert M. Bendich, "Privacy, Poverty, and the Constitution," in Jacob tenBroek, ed., *The Law of the Poor* (San Francisco: Chandler Publishing Co., 1966), pp. 83–84.

45. Kenneth L. Karst and Harold W. Horowitz, "*Reitman v. Mulkey:* A Telophase of Substantive Equal Protection," in Philip B. Kurland, ed., *Supreme Court Review,* 1967, pp. 39–80.

46. San Antonio Independent School District v. Rodriguez, 411 U.S. 1 (1973), J. Marshall, dissenting.

47. Bendich, "Privacy, Poverty, and the Constitution," p. 83.

6

The Constitution, Racial Preference, and the Equal Participation Objective

Robert A. Sedler

The Constitutional Setting

The primary constitutional controversy in the area of racial equality today revolves around the permissibility of racial preference in governmental programs and operations.[1] Such preference means that the status of a person as a black American or member of another racial or ethnic minority is affirmatively taken into account by governmental entities in such matters as determining admission to a publicly supported university,[2] hiring and promotion in public employment,[3] or entitlement to government contracts.[4] The constitutional issue arises because the result of such racial preference and race-conscious official decision making is that persons are subject to differential treatment on the basis of race in the allocation of government benefits and burdens.[5]

The Constitution does not prohibit all use of race-conscious criteria in governmental decision making, including use that may cause detriment to persons because of their race. The Constitution proscribes *invidious* racial discrimination,[6] which may be defined as racial discrimination that cannot be shown to be "necessary to the accomplishment of some permissible state objective, independent of the racial discrimination which it was the object of the Fourteenth Amendment to eliminate."[7] More specifically, invidious racial discrimination is the *unjustifiable* use of race-conscious criteria. Any use of such criteria by the government is subject to "strict scrutiny" and will be held unconstitutional unless (1) it is "justified by a compelling governmental interest" and (2) the particular use is "narrowly tailored to the achievement of that goal."[8] Conversely, where it *is* "narrowly tailored to the advancement of a compelling governmental interest," it

123

does not amount to invidious discrimination and is constitutional despite the detriment caused to persons because of their race.[9]

The Supreme Court has upheld the use of preference for racial minorities in governmental programs and operations where it has the purpose and effect of alleviating the present consequences of identified past discrimination by the governmental entity. In this circumstance the use of racial preference is deemed to advance a compelling governmental interest and so does not constitute invidious discrimination.[10] There is no constitutional requirement that the particular beneficiaries of the racial preference be individual victims of the identified past discrimination.[11] As a practical matter a governmental entity using racial preference will, wherever possible, try to defend its use against constitutional challenge by trying to show that it is designed to overcome identified past discrimination by that governmental entity.[12]

While such use of racial preference has quite properly been held to be constitutional, the constitutional permissibility of using racial preference should not be so circumscribed. Rather, the resolution of the constitutional issue in regard to racial preference should depend on an analysis of constitutional values as those values are understood in a historical context and related to the situation that prevails in contemporary American society. I will set forth here a justification for racial preference in governmental programs and operations that is consistent with and serves to further important constitutional values. Constitutional values may also furnish guidance for policy choices. I will therefore also contend that, in light of the constitutional justification for racial preference advanced here, racial preference in governmental programs and operations should be adopted as a matter of public policy.

The justification for racial preference in governmental programs and operations is that it is necessary to advance what I term the "equal participation objective." I will begin by explaining the meaning of that objective and show why it cannot be realized in American society today except through the use of racial preference. Next I will show why there is a strong societal interest in its realization and explain why this consideration renders the use of racial preference in governmental programs and operations constitutional despite the resulting detriment to adversely affected whites. I will then demonstrate that the equal participation objective is fully consistent with and serves to further important constitutional values embodied in the Fourteenth Amendment and the Reconstruction Amendments taken as a whole.[13] My conclusion, therefore, is that the use of racial preference in governmental programs and operations to advance the equal participation objective both is constitutional and should be adopted as a matter of public policy.

The Equal Participation Objective and the Social History of Racism

The equal participation objective relates to redressing the present consequences of the long and tragic social history of racism in this nation, as a result of which fundamental inequalities between blacks and whites permeate all important aspects of American life. The goal is to end white supremacy and black inequality in all their manifestations and, in the words of Justice Thurgood Marshall, to achieve "genuine equality" between blacks and whites in American society.[14]

The term "social history of racism" is a convenient way of summarizing the history of victimization of blacks in American society.[15] The social history of racism was the aftermath of slavery, and like slavery it was predicated on and justified by the supposed moral inferiority of the black race.[16] It is a history of an official status of inferiority established by law, of rampant discrimination in employment, of ghettoization, of segregated and inadequate schooling, and of the denial of access to political and economic power. Racial discrimination was often commanded by government at all levels and, when not commanded, was tolerated and encouraged. Private entities and individuals added their significant contributions to the pattern of racism. Indeed, only in the past two or three decades has any real progress been made in halting much of the overt discrimination practiced against blacks in the United States.

The consequences of this long and tragic history remain and perpetuate themselves. It is not necessary to review at length the familiar and depressing manifestations of societal racial inequality in the United States today. There is an enormous economic gap between blacks and whites: blacks suffer disproportionate unemployment and underemployment, are concentrated in low-paying and low-prestige occupations, and have a median family income little more than half that of whites.[17] There is likewise a racial education gap: blacks continue to lag significantly behind whites in academic achievement and in the quality of their educational experience.[18] There is also a racial "power gap": blacks are seriously underrepresented in governmental and institutional power positions, in the elite professions, and in the economic mainstream.[19]

Until fairly recently the struggle for racial equality concentrated almost entirely on removing the structural impediments that denied equality to blacks.[20] From a legal standpoint this struggle has been largely successful. The Constitution has been interpreted as prohibiting state-imposed segregation and other traditional forms of intentional discrimination against blacks.[21] Federal laws prohibit racial discrimination in voting, employment, public accommodations, and housing, and similar protection is afforded by the laws of many states. This means that a system of prevention is now in place: the law prohibits present racial discrimination against blacks and provides remedies for such discrimination.

This system of prevention, however, does not purport to deal directly with the present consequences of the social history of racism and is not designed to do so. In a sense it operates prospectively; it prevents future discrimination and victimization but cannot undo what has gone before. It is premised on adherence to *racial neutrality*—the absence of discrimination against blacks—but adherence to racial neutrality, interacting with the consequences of the social history of racism, will often put blacks at a disadvantage in comparison with whites and will thus perpetuate societal racial inequality.

This point may be illustrated by considering the relation between the educational gap and the use of racially neutral criteria for employment or university admission. The educational gap operates to exclude blacks disproportionately whenever eligibility for any position is based on comparative objective indicators of academic achievement, such as standardized employment or admission examinations. Any standardized examination will be testing, to a large degree, the quality of the examinee's prior education. In light of the racial educational gap, the test scores of black applicants as a group are likely to be significantly lower than those of white applicants as a group. Even though the employer or the university is not intentionally discriminating against blacks and the examinations are valid for the purpose for which they are being used, their use to determine job eligibility or university admission will disproportionately exclude blacks.

This example can be multiplied many times over.[22] Because the consequences of the social history of racism are so pervasive and are self-perpetuating and self-reinforcing,[23] the system of prevention, premised as it is on adherence to racial neutrality, should not be expected to do very much to alter the condition of societal racial inequality and the disadvantaged and subordinate position of blacks.[24]

Racial preference—the explicit use of race-conscious criteria designed to benefit blacks as a group—is a positive *intervention* directed against the present consequences of the social history of racism. It is intended to act on and to alleviate those consequences, so as to bring

126

about the equal participation of blacks with whites in all important aspects of American life. It should be clear that the policy choice for American society today cannot properly be analyzed as a choice between racial neutrality on the one hand and racial preference on the other. Rather it is a choice between perpetuating the present consequences of the social history of racism and the continuing disadvantage and subordination of blacks by a policy of racial neutrality that ignores those consequences and trying to overcome those consequences to some degree and to achieve societal racial equality by a policy of preference for blacks. There should be no doubt that in American society today a policy of racial neutrality means a condition of continued societal racial inequality for blacks.

A policy of racial preference indeed has its costs, costs that must be considered from the standpoint both of the Constitution and of public policy. The direct costs are borne by individual whites who would have received the benefit in question—appointment to a government job or admission to law school or the award of a governmental contract—were it not for the preference for blacks. Those whites thus suffer a disadvantage, and it may be assumed that they did not benefit directly from past discrimination against blacks. It cannot be doubted that a policy of racial preference produces unfairness. The injury to these individual whites must be balanced, in both the constitutional and the public policy equations, against the fact that a policy of racial preference is the only realistic way of achieving racial equality in this nation.

The costs of racial preference, however, are not borne by whites as a group. Whites as a group now have full and equal participation in all important aspects of American life and will not be injured if that participation is shared with blacks. Whites as a group can of course have no legitimate interest in maintaining their present position of societal dominance. In the final analysis, what racial preference means is that the burden of the consequences of the social history of racism is shared to some degree by whites, however innocent, instead of falling entirely on blacks. The real unfairness is a generational one, in that this generation is called upon to deal with the present consequences of this nation's long and tragic history of racism.

Overcoming those present consequences means achieving the equal participation objective. The goal is that blacks as well as whites will be significantly involved in societal governance and will share positions of power and prestige in both the public and the private sectors, that blacks will be full participants in all parts of the American economic system, and that blacks will not have disproportionately lower incomes than whites. When this goal is achieved, the consequences of the social history of racism will no longer be so strikingly visible in American society.

Since the objective is to redress the present consequences of the social history of racism, it is necessarily a racial objective, and the frame of reference is necessarily racial. The pervasive racial discrimination and victimization of blacks, predicated on a belief in their moral inferiority, have been qualitatively different from the kind of discrimination practiced in times past against certain white ethnic groups in this nation.[25]

The equal participation objective is not based on any notion of "reparations" or "proportionality." It does not mean that because blacks have been subject to a long history of discrimination and victimization, white society owes them reparations and must now give them benefits at the expense of whites.[26] Nor does it mean that blacks as a group should be entitled to the proportionate share of the benefits of American society that they would have received had it not been for the social history of racism or a share of those benefits in direct proportion to their representation in the general population. The equal participation objective focuses on the situation that now exists in American society and seeks to give blacks as a group some meaningful share of societal participation and to bring them fully into the mainstream of American life.[27]

The Societal Interest in the Equal Participation Objective

One justification of the equal participation objective relates to the interest of blacks as a group in achieving equal participation in important aspects of American life. Under this view the government is justified in using racial preference in its programs and operations to bring about the equal participation of blacks and thus to redress the present consequences of the social history of racism.[28] My focus here, however, is not on the group interest of blacks but on the societal interest in the equal participation objective—the interest of the society itself in the benefits that result from the equal participation of blacks. Sometimes this interest may be a very specific one, such as a university's interest in the enriched educational atmosphere derived from the presence of a "racially and ethnically diverse" student body.[29] More frequently it is a broader interest in the effective functioning of institutions in a pluralistic society. Often the societal interest correlates with the group interest of blacks, in the sense that American society as a whole is well served by the equal participation of all segments of the society. In the final analysis, society has a strong interest in racial equality.

Although the opinion of Justice Lewis F. Powell in the *Bakke* case dealt with a very specific institutional interest in the equal participation objective, it can serve as a starting point to illustrate the larger societal interest. Justice Powell concluded that the medical school could use race-conscious admissions criteria to advance its educational interest in achieving a "racially and ethnically diverse" student body.[30] As one commentator has observed:

> Justice Powell's diversity idea is based on the interest of the *institution*, that is, an enterprise interest in an enriched educational atmosphere—rather than an interest held by the represented minority group. This seems to be Justice Powell's view, despite the fact that the represented groups are the immediate beneficiaries of the policy, and the proximate cause of the hypothesized enrichment.[31]

The justification for the use of race-conscious admissions criteria, then, was the university's institutional interest in improving the quality of its educational program by enrolling a "racially and ethnically diverse" student body. Other social institutions can similarly assert both their particular interest and the broader interest of the society they serve in the equal participation of blacks to justify the use of racial preference in their programs and operations.

It is obvious how a "racially and ethnically diverse" student body contributes to an enriched educational atmosphere. In his opinion in *Bakke* Justice Powell referred to the Harvard College admission program, which states simply that a "black student can usually bring something that a white person cannot offer."[32] That "something" is the perspective that comes from the "experience of being black in America." In the educational context that experience can be shared with white students, so that black and white students, interacting with one another, can "contribute to the robust exchange of ideas"[33] during the educational process. From a constitutional standpoint, therefore, the use of racial preference in determining admission to the medical school advanced a "compelling" governmental interest related to the quality of the medical school's educational program and so was constitutionally permissible. For the same reason, from the standpoint of the medical school, racial preference in admissions was sound as a matter of public policy.

The equal participation objective more frequently advances broader interests related to the effective functioning of societal institutions in a pluralistic society and the interest of society itself in the equal participation of all its elements in the important aspects of societal life. I now proceed to illustrate the societal interest in the equal participation objective in three areas: the functions of government; the power professions, such as law and medicine; and the American economic system.

There appears to be a societal interest in the equal participation objective whenever a "black person can bring something that a white person cannot offer" to any governmental institution, so that the institution will be in a better position to serve its function and to be responsive to the needs of all citizens. Consider first the police function, which "fulfills a fundamental obligation of government to its constituency."[34] Blacks have traditionally been grossly underrepresented in municipal police forces, even in cities having very substantial black populations, and virtually nonexistent in state police forces, again regardless of the size of a state's black population.[35] There can be no doubt that participation by blacks in the all-important police function advances the societal interest in the effective performance of that function. As long as blacks were grossly underrepresented in the police force, the police would be perceived by the black community as an "occupying army," as was so tragically demonstrated in the 1967 riots.[36] According to the President's Commission on Law Enforcement and the Administration of Justice:

> In order to gain confidence and acceptance of a community, personnel within a police department should be representative of the community as a whole. . . . If minority groups are to feel that they are not policed entirely by a white police force, they must see the Negro or other minority officers participate in policymaking and other crucial decisions.[37]

Similarly, as a federal court of appeals put it, when upholding the constitutionality of racial preference in police promotions:

> The argument that police need more minority officers is not simply that blacks communicate better with blacks or that a police department should cater to the public desires. Rather it is that effective crime prevention and solution depend heavily on the public support and confidence in the police. In short, the focus is not on the superior performance of minority officers, but on the public's perception of law enforcement officials and institutions.[38]

Equal participation by blacks in the police function, then, clearly advances the societal interest in effective law enforcement,[39] which justifies the use of racial preference in police hiring and promotions.

Society has the same interest in the equal participation of blacks in all functions of government. The Senate Committee on Labor and Public Welfare, recommending the extension of Title VII to state and local governments, observed: "The exclusion of minorities from effective participation in the bureaucracy not only promotes ignorance of minority problems in that particular community, but also creates mistrust, alienation, and all too often hostility toward the entire process of government."[40] The equal participation of blacks in all functions of government thus serves important societal interests by (1) ensuring that the government will be aware of the problems and needs of the black community, (2) ensuring that the government, while making and implementing policy, will have the benefit of the perspective that comes from "the experience of being black in America," and (3) helping to bring about confidence in the institutions of government on the part of black citizens.[41] Racial preference in governmental hiring and promotions is directly related to achieving the equal participation objective in all governmental operations and so should be held to be constitutionally permissible.[42] For the same reason it should be adopted as a matter of public policy.

We may next consider the societal interest in the equal participation of blacks in the power professions, such as law and medicine, in which blacks are seriously underrepresented.[43] As Justice Marshall argued in *Bakke:* "It is because of a legacy of unequal treatment that we now must permit the institutions of this society to give consideration to race in making the decisions about who will hold the positions of influence, affluence, and prestige in America."[44] The societal interest in the equal participation of blacks in the legal and medical professions is not so much that black lawyers should be available to represent black clients and black physicians to treat black patients as that the exercise of societal power by the power professions will be significantly improved by black participation and the inclusion of the black perspective.

The exercise of societal power and the benefits of black participation in that exercise are more obvious with respect to the legal profession. We are all aware of the power and influence of lawyers as a group in American society, not only through their role in the legal system and the administration of justice but also through their representation in legislatures, governmental bodies, and many other important societal institutions. Being a lawyer means being in a position, by virtue of one's profession, to do significant things in American society.

Once admitted to the legal profession in reasonable numbers, black lawyers will have an influence on the profession and on societal institutions in which lawyers are involved. Blacks, like whites, will be judges and prosecutors and law professors. They will be lawyers for the government, "members of the firm," and bar association officers. They will be in a position to contribute directly to the development of the American legal system and to make that system responsive to the needs of black people. In addition, black citizens will have greater confidence in the administration of justice.

Entry to the legal profession depends entirely on admission to law school. In determining their admission policies, therefore, the law schools should properly take into account the societal interest in the equal participation of blacks in the legal profession.[45] That interest justifies the use of race-conscious admissions criteria and the giving of racial preference to qualified black applicants.[46]

There is likewise a strong societal interest in the equal participation of blacks in the medical profession, which relates to incorporating the "black perspective."[47] The medical profession exercises very significant power by its substantial control over the nation's health care delivery system. Physicians do much more than treat patients. They serve on hospital staffs and medical committees. They take part in decisions that affect the kind of medical services that will be offered and the cost of those services. They influence the distribution of medical resources and the location of health care facilities. They perform substantially the same function with respect to the health care delivery system that lawyers perform with respect to the legal system and the administration of justice.

There is a considerable health gap between blacks and whites in this nation: blacks as a group have higher mortality and morbidity rates than whites as a group, and black communities are being under-represented in the delivery of health care services.[48] There is a societal interest in ending the health gap and in ensuring that the quality of life, reflected in the condition of a person's health and access to adequate medical care, in no way depends on race. It is certainly reasonable to believe that the equal participation of black physicians in the medical profession and in the administration of the health care delivery system would contribute to ending the racial health gap. Black physicians would for the most part be in a better position than white physicians to assess the health care needs of black communities and to understand the difficulties of black people in making use of the traditionally white-dominated health care delivery system. They could also be expected to lobby for adequate health care facilities for underserved black communities. The equal participation of blacks in the health care delivery system, like the equal participation of blacks in the legal system, thus advances a very strong societal interest.

Here too entry into the profession is completely dependent on admission to medical school, and the enormous cost of training physicians constrains the number of new entrants into the profession. The societal interest in the equal participation of blacks justifies the use of race-conscious admissions criteria and the giving of preference to qualified black applicants seeking admission to medical school.

Blacks as a group do not participate equally in any way in the American economic system, and their lack of equal participation correlates directly with the racial economic gap and the condition of racial economic inequality in the United States today.[49] The relatively few black-owned business enterprises generate an insignificant amount of the total business volume.[50] The absence of blacks in the top management of American corporations needs no documentation. Blacks are disproportionately underrepresented in white-collar jobs,[51] and even among blue-collar jobs, where the distribution of blacks and whites is more nearly equal, blacks are disproportionately concentrated in laborer and domestic worker jobs and are underrepresented in skilled and crafts jobs.[52]

Racial economic inequality is perhaps the most enduring and persistent consequence of the social history of racism, and it reinforces other forms of racial disadvantage. It produces alienation on the part of blacks and contributes to socially harmful conditions, such as the disproportionately high rates of black crime and illegitimate birth. The integration of blacks into the mainstream of American society cannot be achieved until race is no longer associated with poverty and low income, as it is today. For all these reasons there is a strong societal interest in the equal participation of blacks economically.

For the equal participation objective to be advanced in the economic area, structural changes must be made in the way that particular forms of economic activity operate, so as to increase black participation in those activities substantially.[53] For example, the underrepresentation of blacks in the skilled crafts can be alleviated by providing blacks with a proportion of the places in union apprenticeship programs, from which they have traditionally been excluded.[54] Likewise, employers can set up in-plant training programs for skilled workers, with black workers guaranteed a proportion of places in the program,[55] and the government can require governmental contractors to establish such programs as a condition for the receipt of government contracts. The situation of minority business enterprises, which are generally unable to compete with white-controlled firms in bidding for government contracts, can be improved by imposing minority business enterprise "set-asides."[56]

The ultimate purpose of these structural changes is to alleviate racial economic inequality, which both reflects and is substantially caused by the lack of equal participation by blacks in the American economic system.[57] The training of blacks as skilled workers will increase the income of blacks as a group. Similarly, since experience indicates that black-owned business enterprises are likely to employ proportionately more blacks than white-owned business enterprises,[58] the continued survival of those enterprises will increase the income of blacks as a group. In addition, an increase in the number of black skilled and craft workers and in the number of viable black-owned enterprises may reduce black unemployment and underemployment and will also have a multiplier effect insofar as those enterprises deal with other black enterprises as suppliers and customers. Finally, the increased participation of blacks in the management of America's corporations may make those corporations more responsive to the interests of blacks as consumers and investors, and blacks will have more confidence in the free enterprise system if blacks, as well as whites, participate in the managerial function. Thus a strong societal interest in the equal participation of blacks in the American economic system justifies racial preference that takes the form of structural changes in the way that particular forms of economic activity operate to increase black participation in those activities.

I have illustrated the societal interest in the equal participation objective in three important areas of American life. It is my thesis that this interest justifies the use of racial preference to advance the equal participation objective in governmental programs and operations.

This justification should counter any constitutional objection to racial preference on the grounds that it causes racial disadvantage to adversely affected whites. From a constitutional standpoint racial preference designed to advance the equal participation objective cannot be analyzed as a conflict between group rights and individual rights.[59] Rather the analysis must be concerned with whether it is permissible to impose "racial burdens" on individuals to advance racial societal interests.

The Constitution does not prohibit all use of race-conscious criteria in governmental decision making, including use that may cause disadvantage to persons because of their race. But since racial preference for blacks does cause disadvantage to some whites, the racial equality value embodied in the Fourteenth Amendment imposes certain constraints on its use. As Justice Powell explained in *Bakke:* "When [classifications] touch upon an individual's race or ethnic background, he is entitled to a judicial determination that the burden he is asked to bear on that basis is precisely tailored to serve a compelling governmental interest."[60] In other words, the interest advanced by the use of racial preference must be a very important one—a "compel-

134

ling" one— to justify the resulting disadvantage to adversely affected whites. In addition, the particular means used must be reasonable and appropriate in the circumstances and must strike a reasonable accommodation between the advancement of the compelling governmental interest and the interest of individual whites in being free from racial disadvantage.[61] As long as these exacting requirements are satisfied, the use of racial preference is constitutionally permissible despite the disadvantage caused to some whites.[62]

The societal interest in achieving the equal participation objective is indeed very important. As I will demonstrate in the next section, that objective is fully consistent with and furthers important constitutional values. It should therefore be found to be a compelling interest for constitutional purposes, and the appropriate use of racial preference to advance the equal participation objective should be upheld as constitutional.

Constitutional Values and the Equal Participation Objective

I have justified racial preference in governmental programs and operations by the equal participation objective and have maintained that there is a strong societal interest in bringing about the equal participation of blacks in all important aspects of American life. The constitutional permissibility of using racial preference to advance the equal participation objective depends analytically on the Court's determination of whether the societal interest in that objective is found to be compelling. When the Court concludes that a particular interest is compelling, it has made the judgment that the interest is of sufficient importance and legitimacy to justify the resulting detriment to adversely affected whites. I have contended here that the societal interest in the equal participation objective is indeed a compelling governmental interest for constitutional purposes, because that objective is fully consistent with and furthers the values embodied in the Fourteenth Amendment and the Reconstruction Amendments.

While the protections of the Fourteenth Amendment are universal and go beyond racial equality,[63] the primary concern of the framers of the Fourteenth Amendment was undoubtedly with racial equality and the protection of the newly emancipated blacks.[64] Given the historical context in which the Fourteenth Amendment and the other Reconstruction Amendments were promulgated[65] and the previous condition of slavery and its consequences that the amendments were designed to remedy, it may properly be said that the broad, organic purpose of those amendments was to bring about a condition of *black freedom* in the United States.

A contemporaneous explication of the purpose of the Reconstruction Amendments is found in the Supreme Court's opinion in the *Slaughter-House* cases.[66] Although the main issue in those cases involved the meaning of the Fourteenth Amendment's privileges and immunities clause, the Court emphasized that the amendment could not be read in isolation from the Reconstruction Amendments taken collectively. The Court reviewed the circumstances leading to the adoption of each of those amendments and explained how they were designed to deal with the consequences of slavery and the position of the newly emancipated blacks in American society.

The Court began by observing that slavery was the "overshadowing and efficient cause of the Civil War"[67] and that at the end of the war in 1865 the Thirteenth Amendment was put into the Constitution as "one of its most fundamental articles" to implement "this main and most valuable result" of the war.[68] The Court referred to the Thirteenth Amendment as "this grand yet simple declaration of the personal freedom of the human race within the jurisdiction of this government."[69] Although slavery had been abolished, there was still massive discrimination against the newly emancipated blacks in the former slave states, so that "something more was necessary in the way of constitutional protection to the unfortunate race who had suffered so much."[70] To this end the Fourteenth Amendment was adopted in 1868. But even that was "inadequate for the protection of life, liberty and property, without which freedom to the slave was no boon," because blacks were being denied the suffrage.[71] Thus the trilogy of constitutional protection for the newly emancipated blacks was completed by the adoption of the Fifteenth Amendment in 1870. As the Court concluded: "It is sure that only the 15th Amendment, in terms, mentions the negro by speaking of his color and his slavery. But it is just as true that each of the other articles was addressed to the grievances of that race and designed to remedy them as the fifteenth."[72]

The Court stated the broad, organic purpose of the Reconstruction Amendments in terms of a constitutional value of black freedom:

> We repeat, then, in the light of this recapitulation of events, almost too recent to be called history, but which are familiar to us all; and on the most casual examination of the language of these amendments, no one can fail to be impressed with the one pervading purpose found in them all, lying at the foundation of each, and without which none of them would have been suggested; we mean the freedom of the slave race, the security and firm establishment of that freedom, and the protection of the newly made freeman and citizen from the

oppressions of those who had formerly exercised unlimited dominion over him.[73]

Professor Arthur Kinoy has related the value of black freedom to the constitutional overturning of the premise of racial inferiority and subordination.

> The main thrust of the Thirteenth, Fourteenth and Fifteenth Amendments was the construction of a penumbra of legal commands which were designed to raise the race of freedmen from the status of inferior beings—a status imposed by the system of chattel slavery—to that of free men and women, equal participants in the hitherto white political community consisting of the "people of the United States." The constitutional right of the black race to this status of freedom was the simple and central objective of the Reconstruction Amendments.[74]

The significance of what Kinoy has called the constitutional right of black freedom was recognized by the Supreme Court when it held that Congress had the power, under the implementing clause of the Thirteenth Amendment, to prohibit all racial discrimination by private persons in the sale and rental of property.[75]

The Reconstruction Amendments, then, embody the value of black freedom. Their broad, organic purpose was to establish black freedom in the United States, to overturn forever the premise that blacks were an inferior and subordinate group, and to make them equal participants in the previously white-dominated American society. The promise of the amendments was lost in the social history of racism and has yet to be realized in this nation, where we still have "two societies, black and white, separate and unequal."[76]

The equal participation objective, then, is fully consistent with the black freedom value embodied in the Fourteenth Amendment and the Reconstruction Amendments. The objective is to achieve a *racially equal society,* a society in which blacks would be full and equal participants with whites in all important aspects of American life and in which black freedom would truly become a reality. The promise of a racially equal society was not realized because of the social history of racism, whose consequences remain. Because those consequences are so pervasive and self-perpetuating and self-reinforcing, they can be significantly alleviated only by the use of racial preference directed toward overcoming them and bringing about the equal participation of blacks. The societal interest in the equal participation objective should be held to be compelling, and the appropriate use of racial preference in governmental programs and operations directed toward the advancement of that interest should be held to be constitutional.

I further submit that constitutional values may furnish guidance for policy changes.[77] Policy makers should take constitutional values into account, and the lack of equal participation by blacks in all important aspects of American life today should strongly influence governmental policy making.

The matter of racial preference bitterly divides American society, mostly on racial lines,[78] and is the subject of intense moral and philosophical debate.[79] The societal dilemma is that racial preference for blacks will benefit blacks as a group, and individual blacks in particular, at the expense of individual whites who will suffer the direct effects of such preference. In this sense racial preference seems unfair. But without it we will not in the remotely foreseeable future be able to attain anything approaching genuine racial equality in American society. I have also demonstrated a strong societal interest in the advancement of the equal participation objective. For these reasons, although racial preference may seem unfair, it is clearly not unjustifiable.

Notes

1. I have discussed the constitutionality of racial preference and many of the ideas leading to the present thesis in three law review articles: "Racial Preference, Reality, and the Constitution: *Bakke* v. *Regents of the University of California*," *Santa Clara Law Review*, vol. 17 (1977), p. 329; "Beyond *Bakke*: The Constitution and Redressing the Social History of Racism," *Harvard Civil Rights–Civil Liberties Law Review*, vol. 14 (1979), p. 133; and "Racial Preference and the Constitution: The Societal Interest in the Equal Participation Objective," *Wayne Law Review*, vol. 26 (1980), p. 1227. I have also discussed racial preference in "The Constitution and the Social History of Racism," *Arkansas Law Review*, vol. 40, Symposium issue in honor of Justice Thurgood Marshall (1987), p. 677.

My colleague Professor Edward J. Littlejohn reviewed an earlier draft of this paper and made a number of valuable suggestions and comments. The views expressed herein, of course, are entirely my own.

2. See, for example, Bakke v. Regents of the University of California, 438 U.S. 265 (1978) (hereafter cited as *Bakke*).

3. See, for example, Detroit Police Officers v. Young, 608 F.2d 671 (6th Cir., 1979).

4. See, for example, Fullilove v. Klutznick, 448 U.S. 448 (1980).

5. See Richard Posner, "The *DeFunis* Case and the Constitutionality of Preferential Treatment of Racial Minorities," *Supreme Court Review* (1974), pp. 1, 25.

6. See the discussion in my article "Racial Preference, Reality, and the Constitution," pp. 329, 368–72.

7. Loving v. Virginia, 388 U.S. 1, 11 (1967).

8. Wygant v. Jackson Board of Education, 106 S.Ct. 1842, 1848 (1986) (Opinion of Powell, J.).

9. See the discussion of this point in Sedler, "Beyond *Bakke*," pp. 157–62.

10. As Justice Lewis F. Powell put it in *Bakke:* "The State certainly has a legitimate interest in ameliorating, or eliminating where feasible, the disabling effects of identified discrimination." *Bakke* at 307 (Opinion of Powell, J.).

11. The past discrimination has violated the rights of blacks as a group, and the racial preference is designed to remedy the injury to group interests. As Justice William J. Brennan observed in *Bakke:* "Such relief does not require as a predicate proof that recipients of preferential treatment have been individually discriminated against; it is enough that each recipient is within a group likely to have been the victims of discrimination." *Bakke* at 363 (Opinion of Brennan, J.).

Similarly, as Justice Sandra Day O'Connor observed in *Wygant:* "It is agreed that a plan need not be limited to the remedying of specific instances of identified discrimination for it to be deemed sufficiently 'narrowly tailored,' or 'substantially related,' to the correction of prior discrimination by the state actor." Wygant v. Jackson Board of Education (Opinion of O'Connor, J.).

12. But see Wygant v. Jackson Board of Education at 1842, where the governmental body failed to make such a showing.

13. The Thirteenth, Fourteenth, and Fifteenth amendments are commonly referred to as the Reconstruction Amendments.

14. *Bakke* at 398 (Opinion of Marshall, J.). "It is inconceivable that the Fourteenth Amendment was intended to prohibit all race-conscious relief measures. . . . Such a result would pervert the intent of the framers by substituting abstract equality for the genuine equality the Amendment was intended to achieve."

15. The social history of racism and its consequences were traced fully in Justice Thurgood Marshall's opinion in *Bakke* at 390–96.

16. As Professor Michael Perry has observed: "The *material inequality* of the races is the objective, concrete, manifestation of the widespread American belief in the *moral inequality* of the races and of racially discriminatory practices reflecting that belief." Perry, "Modern Equal Protection: A Conceptualization and Appraisal," *Columbia Law Review,* vol. 79 (1979), pp. 1023, 1040.

17. The black unemployment rate has been consistently double that of whites. In December 1984 the black rate stood at 14.4 percent and the white rate at 6.0 percent. U.S. Department of Labor, Bureau of Labor Statistics, *Employment and Earnings* (January 1985), table A-6. In 1982 the black unemployment rate was 18.9 percent and the white rate 8.6 percent. U.S. Department of Commerce, Bureau of the Census, *America's Black Population: 1970–1982,* chart 5. In 1976 the unemployment rate stood at 15.9 percent for black males and 5.9 percent for white males; the rates for women were 18.9 percent and 8.7 percent respectively. U.S. Commission on Civil Rights, *Social Indicators of Equality for Minorities and Women* (1978), table 3.1. Among black teenagers in 1982, the unemployment rate reached 48 percent, while the rate for white teen-agers was 20.4 percent. Census Bureau, *America's Black Population,* chart 5. In 1976 the rate for black male teen-agers was 47.8 percent and for

black female teen-agers 51.3 percent while the rates for white were 5.9 percent and 19.2 percent. Civil Rights Commission, *Social Indicators*, table 3.2. The unemployment figures exclude "discouraged workers," a disproportionate number of whom are black, so that the actual gap in employment between blacks and whites is even larger than the statistics indicate. Ibid., pp. 28–29.

A disproportionate number of employed blacks are found in lower-paying, lower-prestige occupational categories; they are underrepresented in the more elite and white-collar jobs. Even in the blue-collar category, where the distribution of blacks and whites is more even, blacks are disproportionately concentrated in the least desirable occupations. The "prestige value" of the average black male worker was only 77 percent that of his white counterpart according to *Social Indicators*, pp. 34–36, table 3.4. In December 1984, for example, 56.8 percent of all white workers and 39.5 percent of all black workers were employed in white-collar jobs (managerial and professional, specialty, and technical, sales, and administrative support). Among blue-collar occupations 13 percent of white workers and 8.5 percent of black workers were employed in the precision, production, craft, and repair category. By contrast, 24.1 percent of black workers and 12.2 percent of white workers were employed in service occupations, and 25 percent of black workers and 15 percent of white workers were employed as operators, fabricators, and laborers. Bureau of Labor Statistics, *Employment and Earnings*, table A-23.

In 1980, when blacks made up 10.1 percent of the civilian labor force, they constituted only 6.1 percent of managerial and professional workers, 8.3 percent of technical, sales, and administrative support workers, and 6.9 percent of precision, production, craft, and repair workers. But they made up 17.6 percent of service workers and 14.5 percent of operators, fabricators, and laborers. They constituted 53.7 percent of private household workers, 33 percent of maids and housemen, 27.4 percent of nursing aides, orderlies, and attendants, 22.1 percent of janitors and cleaners, 34.8 percent of garbage collectors, and 18.7 percent of general laborers but only 4.1 percent of managers and administrators, 2.6 percent of engineers, 4.9 percent of postsecondary teachers, 3.0 percent of sales representatives, and 5 percent of carpenters and electricians. Census Bureau, *America's Black Population*, table 3.

The result is that black family income is little more than half of white family income, a figure that has remained constant for a long time. In 1983 median black family income was $12,429, or approximately 57 percent of the median white family income of $21,902. In 1967 median black family income was $4,325, or 58 percent of the median white family income of $7,449. U.S. Department of Commerce, Bureau of the Census, *1985 Statistical Abstract of the United States*, table 735. In 1981, 34 percent of black families and only 11 percent of white families lived below the federally defined poverty level ($9,287 for a family of four). Census Bureau, *America's Black Population*, chart 4.

The racial difference in median family income is due only in part to the much higher proportion of black families (41 percent in 1982) than of white families (12 percent) headed by women. Among such families black families had a median income of $7,510, or 60 percent of the median of $12,510 for white families. Ibid., chart 2. Among families where the father was the only wage earner, the median income for black families was $14,420, or 61 percent of the median of $23,460 for white families. U.S. Department of Labor, Bureau of Labor Statistics, *Families at Work: The Jobs and the Pay* (August 1984), table 4. Some 24.4 percent of such black families and 9 percent of such white families lived below the poverty level.

The income gap is smaller among married-couple families, the median black family income being $19,620 in 1981, or 77 percent of the $25,470 for white families. Census Bureau, *America's Black Population*, chart 2. But even among married-couple families in 1982, 15.6 percent of the black families and only 6.9 percent of the white families lived below the poverty level. Bureau of Labor Statistics, *Families at Work*, table 4. Only in married-couple families where both spouses are employed is the gap narrowed considerably, since white working wives do not earn very much more than black working wives. In 1982 the median income of working-couple black families was $26,110, or 88 percent of the $29,650 median for working-couple white families. Ibid.

The data indicate that the racial difference in median family income would still be substantial if the proportion of black families headed by women was the same as the proportion of white families headed by women. The gap is worsened because of the much higher proportion of black families than of white families headed by women.

There appears to be little prospect that racial economic inequality will improve in the foreseeable future, and it may even be worsening. As the black population of the nation's central cities increases, for example, the availability of manufacturing and other jobs requiring minimal skills has declined in the central cities. The increase of jobs in the central cities has been primarily in the information-processing and other white-collar areas, which require higher skill and education. See "New Jobs in Cities Little Aid to Poor," *New York Times*, October 22, 1986, p. 1. In the nation's fifty largest cities the percentage of black families living in poverty increased from 1970 to 1980, and the number of blacks living in poverty in those cities exceeded the number of whites. During this period the number of blacks living in poverty increased from 2.6 million to 3.1 million while the number of whites declined from 3.2 million to 2.6 million. See "Poverty of Blacks Spreads in Cities," *New York Times*, January 26, 1987, p. 1.

18. In 1983, 43.2 percent of blacks and 27.9 percent of the general population had not completed high school. Among persons 25–29 years old, the rate was 20.6 percent for blacks and 14.0 percent for the general population. Census Bureau, *1985 Statistical Abstract of the United States*, table 213. In that year 19.5 percent of all whites and 9.5 percent of all blacks had graduated from college. Ibid., table 214. Of persons 14–24 years old, 15.3 percent of blacks and 11.0 percent of whites had dropped out of high school. Ibid., table 243.

When the quality of education received by blacks is considered, the gap grows even wider. Earlier studies in metropolitan areas, where some 80 percent of the black population resides, have shown a marked disparity in educational expenditures between low-income, predominantly nonwhite

141

neighborhoods and wealthier, predominantly white areas, even within the same school districts and even more strikingly between urban and suburban school districts. See, for example, James W. Guthrie, G. Kleindorfer, H. Levin, and R. Stout, *Schools and Inequality* (Cambridge, Mass.: MIT Press, 1971), pp. 34–36; and John D. Owen, *School Inequality and the Welfare State* (Baltimore: Johns Hopkins University Press, 1974), pp. 18–21.

There is little evidence that these inequalities have been reduced in more recent years, and if the experience in Michigan is any indication, they have increased. In the 1981–1982 school year, for example, the Detroit school district, which is about 90 percent black, spent $2,178 per student; two other predominantly black school districts in Wayne County, Highland Park and Inkster, spent $2,350 and $2,061 respectively. Of the thirty-nine districts in Wayne County, Highland Park ranked twenty-sixth, Detroit thirty-second, and Inkster thirty-fifth in per student expenditures. Twelve Wayne County districts that were all white or virtually so spent $3,000 or more per student.

A 1977 study by the U.S. Office of Education found that only 58 percent of black seventeen-year-olds but 87 percent of white seventeen-year-olds were functionally literate. U.S. Congressional Budget Office, *Inequalities in the Educational Experiences of Black and White Americans* (1977), pp. 8–9. In 1978 black males were likely to be two or more school grades behind their white peers by the time they reached high school. Civil Rights Commission, *Social Indicators*, table 2.1.

A recent study by the Rand Corporation found that black students "are disproportionately more likely to be enrolled in special education programs, and are less likely to be enrolled in programs for the gifted and talented" and are "underrepresented in academic programs and overrepresented in vocational-educational programs." The study concludes, "Overall, the evidence suggests that black students are exposed to less challenging educational program offerings, which are less likely to enhance the development of higher cognitive skills and abilities than white students." See "Gains by Blacks in Education Found Eroding," *Chronicle of Higher Education*, April 17, 1985.

The disparity in educational quality carries over into higher education, where blacks are more likely than whites to attend poorly rated schools. The Rand study found that blacks were enrolling in increasing proportions at two-year institutions, where dropout rates, especially for blacks, are higher than at four-year colleges and where fewer resources are available in the most important areas of educational programming. In colleges, as well as in secondary schools, the report concluded, black students on the average "receive educational programs and offerings that differ in kind and content from those of white students." Ibid.

19. Although the black population of the United States is now 12 percent, blacks constitute only 2.6 percent of the lawyers and judges, 5 percent of the physicians, 3.2 percent of the editors and reporters, and 4.7 percent of the college and university teachers.

20. As Justice Powell noted in *Bakke*, at the time the Civil Rights Act of 1964

was enacted, there was no notion of "racial preference" or "affirmative action." "There simply was no reason for Congress to consider the validity of hypothetical preferences that might be accorded minority citizens: the legislators were dealing with the real and pressing problem of how to guarantee those citizens equal treatment." *Bakke* at 285 (Opinion of Powell, J.).

21. While many of the traditional forms of intentional discrimination against blacks, such as discrimination in employment or admission to public universities, resulted in racial preference for whites, as a matter of constitutional analysis there was no need to distinguish such racial preference for whites from the other forms of discrimination against blacks. The use of race-conscious criteria that produced discrimination against blacks was invariably found to be "invidious" and hence unconstitutional, because in no case could it be shown to be "necessary to the accomplishment of some permissible state objective, independent of the racial discrimination which it was the objective of the Fourteenth Amendment to eliminate." Loving v. Virginia.

22. Whenever seniority is used as the criterion for promotion or retention, it will severely curtail the employment opportunities of blacks, because of pervasive past employment discrimination. Since only in recent years have many employers hired blacks in substantial numbers for other than menial jobs, black workers as a group have much less seniority than white workers as a group.

23. The self-perpetuating and self-reinforcing nature of those consequences is illustrated by the relation between the economic gap and the education gap from one generation to another. Because of the economic gap black children come disproportionately from lower-income families and for this reason are likely to have substantially lower academic achievement than white children. Low educational attainment, caused in large part by economic disadvantage and attendance at schools in which economically disadvantaged children predominate, has a severe detrimental effect, when the children become adults, on their economic status, social mobility, and other indicators of social well-being. Thus poorly educated black children find themselves as adults in low-status, low-paying jobs, and their depressed economic condition adversely affects the educational opportunities of their children. The cycle of poverty and inequality is then perpetuated from one generation to another.

24. Most of the system of prevention was in place by the late 1960s. If the removal of structural barriers to equality alone could bring about the equal participation of blacks in American society, the societal position of blacks should have improved significantly in a decade or so. Of course, it has not. While blacks have made some gains according to a number of social indicators, there has been little improvement in their societal position relative to that of whites. See Civil Rights Commission, *Social Indicators*, pp. 89–91.

25. The qualitative difference of racial discrimination from other forms of discrimination was fully explicated in the report of the National Advisory Commission on Civil Disorders, which concluded: "European immigrants too suffered from discrimination, but never was it so pervasive as the prejudice

against color in America, which has formed a bar to advancement, unlike any other." *Report of the National Advisory Commission on Civil Disorders* (New York: Bantam Books, 1968), p. 279.

26. It has been said that "there is the plea from many blacks for reparations in the form of a substantial approximation to ethnic proportionality in the allocation of scarce social goods" and that "a policy of ethnic proportionality that qualifies a person's equality of opportunity has no foundation in our individual rights focused constitutional tradition." Robert Dixon, *"Bakke:* A Constitutional Analysis," *California Law Review,* vol. 67 (1979), pp. 69, 74. Regardless of the validity of the attack on "reparations" and "proportionality," the attack cannot properly be mounted against the equal participation objective.

27. To quote Justice Marshall in *Bakke:* "In light of the sorry history of discrimination and its devastating impact on the lives of Negroes, bringing the Negro into the mainstream of American life should be a state interest of the highest order. To fail to do so is to ensure that America will forever remain a divided society." *Bakke* at 396 (Opinion of Marshall, J.).

28. This justification has been developed fully in Sedler, "Beyond *Bakke,"* pp. 170–71.

29. See *Bakke.* The Court held that the medical school could use race-conscious admissions criteria to advance this objective. This was the basis of Justice Powell's opinion, and the "Brennan four," in a footnote, agreed with Justice Powell on this point. *Bakke* at 326, n.1. Although the holding was relatively narrow in terms of constitutional doctrine, as a practical matter it ensured the continued validity of racially preferential university admissions programs. See the discussion in Sedler, "Beyond *Bakke,"* pp. 141–45.

30. Justice Powell found that the use of race-conscious admissions criteria taking the form of a rigid racial quota was constitutionally impermissible but upheld the use of such criteria taking the form of "competitive consideration of race or ethnic origin."

31. Dixon, *"Bakke,"* pp. 75–76.

32. *Bakke* at 316 (Opinion of Powell, J.).

33. Id. at 313.

34. Foley v. Connelie, 435 U.S. 291, 297 (1978).

35. See *Report of the National Advisory Commission on Civil Disorders,* pp. 315–18. When Detroit adopted a racially preferential hiring and promotion policy for its police department in July 1974, the city had a black population of nearly 50 percent but a police force that was only 17 percent black. Detroit Police Officers Association v. Young. Less than 5 percent of the lieutenants were black. Bratton v. City of Detroit, 704 F.2d 878, 889 (6th Cir., 1983).

The gross underrepresentation of blacks on police forces has often been shown to be the product of unlawful racial discrimination, and in the absence of voluntary action on the part of the responsible governmental body, racially preferential hiring and promotional remedies have been imposed by the courts. See, for example, United States v. City of Chicago, 549 F.2d 415 (7th Cir., 1977); and NAACP v. Allen, 493 F.2d 614 (5th Cir., 1974). The Supreme

Court recently upheld the judicial imposition of a sweeping racially preferential promotional remedy in the face of Alabama's persistent refusal to adopt promotion procedures that would overcome the present effects of its past racial discrimination with respect to hiring and promotions in the state police force. Under the Court's order the state police force was required to promote one qualified black officer for every white officer promoted until 25 percent of the officers in each rank were black or until the state police had developed and implemented a promotional plan without adverse effects on blacks for the relevant rank. United States v. Paradise, 107 S.Ct. 1053 (1987).

36. See *Report of the National Advisory Commission on Civil Disorders*, pp. 299–301.

37. President's Commission on Law Enforcement and the Administration of Justice, *Task Force Report: The Police* (1967), p. 167.

38. Detroit Police Officers v. Young at 696.

39. This point has been demonstrated empirically with respect to Detroit's racially preferential hiring and promotions program for police officers. As the federal district court stated in Baker v. City of Detroit, 483 F.Supp. 930, 1000 (E.D.Mich. 1979), aff'd. sub nom. Bratton v. City of Detroit:

> There is clear evidence in the record that before 1974 there existed enormous tension between the Department and the black community. There is clear evidence in the record that after the institution of the affirmative action prógram, police-community relations improved substantially, crime went down, complaints against the Department went down, and no police officers were killed in the line of duty. . . . Upon careful review of the testimony this Court believes that no reasonable person could fail to conclude that given the history of antagonism between the Department and the black community, the affirmative action plan was a necessary response to what had been an ongoing city crisis.

40. Senate Committee on Labor and Public Welfare, *Legislative History of the Equal Employment Opportunity Act of 1972*, 92d Congress, 2d session, 1972, p. 419.

41. See also the discussion in Ann Ginger, "Who Needs Affirmative Action?" *Harvard Civil Rights–Civil Liberties Law Review*, vol. 14 (1979), pp. 265, 270–73.

42. In practice governmental agencies adopting such programs will assert their own past discrimination to defend them against constitutional challenge. See, for example, Local 526-M, Michigan Corrections Organization, Service Employees International Union v. Civil Service Commission, 110 Mich. App. 546, 313 N.W.2d 143 (1981) (state civil service).

43. Although the black population of the United States is approximately 12 percent, in 1984 only 2.3 percent of lawyers, 5.0 percent of physicians, and less than 1 percent of dentists were black. Bureau of Labor Statistics, *Employment and Earnings* (January 1985), table 22.

44. *Bakke* at 401 (Opinion of Marshall, J.).

45. As Professor Kent Greenawalt has observed:

> Universities and particularly professional schools have long made decisions about who will have the keys to important societal positions through determinations about admissions and scholarships. Implicit in the exercise of such power is some view of the public welfare. It would seem appropriate for a law school to choose not to limit consideration even to such broad concerns as potential ability as a lawyer and likely area of legal employment. . . . It requires no substantial extension of the institutional responsibility to determine who will become members of the profession for institutions to make some judgments about the social desirability of broadening the availability of professional positions, in the belief that a more diverse and representative profession will enrich the understanding of all its members of relevant social problems and will otherwise promote a more harmonious and integrated society.

Kent Greenawalt, "The Unresolved Problems of Reverse Discrimination," *California Law Review,* vol. 67 (1979), pp. 87, 124.

46. The societal interest in the equal participation of blacks in the administration of justice must be distinguished from the law school's institutional interest in achieving a "racially and ethnically diverse" student body, which was recognized in *Bakke.*

47. This societal interest was apparently not asserted by the medical school in *Bakke.* The school's justification for racially preferential admissions was that minority physicians were more likely than whites to serve in underserved minority communities. Justice Powell took the position that the medical school "simply has not carried its burden of demonstrating that it must prefer members of particular ethnic groups over all other individuals in order to promote better health care delivery to deprived citizens." *Bakke* at 311 (Opinion of Powell, J.).

It may be queried whether the Court in *Bakke* would have viewed racially preferential admissions in a different light if that case had involved admission to law school rather than to medical school. The ways in which lawyers exercise societal power would, of course, have been clear to the Court. The ways in which physicians exercise societal power may have been less clear.

48. For a summary of the situation existing in the early 1970s, see Max Seham, *Blacks and American Medical Care* (Minneapolis: University of Minnesota Press, 1973), pp. 9–11. The situation may have improved somewhat in the interim, but it may be assumed that a substantial health gap remains. Black life expectancy, for example, is still four years lower than white life expectancy. Census Bureau, *America's Black Population,* p. 18.

49. See note 17.

50. In 1976, for example, only 3 percent of the 13 million businesses in the United States were owned by blacks and other minority persons, and of the $2.54 trillion in gross business receipts that year, only about $16.6 billion, or 0.65 percent of the total, was realized by minority-owned businesses. *Congressional Record,* vol. 122, p. 13866 (statement of Senator Javits), p. 34754 (statement of Senator Glenn). In 1984 the largest black-owned business, Johnson Publishing, had sales of only $138.9 million. As the president of one black-

owned company observed: "Our figures are not that significant. When you put all of the top black companies' sales together they might equal one of the companies on the bottom of the Fortune 500 list." "Black-owned Companies Gain," *New York Times*, May 8, 1985.

51. See note 17.

52. Ibid.

53. While my focus has been on the use of racial preference in governmental programs and operations, the same policy reasons justify racial preference in the programs and operations of private entities. Since the United States is a free enterprise economy, racial preference on the part of private entities is of the utmost importance in the economic area. Many of the major corporations now have in place affirmative action programs, designed to increase the number of minority and women employees. See "Employers Welcome Ruling Upholding Affirmative Action," *New York Times*, March 27, 1987, p. 17.

54. The exclusion of blacks from the crafts on racial grounds has been so clearly demonstrated as to be now a subject of judicial notice. United Steelworkers of America v. Weber, 443 U.S. 193, 198, n.1 (1979). For a particularly egregious example of such exclusion and a resulting judicially ordered racial admission program, see Local 28 of Sheet Metal Workers Int'l. Ass'n. v. Equal Employment Opportunity Commission, 106 S.Ct. 3019 (1986).

55. This is what was done in the *Weber* case. The Court there held that racial preference by a private employer designed to overcome minority underrepresentation in the employer's work force did not constitute "discrimination on the basis of race" within the meaning of Title VII of the Civil Rights Act of 1964. The holding in *Weber* was reaffirmed and extended to permit the use of gender preference in order to overcome the underutilization of women in Johnson v. Transportation Agency, Santa Clara County, California, 107 S.Ct. 1442 (1987). As the Court explained *Weber:* "Our decision was grounded in the recognition that voluntary employer action can play a crucial role in furthering Title VII's purpose of eliminating the effects of discrimination in the workplace, and that Title VII should not be read to thwart such efforts." Id. at 1451.

56. See Fullilove v. Klutznick.

57. I have suggested that when Congress enacted Title VII of the Civil Rights Act of 1964, it recognized a societal interest in blacks' having a "fair share" of the available jobs in an employer's work force, which in time would alleviate the condition of racial economic inequality. Sedler, "Beyond *Bakke,*" pp. 147–49. As the Court observed in *Weber:*

> Congress' primary concern in enacting the prohibition against racial discrimination in Title VII of the Civil Rights Act of 1964 was with "the plight of the Negro in our economy." . . . It was clear to Congress that "the crux of the problem [was] to open employment opportunities for Negroes in occupations which have been traditionally closed to them," and it was to this problem that Title VII's prohibition against racial discrimination in employment was primarily addressed.

147

United Steelworkers of America v. Weber at 202–3.

58. Blacks are more likely to be aware of jobs that are available in black-owned enterprises and more likely to be hired by those enterprises. A recent Census Bureau study of the hiring practices of smaller companies concluded that "minorities hire minorities." Nearly half the companies owned by blacks and Hispanics had work forces consisting of more than 75 percent minorities, while half of the businesses owned by white men reported no minority workers. See "White Men Found Least Likely to Hire Minorities," *New York Times,* September 18, 1987, p. 15.

59. I have elsewhere taken the position that when the preference for group rights advances a compelling governmental interest, such as overcoming the present consequences of the social history of racism, group rights may be preferred over individual rights in governmental programs and operations. Sedler, "Beyond *Bakke*," pp. 163–71. See also the discussion in Sedler, "Racial Preference, Reality, and the Constitution," pp. 370–80.

60. *Bakke* at 299 (Opinion of Powell, J.).

61. See Carter v. Gallagher, 452 F.2d 315 (7th Cir., 1972), where the lower court, after finding racial discrimination in the hiring practices of a municipal fire department, ordered that the next twenty vacancies be filled by members of racial minorities. This absolute preference for minorities was held to be impermissible, because it completely foreclosed any present opportunity for whites to be hired. The court of appeals directed instead that one of every three new firefighters be a minority person until twenty minority persons had been hired. The Supreme Court recently upheld a judicially imposed one-to-one promotional remedy to overcome identified racial discrimination in the hiring and promotion of blacks in the Alabama state police. United States v. Paradise. From a constitutional standpoint any racially preferential hiring or promotions plan, whether adopted voluntarily or judicially ordered to remedy identified past discrimination, must not "unnecessarily trammel" the interests of whites. Bratton v. City of Detroit at 878, 897. See also the discussion of this point in *Paradise* at 4220 (Opinion of Brennan, J.).

62. As Chief Justice Warren E. Burger stated in the *Fullilove* case, where the Court upheld the constitutionality of minority business enterprise set-asides in governmental contracting: "It is not a constitutional defect in this program that it may disappoint the expectations of non-minority firms. When effectuating a limited and properly tailored remedy to cure the effects of prior discrimination, such 'a sharing of the burden' by innocent parties is not impermissible." Fullilove v. Klutznick at 484 (Opinion of Burger, C.J.).

63. See the discussion of this point in Robert A. Sedler, "The Legitimacy Debate in Constitutional Adjudication: An Assessment and a Different Perspective," *Ohio State Law Journal,* vol. 44 (1983), pp. 93, 129–30.

64. See the discussion in John Frank and Robert Munro, "The Original Understanding of 'Equal Protection of the Laws,'" *Columbia Law Review,* vol. 50 (1950), pp. 131, 132–42. As my colleague Joseph Grano has put it, the framers constitutionalized the value of racial equality in the Fourteenth Amendment. Grano, "Judicial Review and a Written Constitution in a Democratic Society," *Wayne Law Review,* vol. 28 (1981), pp. 1, 70–73.

65. The term "historic context" refers to the "principles and ideas which most importantly influenced the development of [the] constitutional text." Richard Saphire, "Judicial Review in the Name of the Constitution," *University of Dayton Law Review,* vol. 8 (1983), pp. 745, 780. Saphire uses the term "historic context" to avoid the problems associated with ascertaining the framers' intent and notes that the reference to the historic context of a constitutional provision is a reference to "foundational principles and ideas [that] transcend the views expressed by particular persons." These principles and ideas are "epochal" and "must be extrapolated, however imperfectly, from the events of an entire political era." Ibid.

66. 83 U.S. (16 Wall.)36 (1873).

67. Id. at 68.

68. Id.

69. Id. at 69.

70. Id. at 70.

71. Id. at 71.

72. Id. at 71–72.

73. Id. at 71.

74. Arthur Kinoy, "The Constitutional Right of Negro Freedom," *Rutgers Law Review,* vol. 21 (1967), pp. 387, 388.

75. Jones v. Alfred H. Mayer Co., 392 U.S. 409 (1968). As the Court stated in that case:

> And when racial discrimination herds men into ghettos and makes their ability to buy property turn on the color of their skin, then it too is a relic of slavery.
> . . . At the very least, the freedom that Congress is empowered to secure under the Thirteenth Amendment includes the freedom to buy whatever a white man can buy, the freedom to live wherever a white man can live. If Congress cannot say that being a free man means at least this much, then the Thirteenth Amendment has made a promise the Nation cannot keep.

Id. at 442–43.

76. *Report of the National Advisory Commission on Civil Disorders,* p. 1.

77. I do not here suggest that the Constitution should be interpreted as *requiring* the government to provide for racial preference to advance the equal participation objective in governmental programs and operations. My constitutional submission does not go beyond the constitutional *permissibility* of racial preference for this purpose.

78. See Seymour Martin Lipset and William Schneider, "The *Bakke* Case: How Would It Be Decided at the Bar of Public Opinion?" *Public Opinion* (March/April 1978), p. 38.

79. Compare Carl Cohen, "Why Racial Preference Is Illegal and Immoral," *Commentary* (June 1979), p. 40, with James Nickel, "Preferential Policies in Hiring and Admissions: A Jurisprudential Approach," *Columbia Law Review,* vol. 75 (1975), p. 534. See Marshall Cohen, Thomas Nagel, and Thomas Scanlon, eds., *Equality and Preferential Treatment: A Philosophy and Public Affairs Reader* (Princeton, N.J.: Princeton University Press, 1977).

7
"Matters of Color"—
Blacks and
the Constitutional Order

Glenn C. Loury

In his treatise on the early development of American legal doctrine affecting slaves, U.S. Circuit Court Judge Leon Higginbotham observes: "This new nation, 'conceived in liberty and dedicated to the proposition that all men are created equal,' began its experiment in self-government with a legacy of more than one-half million enslaved blacks—persons denied citizenship and enslaved, not for criminal infractions, but solely as a matter of color." The United States, in other words, was born with the burden of a sinful, "peculiar" institution that belied the very ideals the founders sought to affirm. That a group of colonialists, proclaiming themselves fathers of a new nation built on Jefferson's "self-evident truths," were prepared to legitimate in law the brutalities requisite to a commerce in human beings is an irony that forms the heart of a powerful indictment of the American legal tradition by Judge Higginbotham. He goes on to cite a conversation with Earl Warren shortly before the chief justice's death, in which the two jurists agreed that "there is a powerful nexus between the brutal centuries of colonial slavery and the racial polarization and anxieties of today. The poisonous legacy of legalized oppression based upon the matter of color can never be adequately purged from our society if we act as if slave laws had never existed." But no matter what our actions, can this "poisonous legacy" ever be purged from our civic life? Is the Constitution an aid or an obstacle to the removal of this legacy? Are the precepts and structures of American government capable of eradicating the consequences of the "original sin" that was African slavery? This is an old question, raised 150 years ago by Tocqueville, who wrote: "The most formidable of all the ills that threaten the future of the Union arises from the presence of a black

Reprinted with permission of the author from *The Public Interest*, no. 86 (Winter 1987), pp. 109–23. Copyright 1987 by National Affairs Incorporated.

population upon its territory." This astute observer of early American life further noted that the difficulty was more than a legal one, that "the prejudice which repels the Negroes seems to increase in proportion to their emancipation . . . and inequality is sanctioned by the manners while it is effaced from the laws of the country."

Moreover, this question remained unanswered a century after the publication of Tocqueville's *Democracy in America*, when Gunnar Myrdal defined the "American Dilemma" as

> the ever-raging conflict between, on the one hand, the valuations preserved on the general plane which we shall call the "American Creed," where the American thinks, talks and acts under the influence of high national and Christian precepts, and, on the other hand, the valuations on specific planes of individual and group living, where personal and local interests; economic, social and sexual jealousies; considerations of community prestige and conformity; group prejudice against particular persons or types of people; and all sorts of miscellaneous wants, impulses, and habits dominate his outlook.

Myrdal envisioned a fundamental conflict between the civic creed embraced in principle by Americans, and codified in the Constitution and Declaration of Independence, on the one hand, and the social norms and practices that governed the ways in which concrete social intercourse occurred among various groups of Americans, on the other. Neutralization of the legacy of slavery would require, in his view, a bridging of this gap between ideals and customs.

Nor has this question regarding the permanency of that "poisonous legacy" yet been settled, despite the remarkable revolution in our law and politics on the matter of color that has occurred in the past generation. For the considerable merits of this long-overdue reconstruction of the legal status of blacks notwithstanding, a cursory inspection of our contemporary political discourse on "matters of color" would reveal that, for many, it has not been sufficient to vindicate the liberating potential of the American constitutional tradition. Too many black and white Americans—dissatisfied with our slow progress toward racial economic equality, disillusioned with the limited efficacy of public policies (like court-ordered busing for school desegregation) in which they had placed so much hope, disoriented by the now nearly wholesale rejection by blacks of the classical integration ideal, dismayed by the depressing nature of social life among the black underclass—have concluded that it is this tradition itself that has, in view of these developments, been shown to be inadequate.

One indication of this state of affairs is the remarkable argument

of political scientist Jennifer Hochschild's book on school desegregation, *A New American Dilemma*. There she holds that the unwillingness
of the American courts to go any further than they did to override
popular, democratically expressed opposition to massive, cross-district busing is a measure of our nation's limited commitment to the
ideal of equal opportunity. The "new" dilemma that she has discovered is that, given the interests and concerns of whites, democracy
is inconsistent with racial equality of opportunity because the former
too severely constrains those state actions essential for the attainment
of the latter.

This is a far more pessimistic vision than that of Myrdal, though
offered at a time when most of Myrdal's concerns had been legally
addressed, and when attitude surveys revealed a significant increase
in racial tolerance among whites over the past generation. Hochschild
argues that a genuine commitment to equal opportunity would require a willingness to carry on color-conscious pupil assignments
regardless of the ambiguity of the evidence as to the beneficial educational effects of such actions, or the extent or intensity of popular
opposition to such policy—or even whether that opposition comes
from blacks instead of whites. In her view, the "poisonous legacy" of
slavery shall be indefinitely perpetuated precisely because our system
of government accords too much respect to the "will of the people."

Promise and Performance

The not-so-quiet desperation in Hochschild's argument is mirrored in
the public pronouncements of civil rights advocates around this country, where the recalcitrant persistence of racial inequality of results
under conditions of ostensible equality of opportunity is attributed to
the halfhearted or incomplete application of some constitutional
mandate. When a police sergeant's examination was administered in
New York City, using an exam that was explicitly prepared (at a cost of
$500,000, under a court-supervised consent decree) so as to test only
job-relevant skills (in keeping with the Supreme Court's interpretation, in its famous *Griggs* decision, of the requirements of the Civil
Rights Act of 1964), the disappointing result was that 10.1 percent of
the white officers and 1.7 percent of the black officers passed the
exam. Immediately a lawsuit was filed to prevent promotions based
on the exam results, with representatives of the black officers admitting that it was not the *test*, but the *results* of the test that were "unfair."
In due course, the city chose to employ a racial quota instead of
strictly following the results of the exam. But the matter did not end
there; white officers filed countersuits, and the city was forced to
make inquiries into the genealogical backgrounds of officers claiming

152

minority status so as to avail themselves of the benefits of the quota. Despite well-intentioned efforts, the "poisonous legacy" continues to assert itself.

The deep problem posed by persistent racial differences in educational performance, for those who placed their hopes for the attainment of equal educational opportunity on desegregating public schools, is illustrated by the attack on public high schools for the gifted waged by some advocates in New York City. More than three decades after the *Brown* decision, confronted with the depressingly small numbers of black students qualifying for placement at these academically elite institutions, the best these advocates can do is condemn the use of public resources to foster the development of New York City's most talented youngsters. Writing in the *New York Times*, former NAACP official Michael Meyers argued: "The specialized high schools for the 'gifted' should be phased out," for "the mere existence of such schools exacerbates the problem of a racially segregated educational system by serving as havens for many whites." These schools, he insisted, "institutionalize educational racial tracking under the guise of catering to educational elitism." His remedy: close the Bronx High School of Science and like institutions because the low representation of blacks violates the constitutional prohibition against "separate but equal" educational facilities.

But the prohibition against "separate but equal" facilities is irrelevant to the problem at hand, and this argument places far too much weight on constitutional considerations to resolve difficulties that are of social and economic origin. There is every reason to believe that where black parents are intimately involved in their child's education, where adolescent peers accord as much respect to academic as to athletic excellence, and, yes, where teachers hold high expectations for the performance of all their students, black youngsters can attain the highest academic rewards. But how are any of these things to be had by closing the Bronx High School of Science? And who but the poor (who, even when white, deserve our concern) will pay the price for such folly? In view of the fact that (even in New York City) demands such as this are destined to fall on deaf ears, Mr. Meyers, like Professor Hochschild, is left with no recourse other than to decry our nation's limited commitment to the constitutional principles that he mistakenly invokes.

This pessimism among influential advocates for blacks' rights about the ability of the American civic tradition to accommodate the eradication of slavery's legacy is further illustrated by events surrounding the first national celebration of Martin Luther King, Jr., Day. The Rev. Jesse Jackson could then be heard decrying the focus on

King's 1963 "I Have A Dream" speech and belittling King's powerful metaphor—his "dream" that America might yet come to live by the great principles it espoused. Said Jackson: "That so-called 'I have a dream speech' . . . was not a speech about dreamers and dreaming. It was a speech describing nightmare conditions. . . . Dr. King was not assassinated for dreaming." Why, then, was the "dreamer" killed? This is Jackson's "explanation" of the tragedy, as reported in the *Washington Post* during the 1984 presidential campaign:

> He [Jackson] . . . repeated his belief that the Federal Government had taken part in a conspiracy to murder Dr. King. "I went to see James Earl Ray in prison. . . . It was clear he was involved, but it was also clear he wasn't capable of pulling it off himself." The candidate said that the authorities had failed to protect the minister . . . [adding that] the Federal Bureau of Investigation had attempted to impugn his character and divide his family. The FBI saw as its role to disrupt, discredit or destroy a "black messiah," he said. "Given the fact that the CIA will mine harbors and overthrow governments, if they perceived an individual as having the power to offset a war machine, it stands to reason he would be in extreme jeopardy by a mean government," Mr. Jackson concluded.

Such is the "poisonous legacy" of slavery, still alive in our contemporary politics.

Blacks and the Founders' Vision

It is worth noting that, until quite recently, the black champions of the struggle for equal citizenship have placed great faith in the capacity of the Constitution to deliver on its promise. Abolitionist Frederick Douglass, for example, parted company with his mentor William Lloyd Garrison over this issue. Garrison and his followers saw the Constitution as a proslavery document, "a covenant with death," and thought it immoral to vote or to engage in any political activity under this fundamentally unjust framework. Douglass, on the other hand, held "that the Federal Government was never, in its essence, anything but an antislavery government. Abolish slavery tomorrow, and not a sentence or syllable of the Constitution need be altered. . . . If in its origin slavery had any relation to the government, it was only as the scaffolding to the magnificent structure, to be removed as soon as the building was completed." Clearly the decades-long effort of Charles Houston and William Hastie, architects of the NAACP's legal assault on segregation, which culminated in that great victory that was the

Supreme Court's 1954 *Brown* decision, was sustained by an abiding faith in the coherence of the founders' vision. And Martin Luther King, Jr., while leading a mass movement to eradicate Jim Crow in the South, spoke eloquently and often of "that magnificent promissory note," which was the as yet unfulfilled obligation to blacks implicit in the American civic creed.

But has not *that* obligation now been fulfilled? Do not the Civil Rights Acts of the 1960s, the Supreme Court decisions running from *Brown* through *Bakke*, the most recent cases upholding affirmative action, the political failure of those in the Reagan administration to change the direction of the country on civil rights issues, the near-universal affirmation of the inadmissibility of racial prejudice in public political discourse, the broad acceptance throughout the private sector of the legitimacy and necessity of exerting special efforts to include "previously excluded groups" when making employment or educational admissions decisions, even the historic campaign for the presidency of Jesse Jackson himself—do not all of these things, and many more that could be mentioned, confirm that Martin Luther King, Jr., did not "dream" in vain?

Is it not therefore ironic indeed, at the bicentennial of the U.S. Constitution, with the faithful visions of Douglass, Houston, King, and countless others vindicated by the successes of the civil rights movement, that there should be so many questions raised about the ability of the American constitutional order to accommodate an equal citizenship for blacks? For although there can be little question that, on the whole, black Americans have not as yet attained full equality— in economic, social, or political standing—within our society, it is hard to see how the principles of government codified in the Constitution, as now being interpreted and administered throughout the land, can be faulted for this incomplete success. But, if this is so, how can we ever expect to be finally free of the enormous burden arising out of the "original sin" that was black slavery?

Emancipation Is Not Enough

We will never escape the specter of the "original sin" of slavery until we understand that the liberalization of the legal framework—the fulfillment of the promise of equal rights implied in the founders' vision of American government—is a necessary, but not sufficient condition for the attainment of equal citizenship for the descendants of the slaves. As Tocqueville and Myrdal both saw clearly, and as the problem of "white flight"—which has plagued public schools and, to a lesser extent, residential desegregation efforts—further attests, the inequality of condition that black Americans endure is rooted in *social* as much as in *legal* practice. And the ability of the law to undo what the racially discriminatory associational behaviors of white and black Americans have wrought is extremely limited.

We are, of course, intimately familiar with these socially discriminatory behaviors because we all engage in them daily. We choose our friends and neighbors, decide upon our business partners and professional associates, select the schools our children will attend, influence (to the extent we can) the prospective mates of our children, and, of course, choose our own mates. Moreover, for the great majority of us—black and white—race, ethnicity, and religion are factors in these discriminating judgments. The statistics on interracial marriages show this to be so, as does the extent of social segregation in the ostensibly integrated environments of today's colleges and universities. The preservation of our distinct ethnic communities, once thought to be a parochial, even reactionary, objective has, in the wake of the "black power movement," the "rise of the unmeltable ethnics," and the advent of bilingualism, become the respectable (and occasionally government-mandated) pursuit of "pluralism."

While all but the old-style integrationists now celebrate the embrace of diversity implied by this new pluralism, advocates of equality are not always happy with its consequences. For, as a number of writers have observed, there is an inevitable tension between the ideal of equality of opportunity for individuals and the fact of pluralistic social organization along group lines.[1] The fact is that such social clustering has important economic consequences. There is an extensive literature in economics and sociology that documents the importance of family and community background as factors influencing a child's later life success. There is also good reason to think that the attitudes and values communicated to youngsters through the cultural milieux of their particular communities of origin—attitudes about work, family, and education—serve to promote group differences in economic attainment in adulthood. And these factors operate not only between the races, but within racial groups as well. A number of analysts of the black underclass have stressed the debilitating consequences of the social isolation of inner-city communities—isolation from whites and from those black families that, in the post-1960s era of declining housing discrimination, have availed themselves of the opportunity to move out of traditionally black residential areas.[2]

It is crucial to realize that what is involved here is in the main not a legal or even an attitudinal problem, but an inescapable social fact. If people are left with the liberty to choose their social environments, then their exercise of that liberty will inevitably produce a situation in

156

which only mutually advantageous associations can be sustained. As a result, some persons will be deprived of the benefits of an association that, while desirable from their point of view, is perceived as undesirable from the point of view of the other. When the association at issue is that between an employer and an employee, the antidiscrimination mandate of the Civil Rights Acts of 1964 requires that race play no part in the calculation of mutual advantage. But when the association is that between two prospective neighbors, mates, business associates, or friends, no such statutory restraints apply.

Our legal and philosophical traditions are such that we are unwilling to undertake the degree of intrusion into the intimate associational choices of individuals that would be required to achieve a full equality of opportunity between individuals or the members of various ethnic groups. Such choices, in our law and in our ethics, lie beyond the reach of the antidiscrimination mandate. They are private matters that, though susceptible to influence and moral suasion about the tolerance of diversity and the like, are not thought to constitute the proper subject of judicial or legislative decree. Freedom to act on the prejudices and discriminations that induce each of us to seek our identities with and to make our lives among a specific, restricted set of our fellows is among those inalienable rights to life, liberty, and the pursuit of happiness enshrined in the Declaration of Independence.

Nor, given our experience with affirmative action, can the use (within reasonable and constitutional bounds) of preferential treatment hope to offset the effects on individual achievement of racially differential access to those social affiliations that have the greatest impact on subsequent economic success. While we seek to maintain integration through race-conscious allocation of public housing units, it is clear that such practice cannot prevent disgruntled residents from moving away when the racial composition of their neighborhood changes contrary to their liking. And while racial school assignments may be needed, it is also clear that busing for desegregation cannot prevent unhappy parents (those who can afford it!) from sending their children to private schools, or moving to another, more ethnically homogenous district.[3] How intrusive we choose to be in restricting such responses is both a political and a constitutional question, though it seems clear that elimination altogether of this kind of discrimination would be neither feasible nor desirable in a free society.

We will therefore have to live with some of the consequences of it. As a practical matter this means that we will have to accept that some of the inequality results from the fact that even the best Head Start program is an expensive and imperfect substitute for the advantages freely conveyed to a youngster born to middle-class, well-educated, attentive, and concerned parents. And we shall have to live with the fact that some subgroups inculcate attitudes and values that leave their youngsters better prepared, and more inclined, than others to pursue careers as university professors, entrepreneurs, or engineers. This is certainly not to say that one should avoid any effort to stimulate interest in these areas among those who may need such stimulation, or that it is futile to try, through social programs of various kinds, to compensate for disadvantaged backgrounds. My argument is that, having undertaken such stimulative and compensatory efforts to the extent deemed prudent, we should not be surprised if they fall short of achieving the equalitarian result that motivated them. Nor need we infer from the continued existence of inequality in the face of such efforts that we have failed to attain a political and legal order consistent with our highest ideals. For among those ideals is a respect for that very individual autonomy in the sphere of personal associations that makes some disparity in the advantages of social background, and thus in subsequent economic results, inevitable.

Autonomy and Equality

One aspect of the "poisonous legacy" of slavery and the subsequent denial of equal rights has been that blacks are disproportionately represented among those whose "social background resources" are comparatively deficient. In view of this history of racial oppression under which we as a political community labor, the ongoing fact of group disparity is bound to be attributed by those advocating the interests of the dispossessed to a failure to make good on the promise of the American civic creed. Our slavery-laden past will naturally be evoked as cause of our unequal present. And the failure of special actions on behalf of blacks, legitimated by reference to the constitutional requirement of "equal protection," to bring about an equality of status in the present may well be seen as evidence that the process of emancipation remains incomplete.

Yet the existence of racial disparity in contemporary economic circumstances is not, ipso facto, evidence that we have failed to achieve equality before the law for the descendants of slaves. Those who look to the Constitution to provide a remedy for group inequality, which originates in historical discrimination but is perpetuated through social organization, are doomed to be disappointed, and sometimes bitterly so. When opportunity for success in life is linked to parental and communal circumstances, and when individuals employ racial criteria among others in their decisions about private associations, group inequality can go on for a long time, notwithstanding the fact that the original source of the disparity, remediable through the law, has long since been addressed. Complete emancipation, in the sense of the attainment of the full legal rights and privileges associated with citizenship, does not imply an equality of standing in the social and economic order.

Unfortunately this point is not sufficiently well understood or accepted by contemporary advocates of racial equality. They continue to seek a constitutionally secured "freedom and equality" for blacks, as if these goals could be ordained by a government endowed with sufficient nobility of spirit and clarity of purpose. There is something tenuous, and ultimately pathetic, about the position of blacks in this regard. Do not recoil here at the use of the word "pathetic"; that, after all, is what this practice is all about—evoking the pity, and the guilt, of whites. But, for that very reason, the practice is inconsistent with the goal of freedom and equality of blacks. One cannot be the equal of those whose pity, or guilt, one actively seeks.

Booker T. Washington, that much maligned figure who rose to prominence as a black leader and spokesman some ninety years ago, understood this matter clearly. "It is a mistake," Washington wrote, "to assume that the Negro, who had been a slave for two hundred and fifty years, gained his freedom by the signing, on a certain date, of a certain paper by the President of the United States. It is a mistake to assume that one man can, in any true sense, give freedom to another. Freedom, in the larger and higher sense, every man must gain for himself."

How long can blacks continue to evoke the "slavery was terrible and it was your fault" rhetoric and still suppose that dignity and equality can be achieved thereby? Is it not fantastic to suppose that the oppressor, whom strident racial advocates take such joy in denouncing, would, in the interest of decency and upon hearing the extent of his crimes, decide to grant the claimants their every demand? The evocation of slavery in our contemporary discourse has little to do with sociology, or with historical causation. Its main effect is moral. It uses the slave experience in order to establish culpability. Why should others—the vast majority of whom have ancestors who arrived here after the emancipation, or who fought against the institution of slavery, or who endured profound discriminations of their own—permit themselves to be morally blackmailed with such rhetoric? How long can the failures of the present among black Americans be excused and explained by reference to the wrongs of the past? Must not, after some point, there begin to be resentment, contempt, and disdain for a group of people that sees itself in such terms? Consider the contradictions: Blacks seek general recognition of their accomplishments in the past and yet must insist upon the extent to which their ancestors were reduced to helplessness. Blacks must emphasize that they live in a nation that has never respected their humanity, yet expect that by so doing, their fellow countrymen will be moved to come to their assistance.

Self-Emancipation

Although the signs of intellectual exhaustion in this line of advocacy are evident, it continues to be embraced because of the way in which blacks' claims have been most successfully pressed over the past generation. These claims are based, above all else, on the status of blacks as America's historical victims. Maintenance of this declared status requires constant emphasis on the wrongs of the past and exaggeration of present tribulations. He who leads a group of historical victims, as victims, must never let "them" forget what "they" have done; he must renew the indictment and keep alive the moral asymmetry implicit in the respective positions of victim and victimizer. He is the preeminent architect of what Kenneth Minogue has called "suffering situations." The circumstance of his group as "underdog" becomes his most valuable political asset.

But such a posture in the political arena can inhibit the attainment of genuine freedom and equality, for it militates against an emphasis on personal responsibility within the group, inducing those group members who have been successful to attribute their accomplishments to fortuitous circumstance, not to their own abilities and character, and encouraging those who fail to see their failure as the inevitable consequence of historical wrongs. It is difficult to overemphasize the self-defeating dynamic at work here. The dictates of political advocacy require that personal inadequacies among blacks be attributed to the "system" and that emphasis by black leaders on self-improvement be denounced as irrelevant, self-serving, dishonest. Individual black men and women simply cannot fail on their own; they must be seen as never having had a chance. But where failure at the personal level is impossible, there can also be no personal success. For a black to embrace the Horatio Alger myth, to assert as a guide to *personal* action that "there is opportunity in America," becomes a *politically* repugnant act. Each would-be black Horatio Alger indicts as inadequate or incomplete the deeply entrenched (and quite useful) notion that individual effort can never overcome the "poisonous legacy" of slavery.

160

Yet where there can be no black Horatio Algers to celebrate, sustaining an ethos of responsibility that might extract maximal effort from the individual in the face of hardship—that is, that might facilitate his true emancipation—becomes impossible as well. A graphic illustration of this theme is John Edgar Wideman's poignant and brilliantly written account of two brothers, one who is serving a life sentence for murder in a Pennsylvania penitentiary and the other who is the author. In *Brothers and Keepers*, Wideman, a Rhodes scholar and a highly acclaimed novelist and college professor, can find only societal and circumstantial explanations for the difference in outcomes between himself and his brother, assiduously avoiding the possibility that distinctions of character and values might somehow be involved. It is not his brother, but "society" that has failed. In a central passage in the book, after describing the death of Garth, his brother's close friend who had received inadequate care at a public health clinic, Wideman relates his mother's (and, evidently, his own) view of the matter:

> Mom expects the worst now. She peeped their [the system's] hole card. She understands they have a master plan that leaves little to accident, that most of the ugliest things happening to black people are not accidental but the predictable results of the workings of the plan. What she learned about authority, about law and order didn't make sense at first. It went against her instincts, what she wanted to believe. . . . Garth's death and [brother] Robby's troubles were at the center of her new vision. Like a prism, they caught the light, transformed it so she could trace the seemingly random inconveniences and impositions coloring her life to their source in a master plan.

Notice the alternatives: Outcomes are either accidents (possibly fortuitous, as in his own case) or the result of a "master plan" against blacks, but never the consequence of individual, willful acts. Indeed, he seems at one point to be arguing that it was his brother's courage and strength to rebel against the rules laid down by racist whites— rules that he dutifully followed while harboring a resentment and rage barely concealed beneath a veneer of refinement and civility— that accounted for their different circumstances. He offers, in his brother's voice, the following "explanation" of the behavior of "young black men in the streetworld life":

> So this hip guy, this gangster or player or whatever label you give these brothers we like to shun because of the poison that they spread, we, black people, still look at them with some sense of pride and admiration, our children openly, as adults

161

somewhere deep inside. We know they represent rebellion—what little is left in us. Well, having lived in the "life," it becomes very hard—almost impossible—to find any contentment in joining the status quo. Too hard to go back to being nobody in a world that hates you.

The work is suffused with the guilt of the survivor—the agonizing dilemma of those who, having escaped catastrophe intact, are forever plagued with the unanswerable question: "Why was I spared, and not the others?" Wideman's answer, which seems to be "I was just lucky," is belied by the very account he provides. That he manages to effect this moral sleight of hand without fundamentally undermining the literary integrity of his book is testimony to his skill and power as a writer. His evocation of the humiliating plight of those trapped in "the cage" of prison, subject to the near unlimited powers of their "keepers," is simply unforgettable. Yet, though there is little now to be done about the tragedy of brother Robby, consider the message that his book sends to young black men in similar circumstances throughout the country, who might yet avoid his brother's plight: "Your life is not your own to build as you will; they've got 'a master plan.' You can submit, and be 'a nobody in a world that hates you,' or have the courage to rebel, and die in a cage." This seductive intellectual nihilism, inspired by an understandable agony of grief for those lost to the ravaging legacy of racism, throws away the infinite possibilities of the many who, with sustained effort inspired by their loved ones' highest expectations, might yet overcome that legacy.

The Price Extracted

James Baldwin spoke to this problem with great insight long ago (so long, in fact, that he seems to have forgotten his own advice). In his 1949 essay "Everybody's Protest Novel," Baldwin said of the protagonist of Richard Wright's celebrated novel *Native Son:*

> Bigger Thomas stands on a Chicago street corner watching airplanes flown by white men racing against the sun and "Goddamn" he says, the bitterness bubbling up like blood, remembering a million indignities, the terrible, rat-infested house, the humiliation of home-relief, the intense, aimless, ugly bickering, hating it; hatred smoulders through these pages like sulphur fire. All of Bigger's life is controlled, defined by his hatred and his fear. And later, his fear drives him to murder and his hatred to rape; he dies, having come, through this violence, and we are told, for the first time, to a kind of life, having for the first time redeemed his manhood.

But Baldwin rejected this "redemption through rebellion" thesis as untrue to life and unworthy of art. "Bigger's tragedy," he concluded,

> is not that he is cold or black or hungry, not even that he is American, black; but that *he has accepted a theology that denies him life, that he admits the possibility of his being sub-human and feels constrained, therefore, to battle for his humanity according to those brutal criteria bequeathed him at his birth.* But our humanity is our burden, our life; we need not battle for it; we need only to do what is infinitely more difficult—that is, accept it. The failure of the protest novel lies in its rejection of life, the human being, the denial of his beauty, dread, power, in its insistence that it is his categorization alone which is real and which cannot be transcended (emphasis added).

Baldwin's interest was essentially literary; mine is sociopolitical. In either case, however, the struggle is against the deadening effect that emanates from the belief that, for the black man, "it is his categorization alone which is real and cannot be transcended." The spheres of politics and of culture intersect in this understanding of what the existence of systemic constraint implies for the possibilities of individual personality. For too many blacks, dedication to the cause of reform has been allowed to supplant the demand for individual accountability; race, and the historic crimes associated with it, has become the single lens through which to view social experience; the infinite potential of real human beings has been surrendered on the altar of protest. In this way does the prophecy of failure, evoked by those who take the fact of racism as barring forever blacks' access to the rich possibilities of American life, fulfill itself: emphasis on the determinative effects of the "poisonous legacy" in the struggle to secure redress for past oppression requires the sacrifice of a primary instrument through which genuine freedom might yet be attained.

Thus does the decision to play the historical victim extract its price. The acknowledgment by blacks of the possibility, within the American constitutional order, of individual success, and the recognition of the personal traits associated with such success, comes to be seen, quite literally, as a betrayal of the black poor, for it undermines the legitimacy of what has proved to be their most valuable, if too often abused and rapidly depreciating, political asset. There is, hidden in this desperate assertion of victim status by blacks to an increasingly skeptical white polity, an unfolding tragedy of profound proportion. Black leaders, confronting their people's need and their own impotency, believe they must continue to portray blacks as "the conscience of the nation." Yet the price extracted for playing this role, in incompletely fulfilled lives and unrealized personal potential,

163

amounts to a "loss of our own souls." As consummate victims, blacks lay themselves at the feet of their fellows, exhibiting their own lack of achievement as evidence of their countrymen's failure, hoping to wring from the American conscience what we must assume, by the very logic of their claim, lies beyond the ability of individual blacks to attain, all the while bemoaning how limited that sense of conscience seems to be. This way lies not the "freedom" so long sought by our ancestors but, instead, a continuing serfdom.

Notes

1. Nathan Glazer foresaw this conflict, with its powerful implications for the equalitarian aspirations of blacks, *before* the separatist sentiments associated with the black power thrust came to the fore. See his "Negroes and Jews: The New Challenge to Pluralism," *Commentary,* December 1964. The philosophical implications of this tension between communal ties and the ideal of equal opportunity are nicely developed by James Fishkin in *Justice, Equal Opportunity, and the Family* (New Haven: Yale University Press, 1983).

2. Perhaps the most prominent exponent of this thesis is University of Chicago sociologist William Julius Wilson. See his *The Truly Disadvantaged: Essays on Inner City Woes and Public Policy* (Chicago: University of Chicago Press, 1987).

3. The Supreme Court's decision in the Detroit cross-district busing case, Milliken v. Bradley, limiting the use of metropolitan busing to solve the "white flight" problem, gives a classic illustration of this point. For, while it may be argued that the nearly totally black public school system in Detroit is handicapped severely in its ability to prepare its students for competition with suburban whites, the Court decided that without evidence of suburban district complicity in the segregation of city schools, whites who chose to avoid the city's school system by moving to the suburbs could not be forced to lend their children to the project of integration.

Appendix:
Address at Cooper Institute

Abraham Lincoln

February 27, 1860

The facts with which I shall deal this evening are mainly old and familiar; nor is there anything new in the general use I shall make of them. If there shall be any novelty, it will be in the mode of presenting the facts, and the inferences and observations following that presentation.

In his speech last autumn, at Columbus, Ohio, as reported in "The New-York Times," Senator Douglas said:

"Our fathers, when they framed the Government under which we live, understood this question just as well, and even better, than we do now."

I fully indorse this, and I adopt it as a text for this discourse. I so adopt it because it furnishes a precise and an agreed starting point for a discussion between Republicans and that wing of the Democracy headed by Senator Douglas. It simply leaves the inquiry: *"What was the understanding those fathers had of the question mentioned?"*

What is the frame of Government under which we live?

The answer must be: "The Constitution of the United States." That Constitution consists of the original, framed in 1787, (and under which the present government first went into operation,) and twelve subsequently framed amendments, the first ten of which were framed in 1789.

Who were our fathers that framed the Constitution? I suppose the "thirty-nine" who signed the original instrument may be fairly called our fathers who framed that part of the present Government. It is almost exactly true to say they framed it, and it is altogether true to say they fairly represented the opinion and sentiment of the whole nation at that time. Their names, being familiar to nearly all, and accessible to quite all, need not now be repeated.

I take these "thirty-nine" for the present, as being "our fathers who framed the Government under which we live."

What is the question which, according to the text, those fathers understood "just as well, and even better than we do now?"

It is this: Does the proper division of local from federal authority, or anything in the Constitution, forbid *our Federal Government* to control as to slavery in *our Federal Territories?*

Upon this, Senator Douglas holds the affirmative, and Republicans the negative. This affirmation and denial form an issue; and this issue—this question—is precisely what the text declares our fathers understood "better than we."

Let us now inquire whether the "thirty-nine," or any of them, ever acted upon this question; and if they did, how they acted upon it—how they expressed that better understanding?

In 1784, three years before the Constitution—the United States then owning the Northwestern Territory, and no other, the Congress of the Confederation had before them the question of prohibiting slavery in that Territory; and four of the "thirty-nine," who afterward framed the Constitution, were in that Congress, and voted on that question. Of these, Roger Sherman, Thomas Mifflin, and Hugh Williamson voted for the prohibition, thus showing that, in their understanding, no line dividing local from federal authority, nor anything else, properly forbade the Federal Government to control as to slavery in federal territory. The other of the four—James M'Henry—voted against the prohibition, showing that, for some cause, he thought it improper to vote for it.

In 1787, still before the Constitution, but while the Convention was in session framing it, and while the Northwestern Territory still was the only territory owned by the United States, the same question of prohibiting slavery in the territory again came before the Congress of the Confederation; and two more of the "thirty-nine" who afterward signed the Constitution, were in that Congress, and voted on the question. They were William Blount and William Few; and they both voted for the prohibition—thus showing that, in their understanding, no line dividing local from federal authority, nor anything else, properly forbade the Federal Government to control as to slavery in federal territory. This time the prohibition became a law, being part of what is now well known as the Ordinance of '87.

The question of federal control of slavery in the territories, seems not to have been directly before the Convention which framed the original Constitution; and hence it is not recorded that the "thirty-nine," or any of them, while engaged on that instrument, expressed any opinion of that precise question.

In 1789, by the first Congress which sat under the Constitution, an act was passed to enforce the Ordinance of '87, including the prohibition of slavery in the Northwestern Territory. The bill for this act was reported by one of the "thirty-nine," Thomas Fitzsimmons, then a member of the House of Representatives from Pennsylvania. It went through all its stages without a word of opposition, and finally passed both branches without yeas and nays, which is equivalent to an unanimous passage. In this Congress there were sixteen of the thirty-nine fathers who framed the original Constitution. They were John Langdon, Nicholas Gilman, Wm. S. Johnson, Roger Sherman, Robert Morris, Thos. Fitzsimmons, William Few, Abraham Baldwin, Rufus King, William Paterson, George Clymer, Richard Bassett, George Reed, Pierce Butler, Daniel Carroll, James Madison.

This shows that, in their understanding, no line dividing local from federal authority, nor anything in the Constitution, properly forbade Congress to prohibit slavery in the federal territory; else both their fidelity to correct principle, and their oath to support the Constitution, would have constrained them to oppose the prohibition.

Again, George Washington, another of the "thirty-nine," was then President of the United States, and, as such, approved and signed the bill; thus completing its validity as a law, and thus showing that, in his understanding, no line dividing local from federal authority, nor anything in the Constitution, forbade the Federal Government, to control as to slavery in federal territory.

No great while after the adoption of the original Constitution, North Carolina ceded to the Federal Government the country now constituting the State of Tennessee; and a few years later Georgia ceded that which now constitutes the States of Mississippi and Alabama. In both deeds of cession it was made a condition by the ceding States that the Federal Government should not prohibit slavery in the ceded country. Besides this, slavery was then actually in the ceded country. Under these circumstances, Congress, on taking charge of these countries, did not absolutely prohibit slavery within them. But they did interfere with it—take control of it—even there, to a certain extent. In 1798, Congress organized the Territory of Mississippi. In the act of organization, they prohibited the bringing of slaves into the Territory, from any place without the United States, by fine, and giving freedom to slaves so brought. This act passed both branches of Congress without yeas and nays. In that Congress were three of the "thirty-nine" who framed the original Constitution. They were John Langdon, George Read and Abraham Baldwin. They all, probably, voted for it. Certainly they would have placed their opposition to it upon record, if, in their understanding, any line dividing local from federal authority, or anything in the Constitution, properly forbade the Federal Government to control as to slavery in federal territory.

In 1803, the Federal Government purchased the Louisiana country. Our former territorial acquisitions came from certain of our own States; but this Louisiana country was acquired from a foreign nation. In 1804, Congress gave a territorial organization to that part of it which now constitutes the State of Louisiana. New Orleans, lying within that part, was an old and comparatively large city. There were other considerable towns and settlements, and slavery was extensively and thoroughly intermingled with the people. Congress did not, in the Territorial Act, prohibit slavery; but they did interfere with it—take control of it—in a more marked and extensive way than they did in the case of Mississippi. The substance of the provision therein made, in relation to slaves, was:

First. That no slave should be imported into the territory from foreign parts.

Second. That no slave should be carried into it who had been imported into the United States since the first day of May, 1798.

Third. That no slave should be carried into it, except by the owner, and for his own use as a settler; the penalty in all the cases being a fine upon the violator of the law, and freedom to the slave.

This act also was passed without yeas and nays. In the Congress which passed it, there were two of the "thirty-nine." They were Abraham Baldwin and Jonathan Dayton. As stated in the case of Mississippi, it is probable they both voted for it. They would not have allowed it to pass without recording their opposition to it, if, in their understanding, it violated either the line properly dividing local from federal authority, or any provision of the Constitution.

In 1819–20, came and passed the Missouri question. Many votes were taken, by yeas and nays, in both branches of Congress, upon the various phases of the general question. Two of the "thirty-nine"— Rufus King and Charles Pinckney—were members of that Congress. Mr. King steadily voted for slavery prohibition and against all compromises, while Mr. Pinckney as steadily voted against slavery prohibition and against all compromises. By this, Mr. King showed that, in his understanding, no line dividing local from federal authority, nor anything in the Constitution, was violated by Congress prohibiting slavery in federal territory; while Mr. Pinckney, by his votes, showed that, in his understanding, there was some sufficient reason for opposing such prohibition in that case.

The cases I have mentioned are the only acts of the "thirty-nine," or of any of them, upon the direct issue, which I have been able to discover.

To enumerate the persons who thus acted, as being four in 1784, two in 1787, seventeen in 1789, three in 1798, two in 1804, and two in

1819–20—there would be thirty of them. But this would be counting John Langdon, Roger Sherman, William Few, Rufus King, and George Read, each twice, and Abraham Baldwin, three times. The true number of those of the "thirty-nine" whom I have shown to have acted upon the question, which, by the text, they understood better than we, is twenty-three, leaving sixteen not shown to have acted upon it in any way.

Here, then, we have twenty-three out of our thirty-nine fathers "who framed the Government under which we live," who have, upon their official responsibility and their corporal oaths, acted upon the very question which the text affirms they "understood just as well, and even better than we do now;" and twenty-one of them—a clear majority of the whole "thirty-nine"—so acting upon it as to make them guilty of gross political impropriety and wilful perjury, if, in their understanding, any proper division between local and federal authority, or anything in the Constitution they had made themselves, and sworn to support, forbade the Federal Government to control as to slavery in the federal territories. Thus the twenty-one acted; and, as actions speak louder than words, so actions, under such responsibility, speak still louder.

Two of the twenty-three voted against Congressional prohibition of slavery in the federal territories, in the instances in which they acted upon the question. But for what reasons they so voted is not known. They may have done so because they thought a proper division of local from federal authority, or some provision or principle of the Constitution, stood in the way; or they may, without any such question, have voted against the prohibition, on what appeared to them to be sufficient grounds of expediency. No one who has sworn to support the Constitution, can conscientiously vote for what he understands to be an unconstitutional measure, however expedient he may think it; but one may and ought to vote against a measure which he deems constitutional, if, at the same time, he deems it inexpedient. It, therefore, would be unsafe to set down even the two who voted against the prohibition, as having done so because, in their understanding, any proper division of local from federal authority, or anything in the Constitution, forbade the Federal Government to control as to slavery in federal territory.

The remaining sixteen of the "thirty-nine," so far as I have discovered, have left no record of their understanding upon the direct question of federal control of slavery in the federal territories. But there is much reason to believe that their understanding upon that question would not have appeared different from that of their twenty-three compeers, had it been manifested at all.

169

For the purpose of adhering rigidly to the text, I have purposely omitted whatever understanding may have been manifested by any person, however distinguished, other than the thirty-nine fathers who framed the original Constitution; and, for the same reason, I have also omitted whatever understanding may have been manifested by any of the "thirty-nine" even, on any other phase of the general question of slavery. If we should look into their acts and declarations on those other phases, as the foreign slave trade, and the morality and policy of slavery generally, it would appear to us that on the direct question of federal control of slavery in federal territories, the sixteen, if they had acted at all, would probably have acted just as the twenty-three did. Among that sixteen were several of the most noted anti-slavery men of those times—as Dr. Franklin, Alexander Hamilton and Gouverneur Morris—while there was not one now known to have been otherwise, unless it may be John Rutledge, of South Carolina.

The sum of the whole is, that of our thirty-nine fathers who framed the original Constitution, twenty-one—a clear majority of the whole—certainly understood that no proper division of local from federal authority, nor any part of the Constitution, forbade the Federal Government to control slavery in the federal territories; while all the rest probably had the same understanding. Such, unquestionably, was the understanding of our fathers who framed the original Constitution; and the text affirms that they understood the question "better than we."

But, so far, I have been considering the understanding of the question manifested by the framers of the original Constitution. In and by the original instrument, a mode was provided for amending it; and, as I have already stated, the present frame of "the Government under which we live" consists of that original, and twelve amendatory articles framed and adopted since. Those who now insist that federal control of slavery in federal territories violates the Constitution, point us to the provisions which they suppose it thus violates; and, as I understand, they all fix upon provisions in these amendatory articles, and not in the original instrument. The Supreme Court, in the Dred Scott case, plant themselves upon the fifth amendment, which provides that no person shall be deprived of "life, liberty or property without due process of law;" while Senator Douglas and his peculiar adherents plant themselves upon the tenth amendment, providing that "the powers not delegated to the United States by the Constitution," "are reserved to the States respectively, or to the people."

Now, it so happens that these amendments were framed by the first Congress which sat under the Constitution—the identical Congress which passed the act already mentioned, enforcing the prohibition of slavery in the Northwestern Territory. Not only was it the same Congress, but they were the identical, same individual men who, at the same session, and at the same time within the session, had under consideration, and in progress toward maturity, these Constitutional amendments, and this act prohibiting slavery in all the territory the nation then owned. The Constitutional amendments were introduced before, and passed after the act enforcing the Ordinance of '87; so that, during the whole pendency of the act to enforce the Ordinance, the Constitutional amendments were also pending.

The seventy-six members of that Congress, including sixteen of the framers of the original Constitution, as before stated, were preeminently our fathers who framed that part of "the Government under which we live," which is now claimed as forbidding the Federal Government to control slavery in the federal territories.

Is it not a little presumptuous in any one at this day to affirm that the two things which that Congress deliberately framed, and carried to maturity at the same time, are absolutely inconsistent with each other? And does not such affirmation become impudently absurd when coupled with the other affirmation from the same mouth, that those who did the two things, alleged to be inconsistent, understood whether they really were inconsistent better than we—better than he who affirms that they are inconsistent?

It is surely safe to assume that the thirty-nine framers of the original Constitution, and the seventy-six members of the Congress which framed the amendments thereto, taken together, do certainly include those who may be fairly called "our fathers who framed the Government under which we live." And so assuming, I defy any man to show that any one of them ever, in his whole life, declared that, in his understanding, any proper division of local from federal authority, or any part of the Constitution, forbade the Federal Government to control as to slavery in the federal territories. I go a step further. I defy any one to show that any living man in the whole world ever did, prior to the beginning of the present century, (and I might almost say prior to the beginning of the last half of the present century), declare that, in his understanding, any proper division of local from federal authority, or any part of the Constitution, forbade the Federal Government to control as to slavery in the federal territories. To those who now so declare, I give, not only "our fathers who framed the Government under which we live," but with them all other living men within the century in which it was framed, among whom to search, and they shall not be able to find the evidence of a single man agreeing with them.

171

Now, and here, let me guard a little against being misunderstood. I do not mean to say we are bound to follow implicitly in whatever our fathers did. To do so, would be to discard all the lights of current experience—to reject all progress—all improvement. What I do say is, that if we would supplant the opinions and policy of our fathers in any case, we should do so upon evidence so conclusive, and argument so clear, that even their great authority, fairly considered and weighed, cannot stand; and most surely not in a case whereof we ourselves declare they understood the question better than we.

If any man at this day sincerely believes that a proper division of local from federal authority, or any part of the Constitution, forbids the Federal Government to control as to slavery in the federal territories, he is right to say so, and to enforce his position by all truthful evidence and fair argument which he can. But he has no right to mislead others, who have less access to history, and less leisure to study it, into the false belief that "our fathers, who framed the Government under which we live," were of the same opinion—thus substituting falsehood and deception for truthful evidence and fair argument. If any man at this day sincerely believes "our fathers who framed the Government under which we live," used and applied principles, in other cases, which ought to have led them to understand that a proper division of local from federal authority or some part of the Constitution, forbids the Federal Government to control as to slavery in the federal territories, he is right to say so. But he should, at the same time, brave the responsibility of declaring that, in his opinion, he understands their principles better than they did themselves; and especially should he not shirk that responsibility by asserting that they "understood the question just as well, and even better, than we do now."

But enough! *Let all who believe that "our fathers, who framed the Government under which we live, understood this question just as well, and even better, than we do now," speak as they spoke, and act as they acted upon it. This is all Republicans ask—all Republicans desire—in relation to slavery. As those fathers marked it, so let it be again marked, as an evil not to be extended, but to be tolerated and protected only because of and so far as its actual presence among us makes that toleration and protection a necessity. Let all the guaranties those fathers gave it, be, not grudgingly, but fully and fairly maintained.* For this Republicans contend, and with this, so far as I know or believe, they will be content.

And now, if they would listen—as I suppose they will not—I would address a few words to the Southern people.

I would say to them:—You consider yourselves a reasonable and a just people; and I consider that in the general qualities of reason and

172

justice you are not inferior to any other people. Still, when you speak of us Republicans, you do so only to denounce us as reptiles, or, at the best, as no better than outlaws. You will grant a hearing to pirates or murderers, but nothing like it to "Black Republicans." In all your contentions with one another, each of you deems an unconditional condemnation of "Black Republicanism" as the first thing to be attended to. Indeed, such condemnation of us seems to be an indispensable prerequisite—license, so to speak—among you to be admitted or permitted to speak at all. Now, can you, or not, be prevailed upon to pause and to consider whether this is quite just to us, or even to yourselves? Bring forward your charges and specifications, and then be patient long enough to hear us deny or justify.

You say we are sectional. We deny it. That makes an issue; and the burden of proof is upon you. You produce your proof; and what is it? Why, that our party has no existence in your section—gets no votes in your section. The fact is substantially true; but does it prove the issue? If it does, then in case we should, without change of principle, begin to get votes in your section, we should thereby cease to be sectional. You cannot escape this conclusion; and yet, are you willing to abide by it? If you are, you will probably soon find that we have ceased to be sectional, for we shall get votes in your section this very year. You will then begin to discover, as the truth plainly is, that your proof does not touch the issue. The fact that we get no votes in your section, is a fact of your making, and not of ours. And if there be fault in that fact, that fault is primarily yours, and remains so until you show that we repel you by some wrong principle or practice. If we do repel you by any wrong principle or practice, the fault is ours; but this brings you to where you ought to have started—to a discussion of the right or wrong of our principle. If our principle, put in practice, would wrong your section for the benefit of ours, or for any other object, then our principle, and we with it, are sectional, and are justly opposed and denounced as such. Meet us, then, on the question of whether our principle, put in practice, would wrong your section; and so meet us as if it were possible that something may be said on our side. Do you accept the challenge? No! Then you really believe that the principle which "our fathers who framed the Government under which we live" thought so clearly right as to adopt it, and indorse it again and again, upon their official oaths, is in fact so clearly wrong as to demand your condemnation without a moment's consideration.

Some of you delight to flaunt in our faces the warning against sectional parties given by Washington in his Farewell Address. Less than eight years before Washington gave that warning, he had, as President of the United States, approved and signed an act of Congress, enforcing the prohibition of slavery in the Northwestern Territory, which act embodied the policy of the Government upon that subject up to and at the very moment he penned that warning; and about one year after he penned it, he wrote La Fayette that he considered that prohibition a wise measure, expressing in the same connection his hope that we should at some time have a confederacy of free States.

Bearing this in mind, and seeing that sectionalism has since arisen upon this same subject, is that warning a weapon in your hands against us, or in our hands against you? Could Washington himself speak, would he cast the blame of that sectionalism upon us, who sustain his policy, or upon you who repudiate it? We respect that warning of Washington, and we commend it to you, together with his example pointing to the right application of it.

But you say you are conservative—eminently conservative— while we are revolutionary, destructive, or something of the sort. What is conservatism? Is it not adherence to the old and tried, against the new and untried? We stick to, contend for, the identical old policy on the point in controversy which was adopted by "our fathers who framed the Government under which we live;" while you with one accord reject, and scout, and spit upon that old policy, and insist upon substituting something new. True, you disagree among yourselves as to what that substitute shall be. You are divided on new propositions and plans, but you are unanimous in rejecting and denouncing the old policy of the fathers. Some of you are for reviving the foreign slave trade; some for a Congressional Slave-Code for the Territories; some for Congress forbidding the Territories to prohibit Slavery within their limits; some for maintaining Slavery in the Territories through the judiciary; some for the "gur-reat pur-rinciple" that "if one man would enslave another, no third man should object," fantastically called "Popular Sovereignty;" but never a man among you in favor of federal prohibition of slavery in federal territories, according to the practice of "our fathers who framed the Government under which we live." Not one of all your various plans can show a precedent or an advocate in the century within which our Government originated. Consider, then, whether your claim of conservatism for yourselves, and your charge of destructiveness against us, are based on the most clear and stable foundations.

Again, you say we have made the slavery question more prominent than it formerly was. We deny it. We admit that it is more prominent, but we deny that we made it so. It was not we, but you, who discarded the old policy of the fathers. We resisted, and still resist, your innovation; and thence comes the greater prominence of the question. Would you have that question reduced to its former proportions? Go back to that old policy. What has been will be again, under the same conditions. If you would have the peace of the old times, readopt the precepts and policy of the old times.

You charge that we stir up insurrections among your slaves. We deny it; and what is your proof? Harper's Ferry! John Brown!! John Brown was no Republican; and you have failed to implicate a single Republican in his Harper's Ferry enterprise. If any member of our party is guilty in that matter, you know it or you do not know it. If you do know it, you are inexcusable for not designating the man and proving the fact. If you do not know it, you are inexcusable for asserting it, and especially for persisting in the assertion after you have tried and failed to make the proof. You need not be told that persisting in a charge which one does not know to be true, is simply malicious slander.

Some of you admit that no Republican designedly aided or encouraged the Harper's Ferry affair; but still insist that our doctrines and declarations necessarily lead to such results. We do not believe it. We know we hold to no doctrine, and make no declaration, which were not held to and made by "our fathers who framed the Government under which we live." You never dealt fairly by us in relation to this affair. When it occurred, some important State elections were near at hand, and you were in evident glee with the belief that, by charging the blame upon us, you could get an advantage of us in those elections. The elections came, and your expectations were not quite fulfilled. Every Republican man knew that, as to himself at least, your charge was a slander, and he was not much inclined by it to cast his vote in your favor. Republican doctrines and declarations are accompanied with a continued protest against any interference whatever with your slaves, or with you about your slaves. Surely, this does not encourage them to revolt. True, we do, in common with "our fathers, who framed the Government under which we live," declare our belief that slavery is wrong; but the slaves do not hear us declare even this. For anything we say or do, the slaves would scarcely know there is a Republican party. I believe they would not, in fact, generally know it but for your misrepresentations of us, in their hearing. In your political contests among yourselves, each faction charges the other with sympathy with Black Republicanism; and then, to give point to the charge, defines Black Republicanism to simply be insurrection, blood and thunder among the slaves.

Slave insurrections are no more common now than they were before the Republican party was organized. What induced the Southampton insurrection, twenty-eight years ago, in which, at least, three

175

times as many lives were lost as at Harper's Ferry? You can scarcely stretch your very elastic fancy to the conclusion that Southampton was "got up by Black Republicanism." In the present state of things in the United States, I do not think a general, or even a very extensive slave insurrection, is possible. The indispensable concert of action cannot be attained. The slaves have no means of rapid communication; nor can incendiary freemen, black or white, supply it. The explosive materials are everywhere in parcels; but there neither are, nor can be supplied, the indispensable connecting trains.

Much is said by Southern people about the affection of slaves for their masters and mistresses; and a part of it, at least, is true. A plot for an uprising could scarcely be devised and communicated to twenty individuals before some of them, to save the life of a favorite master or mistress, would divulge it. This is the rule; and the slave revolution in Hayti was not an exception to it, but a case occurring under peculiar circumstances. The gunpowder plot of British history, though not connected with slaves, was more in point. In that case, only about twenty were admitted to the secret; and yet one of them, in his anxiety to save a friend, betrayed the plot to that friend, and, by consequence, averted the calamity. Occasional poisonings from the kitchen, and open or stealthy assassinations in the field, and local revolts extending to a score or so, will continue to occur as the natural results of slavery; but no general insurrection of slaves, as I think, can happen in this country for a long time. Whoever much fears, or much hopes for such an event, will be alike disappointed.

In the language of Mr. Jefferson, uttered many years ago, "It is still in our power to direct the process of emancipation, and deportation, peaceably, and in such slow degrees, as that the evil will wear off insensibly; and their places be, *pari passu,* filled up by free white laborers. If, on the contrary, it is left to force itself on, human nature must shudder at the prospect held up."

Mr. Jefferson did not mean to say, nor do I, that the power of emancipation is in the Federal Government. He spoke of Virginia; and, as to the power of emancipation, I speak of the slaveholding States only. The Federal Government, however, as we insist, has the power of restraining the extension of the institution—the power to insure that a slave insurrection shall never occur on any American soil which is now free from slavery.

John Brown's effort was peculiar. It was not a slave insurrection. It was an attempt by white men to get up a revolt among slaves, in which the slaves refused to participate. In fact, it was so absurd that the slaves, with all their ignorance, saw plainly enough it could not succeed. That affair, in its philosophy, corresponds with the many attempts, related in history, at the assassination of kings and emperors. An enthusiast broods over the oppression of a people till he fancies himself commissioned by Heaven to liberate them. He ventures the attempt, which ends in little else than his own execution. Orsini's attempt on Louis Napoleon, and John Brown's attempt at Harper's Ferry were, in their philosophy, precisely the same. The eagerness to cast blame on old England in the one case, and on New England in the other, does not disprove the sameness of the two things.

And how much would it avail you, if you could, by the use of John Brown, Helper's Book, and the like, break up the Republican organization? Human action can be modified to some extent, but human nature cannot be changed. There is a judgment and a feeling against slavery in this nation, which cast at least a million and a half of votes. You cannot destroy that judgment and feeling—that sentiment—by breaking up the political organization which rallies around it. You can scarcely scatter and disperse an army which has been formed into order in the face of your heaviest fire; but if you could, how much would you gain by forcing the sentiment which created it out of the peaceful channel of the ballot-box, into some other channel? What would that other channel probably be? Would the number of John Browns be lessened or enlarged by the operation?

But you will break up the Union rather than submit to a denial of your Constitutional rights.

That has a somewhat reckless sound; but it would be palliated, if not fully justified, were we proposing, by the mere force of numbers, to deprive you of some right, plainly written down in the Constitution. But we are proposing no such thing.

When you make these declarations, you have a specific and well-understood allusion to an assumed Constitutional right of yours, to take slaves into the federal territories, and to hold them there as property. But no such right is specifically written in the Constitution. That instrument is literally silent about any such right. We, on the contrary, deny that such a right has any existence in the Constitution, even by implication.

Your purpose, then, plainly stated, is, that you will destroy the Government, unless you be allowed to construe and enforce the Constitution as you please, on all points in dispute between you and us. You will rule or ruin in all events.

This, plainly stated, is your language. Perhaps you will say the Supreme Court has decided the disputed Constitutional question in your favor. Not quite so. But waiving the lawyer's distinction between dictum and decision, the Court have decided the question for you in a sort of way. The Court have substantially said, it is your Constitutional right to take slaves into the federal territories, and to hold them there as property. When I say the decision was made in a sort of way, I mean it was made in a divided Court, by a bare majority of the Judges, and they not quite agreeing with one another in the reasons for making it, that it is so made as that its avowed supporters disagree with one another about its meaning, and that it was mainly based upon a mistaken statement of fact—the statement in the opinion that "the right of property in a slave is distinctly and expressly affirmed in the Constitution."

An inspection of the Constitution will show that the right of property in a slave is not "*distinctly* and *expressly* affirmed" in it. Bear in mind, the Judges do not pledge their judicial opinion that such right is *impliedly* affirmed in the Constitution; but they pledge their veracity that it is "*distinctly* and *expressly*" affirmed there—"distinctly," that is, not mingled with anything else—"expressly," that is, in words meaning just that, without the aid of any inference, and susceptible of no other meaning.

If they had only pledged their judicial opinion that such right is affirmed in the instrument by implication, it would be open to others to show that neither the word "slave" nor "slavery" is to be found in the Constitution, nor the word "property" even, in any connection with language alluding to the things slave, or slavery, and that wherever in that instrument the slave is alluded to, he is called a "person;"—and wherever his master's legal right in relation to him is alluded to, it is spoken of as "service or labor which may be due,"—as a debt payable in service or labor. Also, it would be open to show, by contemporaneous history, that this mode of alluding to slaves and slavery, instead of speaking of them, was employed on purpose to exclude from the Constitution the idea that there could be property in man.

To show all this, is easy and certain.

When this obvious mistake of the Judges shall be brought to their notice, is it not reasonable to expect that they will withdraw the mistaken statement, and reconsider the conclusion based upon it?

And then it is to be remembered that "our fathers, who framed the Government under which we live"—the men who made the Constitution—decided this same Constitutional question in our favor, long ago—decided it without division among themselves, when making the decision; without division among themselves about the meaning of it after it was made, and, so far as any evidence is left, without basing it upon any mistaken statement of facts.

Under all these circumstances, do you really feel yourselves justified to break up this Government, unless such a court decision as yours is, shall be at once submitted to as a conclusive and final rule of political action? But you will not abide the election of a Republican President! In that supposed event, you say, you will destroy the Union; and then, you say, the great crime of having destroyed it will be upon us! That is cool. A highwayman holds a pistol to my ear, and mutters through his teeth, "Stand and deliver, or I shall kill you, and then you will be a murderer!"

To be sure, what the robber demanded of me—my money—was my own; and I have a clear right to keep it; but it was no more my own than my vote is my own; and the threat of death to me, to extort my money, and the threat of destruction to the Union, to extort my vote, can scarcely be distinguished in principle.

A few words now to Republicans. *It is exceedingly desirable that all parts of this great Confederacy shall be at peace, and in harmony, one with another. Let us Republicans do our part to have it so. Even though much provoked, let us do nothing through passion and ill temper. Even though the southern people will not so much as listen to us, let us calmly consider their demands, and yield to them if, in our deliberate view of our duty, we possibly can.* Judging by all they say and do, and by the subject and nature of their controversy with us, let us determine, if we can, what will satisfy them.

Will they be satisfied if the Territories be unconditionally surrendered to them? We know they will not. In all their present complaints against us, the Territories are scarcely mentioned. Invasions and insurrections are the rage now. Will it satisfy them, if, in the future, we have nothing to do with invasions and insurrections? We know it will not. We so know, because we know we never had anything to do with invasions and insurrections; and yet this total abstaining does not exempt us from the charge and the denunciation.

The question recurs, what will satisfy them? Simply this: We must not only let them alone, but we must, somehow, convince them that we do let them alone. This, we know by experience, is no easy task. We have been so trying to convince them from the very beginning of our organization, but with no success. In all our platforms and speeches we have constantly protested our purpose to let them alone; but this has had no tendency to convince them. Alike unavailing to convince them, is the fact that they have never detected a man of us in any attempt to disturb them.

These natural, and apparently adequate means all failing, what will convince them? This, and this only: cease to call slavery *wrong,* and join them in calling it *right.* And this must be done thoroughly— done in *acts* as well as in *words.* Silence will not be tolerated—we must place ourselves avowedly with them. Senator Douglas's new sedition law must be enacted and enforced, suppressing all declarations that slavery is wrong, whether made in politics, in presses, in pulpits, or in private. We must arrest and return their fugitive slaves with greedy pleasure. We must pull down our Free State constitutions. The whole atmosphere must be disinfected from all taint of opposition to slavery, before they will cease to believe that all their troubles proceed from us.

I am quite aware they do not state their case precisely in this way. Most of them would probably say to us, "Let us alone, *do* nothing to us, and *say* what you please about slavery." But we do let them alone—have never disturbed them—so that, after all, it is what we say, which dissatisfies them. They will continue to accuse us of doing, until we cease saying.

I am also aware they have not, as yet, in terms, demanded the overthrow of our Free-State Constitutions. Yet those Constitutions declare the wrong of slavery, with more solemn emphasis, than do all other sayings against it; and when all these other sayings shall have been silenced, the overthrow of these Constitutions will be demanded, and nothing be left to resist the demand. It is nothing to the contrary, that they do not demand the whole of this just now. Demanding what they do, and for the reason they do, they can voluntarily stop nowhere short of this consummation. Holding, as they do, that slavery is morally right, and socially elevating, they cannot cease to demand a full national recognition of it, as a legal right, and a social blessing.

Nor can we justifiably withhold this, on any ground save our conviction that slavery is wrong. If slavery is right, all words, acts, laws, and constitutions against it, are themselves wrong, and should be silenced, and swept away. If it is right, we cannot justly object to its nationality—its universality; if it is wrong, they cannot justly insist upon its extension—its enlargement. All they ask, we could readily grant, if we thought slavery right; all we ask, they could as readily grant, if they thought it wrong. Their thinking it right, and our thinking it wrong, is the precise fact upon which depends the whole controversy. Thinking it right, as they do, they are not to blame for desiring its full recognition, as being right; but, thinking it wrong, as we do, can we yield to them? Can we cast our votes with their view, and against our own? In view of our moral, social, and political responsibilities, can we do this?

Wrong as we think slavery is, we can yet afford to let it alone where it is, because that much is due to the necessity arising from its actual presence in the nation; but can we, while our votes will prevent it, allow it to spread into the National Territories, and to overrun us here in these Free States? If our sense of duty forbids this, then let us stand by our duty, fearlessly and effectively. Let us be diverted by none of those sophistical contrivances wherewith we are so industriously plied and belabored—contrivances such as groping for some middle ground between the right and the wrong, vain as the search for a man who should be neither a living man nor a dead man—such as a policy of "don't care" on a question about which all true men do care—such as Union appeals beseeching true Union men to yield to Disunionists, reversing the divine rule, and calling, not the sinners, but the righteous to repentance—such as invocations to Washington, imploring men to unsay what Washington said, and undo what Washington did.

Neither let us be slandered from our duty by false accusations against us, nor frightened from it by menaces of destruction to the Government nor of dungeons to ourselves. LET US HAVE FAITH THAT RIGHT MAKES MIGHT, AND IN THAT FAITH, LET US, TO THE END, DARE TO DO OUR DUTY AS WE UNDERSTAND IT.

A Note on the Book

This book was edited by Trudy Kaplan, Dana Lane, and
Janet Schilling of the publications staff
of the American Enterprise Institute.
The text was set in Palatino, a typeface designed by Hermann Zapf.